SOCIAL CLASS IN APPLIED LINGUISTICS

'Social class has finally emerged from the shadows in the field of applied linguistics. There is no scholar better qualified than David Block to undertake a rigorous examination of this important and complex topic. *Social Class in Applied Linguistics* is groundbreaking.'

Bonny Norton, *University of British Columbia, Canada*

'This is a fascinating, sometimes provocative, and often innovative book, which brings together concepts and ideas that have been begging to be discussed in their interconnection for a very long while... *Social Class in Applied Linguistics* is a timely book as indeed many applied linguists are increasingly bringing aspects of social class to their analyses. This book will provide a scholarly and stimulating set of building blocks from which to develop the discussions.'

Clare Mar-Molinero, *University of Southampton, UK*

In this ground breaking book David Block proposes a new working definition of social class in applied linguistics.

Traditionally, research on language and identity has focused on aspects such as race, ethnicity, nationality, gender, religion and sexuality. Political economy, and social class, as an identity inscription, have been undervalued. This book argues that increasing socio-economic inequality, which has come with the consolidation of neoliberal policies and practices worldwide, requires changes in how we think about identity and proposes that social class should be brought to the fore as a key construct.

Social Class in Applied Linguistics begins with an in-depth theoretical discussion of social class before considering the extent to which social class has been a key construct in three general areas of applied linguistics: sociolinguistics, bi/multilingualism and second language acquisition and learning research. Throughout the book, Block suggests ways in which social class might be incorporated into future applied linguistics research.

A critical read for postgraduate students and researchers in the areas of applied linguistics, language education and TESOL.

David Block is Research Professor in Sociolinguistics for the Institució Catalana de Recerca i Estudis Avançats (ICREA) and works in the Department d'Anglès i Lingüística at the Universitat de Lleida, Spain. He is co-author of *Neoliberalism and Applied Linguistics* (Routledge, 2012)

SOCIAL CLASS IN APPLIED LINGUISTICS

David Block

Routledge
Taylor & Francis Group

LONDON AND NEW YORK

First published 2014
by Routledge
2 Park Square, Milton Park, Abingdon, Oxon OX14 4RN

and by Routledge
711 Third Avenue, New York, NY 10017

Routledge is an imprint of the Taylor & Francis Group, an informa business

British Library Cataloguing in Publication Data
A catalogue record for this book is available from the British Library

Library of Congress Cataloging in Publication Data
Block, David, 1956–
Social class in applied linguistics / David Block.
page cm.
1. Applied linguistics–Social aspects. 2. Language and languages–Study and teaching–Social aspects. 3. Language and languages–Study and teaching–Economic aspects.
4. Language and culture–Social aspects. 5. Social interaction. 6. Sociolinguistics. I. Title.
P53.8.B59 2013
306.44–dc23
2013019146

ISBN: 978-0-415-54817-5 (hbk)
ISBN: 978-0-415-54818-2 (pbk)
ISBN: 978-1-315-87114-1 (ebk)

Typeset in Bembo
by Taylor and Francis Books

MIX
Paper from responsible sources
FSC
www.fsc.org   FSC® C013604

Printed and bound by CPI Group (UK) Ltd, Croydon, CR0 4YY

CONTENTS

LIST OF TABLES

PROLOGUE

A prologue can serve many purposes, from being a brief introduction to the topics and arguments to be covered in a book, to being the place where thanks can be given to those who have helped the author during the book-writing process. These things and more appear in this prologue as I take it as an opportunity to do some general housekeeping. Thus I start with terminological issues, which are important to dispatch at this early stage so as to avoid reader confusion later in the book, before moving to consider a few scholarship issues. I end with acknowledgements.

Terminological issues

As regards terminology, there is first and foremost **social class** to consider, the key term in the title and the main focus of this book. However, I mention it here not to define it (an effort in this direction can be found in Chapter 2), but to justify its use. In an earlier publication on the topic of social class and how it might be a useful construct in second language acquisition and learning research, I used not 'social class', but 'class', writing the following as a reason for my choice:

> Authors interested in social stratification in societies use two terms: 'class' and 'social class'. In this article, I use the former term, following the general trend in sociology.
>
> *(Block, 2012a: 203)*

Some two years later, as I write this book, I find myself in somewhat of a dilemma and considerably less sure about this choice: while using 'class' (and not 'social class') might be a general trend in sociology today, it is certainly not the case that all sociologists eschew 'social class'. Indeed, there is a tendency to use the two terms interchangeably. In applied linguistics, there has been a tradition of using 'social class' which goes back to William Labov's early variationist work in sociolinguistics, even if this term appears relatively little in his work as the majority of the occurrences of 'class' are preceded by the adjectives 'middle', 'working' and 'lower'. Some four decades later, we see how in Ben Rampton's (2006) *Language in Late Modernity* matters have evolved to the extent that 'class' and 'social class' seem to be used interchangeably. All of this leaves the matter pretty much up in the air. But there is more.

When discussing the book title with Louisa Semlyen and Sophie Jaques at Routledge, as well as several colleagues and associates, I have become even less sure about what to do. 'Class' alone, as in a title such as *Class in Applied Linguistics*, presents a certain ambiguity. There is 'class' as in 'classroom' or group of students, which is very common in that part of applied linguistics that is devoted to second language acquisition and learning. And, as Sophie pointed out to me at a time when I was arguing for 'class' over 'social class', the former also has connotations of distinction and taste, if not in the world of Bourdieu (1984), then in the more prosaic world of expressions such as 'a touch of class' and 'he/she has no class'. In such circumstances, 'social class' seems to be a clearer term, which conveys immediately what the main focus of the book is.

And so, it is 'social class' that appears in the title of the book and that I use throughout the book. However, it should be noted that when I have needed an adjectival form, as in 'class position' or 'class thinking', I have used 'class' without the 'social' for stylistic reasons. Equally with style in mind, I have at times plumped for 'class' over 'social class' in places where I have used the latter term several times in rapid succession. In a sense, there is a kind of feel factor at work which makes me use 'class' instead of 'social class' on some occasions.

The other big term in the title of this book is **applied linguistics**. I will not rehearse here a discussion of this term, which appears in Block, Gray and Holborow (2012), to say nothing of the numerous articles, chapters, monographs and collections that have discussed in detail the exact meaning of the term and defined what it is that applied linguistics does (e.g. Simpson, 2011a). Chris Brumfit's (1991: 46) succinct definition of the field as 'the study of real world problems in which language is a central issue' has always seemed appropriate; it certainly is to the point. The same can be said of James Simpson's more recent definition, which appears in his introduction to *The Routledge Handbook of Applied Linguistics*:

> Applied linguistics is the academic field which connects knowledge about language to decision-making in the real world. Generally speaking, the role of applied linguistics is to make insights drawn from areas of language study relevant to such decision-making. In this sense applied linguistics mediates between theory and practice.
>
> *(Simpson, 2011: 1)*

The definition subsumes Brumfit's and adds to it a reference to the 'applied' part of the term, as Simpson sees a need for 'relevan[ce] to ... decision-making'. However, missing here is an explicit statement about how applied linguistics has always situated itself at the crossroads of a multitude of disciplines in the social sciences and the humanities. William Grabe sums up this characteristic of the field nicely in the following quote from his introduction to a predecessor to Simpson's collection, *The Oxford Handbook of Applied Linguistics* (Kaplan, 2002), as follows:

> By the close of the 1980s, a common trend was to view applied linguistics as incorporating many subfields (as indicated earlier) and as drawing on many supporting disciplines in addition to linguistics (e.g. psychology, education, anthropology, sociology, political science, policy studies and public adminis-tration, and English studies, including composition, rhetoric, and literary studies). Combined with these two foundations (subfields and supporting disciplines) was the view of applied linguistics as problem driven and real-world based rather than theory driven and discounted from real language use.
>
> *(Grabe, 2002: 4–5)*

In this book, I follow scholars like Brumfit, Simpson and Grabe and understand applied linguistics as a broad field that draws on multiple source disciplines in the social sciences and the humanities. From this perspective, I feel justified in making the implicit claim that 'sociolinguistics', 'bi/multilingualism research' and 'second language acquisition and learning', all of which are used as referents to bodies of research in this book, constitute subfields of a bigger entity called applied linguis-tics. Some may contest the kind of divisions I make here and indeed I often found it hard to write about the work of some authors under one heading and not another one. Suffice it to say that I am aware of the many problems in the choices I have made and that I have used such general terms as working categories which have allowed me a fair amount of wiggle room as I develop my discussion of how social class has and has not figured as a key construct in applied linguistics. For example in Chapter 4, entitled 'Social class in bi/multilingualism research', I frame English language learners around the world as bi/multilinguals and therefore include discussions of material which some might see as part of 'world Englishes'.

Another term I would like to clarify here is **erasure**, defined by Judith Irvine and Susan Gal as follows:

> Erasure is the process in which ideology, in simplifying the sociolinguist field, renders some persons or activities (or sociolinguistic phenomena) invisible. Facts that are inconsistent with the ideological scheme either go unnoticed or get explained away. So, for example, a social group or a language may be imagined as homogenous, its internal variation disregarded.
>
> *(Irvine and Gal, 2000: 38)*

Although not in the title of the book, erasure is a concept that underlies my chief motivation for writing it, that is, the substantial and sometimes complete erasure of social class in applied linguistics research due to the ways in which applied linguists frame their discussions of issues such as identity, inequality, disadvantage and exclusion. My main point here is that social class has for the most part been the object of erasure in applied linguistics when it should have a place as a key construct. I should add, however, that I attribute no bad faith to applied linguists who have paid no attention to social class in their work, not least because I can count myself among them, particularly in my early work on identity (e.g. Block, 2002, 2005). As I explain in the Epilogue of this book, there are all kinds of reasons why this has been the case, and these reasons have more to do with the dominant trends in which academics work than individual agency.

Scholarship issues

In this book, I cite a good number of sources from decades ago and in some cases, even from well over a century ago. Following the canons of English language prose at the time of writing, authors and translators producing their work before the 1970s tended to use generic masculine pronouns, which have all but disappeared from academic writing in the Anglophone world in recent years. When citing such work, I will leave quoted material intact, and as a consequence, the reader will see a lot of 'he' and 'his'. In all such cases, masculine pronouns should be understood to refer to all human beings.

A second issue, and one that also relates to older sources, is what to do about publishing years. The works of scholars such as Marx have come out in different editions not only over decades but over a century and a half. As a way of avoiding clutter in the main text, I have adopted the policy of providing the year in which the publication being cited actually appeared in print. However, in the references list of this book, I have provided the original year of publication so that the reader will have more accurate information and a sense of history about when ideas were first disseminated. Thus for the often cited *Capital: A Critique of Political Economy, Volume 1*, I write Marx, 1976, because this is the year of the Penguin edition I am citing. However, in the references list, I include the original publishing year (according to Marxist historians), writing: Marx, K. (1976 [1867]).

A third issue has to do with the citation of sources, again including Marx, that may be seen as falling outside the typical and expected ambit of applied linguistics. As I develop the main argument of this book, and in doing so draw on the work of a wide range of authors in well-established social sciences disciplines, I am all too aware that I am fair game for a criticism articulated by Kat Woolard some three decades ago:

> Sociolinguists have often borrowed social concepts in an ad hoc and unreflecting fashion, not usually considering critically the implicit theoretical frameworks that are imported wholesale along with such convenient constructs.
>
> *(Woolard 1985: 738)*

All I can say about this issue is that I have had a long time to think about what I have written here and I have relied on specialists in political economy to help me through some of the more complex material covered in Chapters 1 and 2 and specialists in applied linguistics in general to help me with the material covered in Chapters 3, 4 and 5. For some readers, there will be the odd clanger (I do hope that 'odd' is the appropriate adjective here, as opposed to 'frequent'!), but, on the whole, I think I have done justice to the work that I have cited.

Another potential problem arises with regard to the more recent sources I cite as the book's narrative unfolds. Most of these sources are very firmly based in the Anglophone world, with the United States and the UK being over-represented. However, I am not sure how things could have panned out differently as I have tended to follow what pitches up on my doorstep via the reading of 'international' journals and books and my attendance at 'international' conferences (all of which are far more parochially Anglophone – and often American and British domi-nated – than many would perhaps care to admit). But there is another issue related to sources, which is perhaps more important, and this is the relevance that researcher findings and arguments from one context have vis-à-vis another context.

Upon completion of this book, I realised that I had fallen into the age-old trap of often leaving to the side a basic fact about all research and argument, that is, that they are always rooted very much in the who, what, where, why, when and how of their making. I have but one defence in this case and it relates to what I see as an underlying (and often implicit) theme of this book, namely, that social class is a universal that applies to all places in the world in which there is an economy involving production and exchange of goods. And this means that social class is a fundamental way of understanding virtually all twenty-first-century societies, although, it should be noted, not ever in exactly the same way in any two societies.

As was the case with my part in the writing of *Neoliberalism and Applied Linguistics* (Block, Gray and Holborow, 2012), I have taken on the task of writing this book at a time when I am shifting my epistemological moorings, moving from a broadly poststructuralist approach to reality (what some would call a *postmodern* approach), such as that which I described in my publications on second language identities (e.g. Block, 2007a, 2007b, 2009, 2010a) to one that is more associated with critical realism (Bhaskar, 1998). I therefore find myself increasingly aligned with views such as the following, expressed by Harriet Bradley in her book *Fractured Identities*:

> Postmodern approaches sit uneasily with study of material factors such as inequality and deprivation, and those influenced by the ideas of post-modernism have tended to avoid these topics. Indeed, it is not quite clear whether such study can legitimately be carried out, certainly within existing frameworks, since postmodernism opposes itself to 'foundationalist' accounts of society (that is, accounts which seek to identify the bases of underlying structures upon which society is founded and which generate specific patterns of social behaviour), and to 'totalizing' narratives about society.
>
> *(Bradley, 1996: 3)*

I explain the reason for this transformation in my thinking in Block *et al.* (2012) and I will discuss this matter further in Chapters 1 and 2 of this book. What I will say here is simply that my move to a stance which is more aligned with critical realism does not mean that I have become a hard-core 'essentialist' or 'structuralist' (two words that have become serious epithets in applied linguistics in recent years); I have not. But my reading and rereading of the work of nineteenth-century scholars, for example Karl Marx and Friedrich Engels, and more recent ones such as Pierre Bourdieu and Nancy Fraser, has had a profound effect on my way of seeing the world and events going on in it.

Finally, I am aware that although I incorporate a great deal of material from many disciplines in this book, some readers will find themselves saying on occasion: 'Yes, but what about X?' I harbour no delusions about my ability to cover *everything* that has been written or said about social class both in the social sciences in general and in applied linguistics in particular. I see this book as I see everything I have ever published, as the momentary capture of my thinking on a topic, one which is partial, both as incomplete and as reflecting my personal biases.

Acknowledgements

I would like to thank the many people who have either directly or indirectly helped me develop my ideas about social class and its relevance to issues in applied linguistics or have simply helped me with the process of writing this book.

I thank Victoria Castillo Austrich and Adrià Block Castillo, my family, for putting up with me, particularly during the final stretch of the writing process.

Equally big thanks go to Louisa Semlyen and Sophie Jacques at Routledge for their unflagging support for this book over a timeframe that was far longer than I (or they!) had originally envisaged.

As regards help with the development of my ideas about social class, I especially thank John Gray and Marnie Holborow for their support over the past several years. Co-authors of *Neoliberalism and Applied Linguistics* and frequent co-panellists in recent years at conferences, they read through several drafts of the different chapters of this book (too often at short notice!). Their comments and influence are obviously at work in much of what I have written here, but equally obviously, any deficiencies in this book are down to me and me alone.

Carles Feixa, Hartmut Haberland, Adam Jaworski, Celeste Kinginger, John O'Regan, Siân Preece and Cathie Wallace also read and commented on two or more chapters and I am extremely grateful to them for having done so.

Over the years I have benefited greatly from informal conversations with Pepe Sanchez (AKA *el Schwarzenegger de bolsillo*) about neoliberalism and its effects.

I thank my colleagues in the *Cercle de Lingüística Aplicada* at the Universitat de Lleida, for discussions, both formal and informal, of some of the topics covered in this book: Lourdes Armengol, Josep Maria Cots, Angèls Llanes, Enric Llurda and Guzman Mancho. I also thank a group of Universitat de Lleida research students with whom I meet on a regular basis to discuss various issues related to research in the social sciences in general and applied linguistics in particular, including social class: Graham Evans, Lídia Gallego Balsà, Sònia Mas, Tanja Strecker and Julia Lettenstrom. And I am very grateful to my employer, the Institució Catalana de Recerca i Estudis Avançats (ICREA) for providing the work conditions that have made possible the completion of this book.

The germination of many of the ideas expressed here arose in sessions of the Marx Reading Group, which I attended in London over a period of three years – 2010–2012. I thank fellow members Melanie Cooke, John Gray, John O'Regan, Siân Preece and Cathie Wallace for conversations about all things related to Marxism taking place during that time.

Over the past several years I have also benefited from helpful conversations with fellow academics and their students, which have been possible because of invitations to give talks on social class in applied linguistics (as well as talks which included the discussion of social class in applied linguistics) at the following universities: University of Birmingham (April 2013); University of Bristol (December 2011); University of Cambridge (June 2010; March 2013); University College London (October 2011); Hong Kong Polytechnic University (May 2011); Institute of Education, University of London (October 2012); Kings College, London (November 2011); Universitat Oberta de Catalunya (September 2012); Oxford Brookes University (May 2012); Universitat Pompeu i Fabra (May 2012); University of Sheffield (October 2012); and University of Stockholm (November 2012).

Equally useful have been individual papers and my participation in panels at conferences, which include: the Association Internationale de Linguistique Appliquée (Beijing, August 2011); three American Association of Applied Linguistics conferences (Chicago, March 2011; Boston, March 2012; Dallas, March 2013); the British Association of Applied Linguistics conference (Newcastle, September 2009); the Cognitive-interactional and Socio-cultural Perspectives on L2 Learning, Teaching, and Assessment conference (London, July 2010); the Discourse and Transnational Identities conference (Hong Kong, May 2011); two English in Europe conferences (Sheffield, April 2012; Copenhagen, April 2013); the International Colloquium on Language Education – Questions of Identity, Teaching and Evaluation (Porto, November 2011); the International Symposium of Bilingualism (Oslo, July 2011); the Learning beyond the Classroom: Gendered and Ethnicised Constructions of Learner Identities conference (London, February 2010); the Multilingual and International Universities: Policies and Practices conference (Lleida, November 2011); the Plurilingualism and Pluriculturalism in a Globalised World: Which Pedagogy? conference (Paris, June 2010); and the Sociolinguistics Symposium (Berlin, August 2012). I am grateful to all of my co-panellists and anyone with whom I have discussed matters related to social class in applied linguistics for helping me think about the arguments developed in this book.

Finally, the 20th anniversary of my father's death came on 12 March 2013, as I was completing the manuscript of this book. Farris Frederick Block died far too young to witness the big events in my life that have taken place in the past 20 years, not least the completion of my PhD, just about all of my academic career and above all books like this one, which I think he just might have enjoyed reading. I think about him often and I dedicate this book to his memory.

David Block
Barcelona
May 2013

1

SETTING THE SCENE

Introduction: some quotes and a life story

> It is acceptable to show up sexism – as it is to show up racism – because to eliminate sexual and racial bias would pose no threat to the existing social order: capitalist society could thrive perfectly well without sexual discrimination and without racial discrimination. But it is not acceptable to show up classism, especially by objective linguistics analysis ... because capitalist society could not exist without discrimination between classes. Such work could, ultimately, threaten the order of society.
>
> (Halliday, 1990: 17)

> Class matters. Race and gender can be used as screens to deflect attention away from the harsh realities class politics exposes. Clearly, just when we should all be paying attention to class, using race and gender to understand and explain its new dimensions, society, even our government, says let's talk about race and racial injustice. It is impossible to talk meaningfully about ending racism without talking about class. Let us not be duped.
>
> (hooks, 2000: 7)

> Unfortunately, educational discourse on the 'left' has been awash in 'postmodern' platitudes that sublimate class and valorize uncritical and fetishized notions of 'difference' while marginalizing socialist alternatives to the social universe of capital.
>
> (McLaren and Scatamburlo-D'Annibale, 2004: 47)

These are three comments about the lack of class thinking in different domains of society and academia that I have come across in my reading over the past several years. The Michael Halliday quote is taken from his position paper on the present and future of applied linguistics, *circa* 1990. In this paper, Halliday comments on how social class is missing as a key construct in applied linguistics research on issues ranging from language policy to language teaching. He positions applied linguistics as complicit in the maintenance of the status quo of socioeconomic stratification worldwide because of the lack of attention to economics and ultimately class politics and practice in different societies around the world. Meanwhile, in a book published some 10 years after the appearance of Halliday's article, bell hooks writes about how, in American society at the end of the twentieth century, there was little or no discussion of inequality in the US in terms of class. A feminist social critic who has written extensively about race and gender in contemporary American society, hooks here criticises how the emphasis on these two key identity inscriptions can make activists complicit in the ongoing exploitation of the working and lower classes of American society, independently of the race and gender of the individuals and collectives concerned. In the third and final quote, critical educationalists Peter McLaren and Valerie Scatamburlo-D'Annibale argue that in educational research, those who position themselves as 'left' have abandoned socialist principles in favour of a 'postmodern' sensibility, which rightfully focuses on inequality in terms of race and gender, but which seems oblivious to the economic realities and class-based stratification existent in twenty-first-century societies around the world.

This book is, in its foundations, about social class as a construct and my argument throughout will be that it is a construct which is highly useful to those who wish to make sense of the social realities of twenty-first-century societies, and especially for those who wish to do so within the general realm of applied linguistics. In making this point, I will take a critical realist position, which I outline later in this chapter, a position aligning me with Helen Meskins Wood, who writes that '[t]he absence of explicit class "discourses" does not betoken the absence of class realities and their effects in shaping the life-conditions and consciousness of the people who come within their field of force' (Wood, 1998: 97). As hooks writes, 'class matters', and those who wish to comment on and act against inequality in contemporary societies would do well to embrace this reality. Nevertheless, it has not always been thus, that is, I have not always thought about society or even my own life in class terms. Indeed, growing up in the southeast Texas city of Houston in the 1960s, I do not recall ever being exposed to the notion of social class in an explicit manner, neither do I recall ever hearing anyone say that people should talk more about social class, as Halliday, hooks and McLaren and Scatamburlo-D'Annibale have suggested. In this sense, I suppose my upbringing was not unlike that of many white middle class Americans in the post-World War 2 era. As they moved into the 1960s, white middle class Americans were relatively optimistic about the future and if they did take note of inequality in the US, they tended to put it down to the deficiencies in the character of those who had not been successful.

However, as the decade unfolded white Americans of a more liberal mindset, like my parents, also showed an awareness of the serious racial divide in America between African Americans and whites. I recall how as I grew up during the 1960s (I was four when the decade began and 14 when it ended), the civil rights movement dominated the media and had an effect on my emergent views about right and wrong, and politics in general. And like so many Americans then (and to this day), I tended to see issues of inequality and difference exclusively in terms of race and ethnicity (gender would be added as an important site of inequality and difference as the decade progressed). Social class, as a way of understanding how people lived, was seldom if ever invoked as *social class*, and it tended to appear indirectly in expressions like 'people like us' and 'people like that' rather than through the kind of indicators I shall discuss in detail in Chapter 2 of this book.

The middle class neighbourhood in which I lived from the age of seven was a small development of about 120 homes, nestled between one of Houston's ubiquitous bayous and the University of Houston campus, just south of downtown Houston. It was located relatively far from schools, which meant that my educational options could go in any of three directions. For elementary school, I was sent south of where I lived. At the time, I probably took for granted that everyone in the school was white, and I did not notice that some of my classmates were, like me, from middle class families and others, those who lived in the area immediately surrounding the school, were working class. I also did not notice that a good proportion of the middle class children were, unlike me, Jewish. This may have been because I was raised in a conscientiously agnostic household in which religion was seldom discussed. During my elementary school years, class differences were constantly right in front of my eyes, for example in the streaming of students (middle class kids tended to dominate the top set) and above all, in the different ways that we lived our lives away from school.

As regards the last point, I recall that when one Saturday I went to visit a classmate, I noticed that his house was much smaller than the one I lived in, that it was far more spartanly furnished than the one I lived in and that the food offered to me at lunchtime, while abundant, was of a lower quality (e.g. beef with a great deal of fat on it) than that which I normally ate in my house. I noticed that these people spoke an English that would have been corrected in my house (e.g. frequent use of ain't and double modals) and, above all, that there was racist language about African American people, which would not have been allowed by my liberal parents. The boy's father worked in construction and when I met him, I noticed how he was physically much more imposing than my own father and how he wore blue jeans and a white t-shirt, not the normal work attire of the public relations officer of a university.

On another occasion, I visited another classmate's home, this time for the birthday party of a girl who lived in an upper middle class area located about a mile from the school. This area was, at the time, where a good proportion of Houston's Jewish community lived because their entry into certain affluent areas in the western part of the city was limited by the systemic anti-Semitism of that time. I recall noticing during my visit that my classmate's home was far larger than the one in which I lived, that the furnishings seemed far more ornate and that both parents were well dressed and spoke in a very educated manner. As in the first case, I was, without realising it at the time, once again in contact with subtle social class markers, such as education, housing, food, dress, language and so on. I certainly noticed these differences, which explains why I can remember them to this day; however, I had no clear way to understand them as 'socioeconomic stratification' or even 'social class'.

In coming years, 'white flight' came into my life. In its earliest usage, 'white flight' was a term used to describe the large-scale migration taking place in the 1950s and 1960s of white Americans (Americans of European ancestry) from inner city neighbourhoods experiencing an influx of African American residents, to racially homogeneous (white) suburban neighbourhoods, away from the inner city.[1] It occurred rapidly in South Houston in the 1960s as a huge section of the city changed demographically from being predominately white to being predominately African American. In my elementary school, the middle class white children (including the majority of the more upper middle class Jewish children) began to disappear, although I do not recall being aware at the time that it was primarily the middle class children or wealthier Jewish children who were leaving the school. In autumn 1967 I began the sixth grade, my last year of elementary school. By this time my class was roughly 50 per cent African American and 50 per cent white, and my teacher was African American. And the vast majority of both the African American children and the white children now lived in the area immediately surrounding the school and were from families with parents holding blue collar jobs. This was confirmed very clearly when I spent a day with one of my African American classmates. I had a very similar experience to the one with my white classmate several years earlier in that the house, the family environment, the food and the language spoken (except for the racist language, which in this case was absent) were all very similar, *and* it should be added, different from what I would have experienced at home. However, given thinking in vogue at the time (1967), I probably attributed these differences to race and not social class.

Junior high school, composed of three grades for children 12–15 years of age, meant going to a new school. It also meant that I was in another type of classed environment, but again without a means of understanding my life in terms of social class. The school was located in a traditional southeast Houston working class neighbourhood where there were good number children from Irish, Italian and other European backgrounds mixed with a rapidly growing Latino population from Mexico. Here I became conscious of the clearly articulated manifestations of tough working class masculinities, which were more often than not about ways of dress, walking and talking and activities like smoking cigarettes, all in combination with a general lack of interest in school activities. At times, these masculinities led to confrontations between groups and during my time at the school, I witnessed several fights involving 'Irish' and 'Mexican' boys (as they would have been labelled at the time). However, I was not generally in direct contact with such goings on as the school's streaming policy meant that I was placed in classes with students who were more academically oriented (although unlike my elementary school, this school had a very low proportion of middle class students).

The third stage of my schooling took place in two schools, one attended in 10th and 12th grade, in which I was a member of a miniscule white minority (when

I graduated in 1974, I was one of five white students among a student body of some 2,000 African American students), and the other, which I attended in the 11th grade, the Houston High School of the Performing and Visual Arts, where the racial and ethnic makeup of the students body was proportional to the demographics of Houston at the time. The latter was far more of a middle class school than any other that I had attended, while the predominantly African American school was similar in some ways to my junior high school in that there were very few middle class children and I was streamed into classes with other academically oriented students, which, in this case, meant just about all of the middle class students who attended the school. It was quite clear that my classmates were members of what amounted to a separate community within the school when it came to their dedication to their studies and their participation in extracurricular activities (e.g. cheerleading, academic clubs, the school newspaper). Most of them had parents working in the professions and at home there was the expectation that they would attend a good university on finishing high school.

Meanwhile, the vast majority of students in the school were from working class households struggling to retain this class position or from poorer households in which a single parent (usually a mother) was often unemployed and received some form of assistance from the government. Here once again I encountered working class toughness in all of its manifestations and there was often a violent tension just under the surface as ongoing school events unfolded. And although I was a marginalised from most of this tension by virtue of my skin colour and my attendance in high stream classes, I was on occasion reminded of the precariousness of the life conditions of a good number of my schoolmates. For example, I witnessed a fair number of fights among students (boys and girls) during breaks or after school. And on other occasions, I would hear about shocking events taking place away from school, such as the time I learned that one of my classmates in Homeroom[2] would no longer be coming to school because the previous evening he had been shot and killed while attempting to rob a convenience store.[3]

Throughout these school years, I was also experiencing social class in my immediate friendship and family circles. My neighbourhood-based friends were all white males from similar middle class backgrounds and as we moved into adolescence we had a fair few things in common, even if we all went to different high schools. During these years, drug use and musical tastes converged and we all were big fans of various strands of British rock music. Confirming the notion that identity is as much about disaffiliation as it is about affiliation and that one often engages in the 'practice of defining one's identity through a contrast with a stigmatised other' (Sayer, 2005: 54), my friends and I distinguished ourselves clearly from white working class culture which in many parts of the city was associated with country music (which we all despised), cowboy-style dress (a sartorial abomination for us), short hair (at a time when our long hair indexed 'coolness') and reactionary (i.e. which we would have called 'redneck'[4]) lifestyles (which we rejected outright).[5] Other friends I made through my school attendance, primarily African American males, were not interested in British rock music, but they did affiliate to other aspects of my lifestyle, such as smoking marijuana, playing basketball and an identification with inner city life, including African American culture. And they certainly shared my wholesale rejection of country music, cowboy-style dress and redneck culture, all associated with the white working class (and indeed, whites of all class positions). However, it should be noted that their social class position, which was generally middle class or upper working class (e.g. my best friend's father and mother worked as a Houston city police officer and a part-time housekeeper, respectively), was not salient to me as an identity marker, while their race certainly was, racial consciousness being what it was in the US in the early 1970s.

In my immediate family environment, my siblings and I distinguished ourselves from redneck white working class culture when we had contact with our father's considerable extended family in East Texas.[6] Most of these relatives worked in the many oil refineries that line the southernmost part of the Louisiana–Texas border, and there was very much the sense that these jobs would pass from generation to generation. Indeed, my father was a member of the small minority of East Texans of his generation who managed to get a university education, and consequently a ticket out of the area to another type of professional and personal life. For big events like Thanksgiving, Christmas and the 4th of July, my father was a big fan of taking us to see as many members of his family as possible and these visits were sometimes the source of great conflict in our family. The basic problem was that my siblings and I were not interested in these contacts with the extended family and we did not want to engage with *their* 'redneck' values and country western lifestyle, which for us stood in stark contrast with *our* urban sophistication and liberalism. I write these words with no sense of pride, so many years later, but I feel I should include them in this book-opening narrative as they form a part of how social class has always been part of my life. Indeed, not only was my life inflected with social class, but I embodied a great deal of class prejudice. And while among many of my friends and my siblings there was a generally held belief that racism was unacceptable and a sign of ignorance and backwardness, class prejudice was perfectly acceptable, although this latter position was usually effective by default rather than in a conscious manner. Interestingly enough, this sentiment seems to be shared and accepted by far too many people working in the social sciences today, again more by default than consciously, as I shall argue in the final chapter of this book.

In 1974 I finished high school and went to study at the University of Texas in Austin. There I came into contact with a very different environment, one that was predominantly (and indeed, overwhelmingly) white, and, although I did not think about it at the time, very middle class. My own middle class *habitus*, that is 'my systems of durable, transposable [middle class] *dispositions*, ... predisposed to function as ... principles of generation and structuring of practices and representations' (Bourdieu, 1977a: 72, emphasis in original), meant that I should have taken to the University of Texas like a fish to water, that I should have had a well-developed 'feel for the game' (Bourdieu, 1990: 66). However, years of living in what we might call an African American-inflected environment, and one in which I was often immersed in working class and economically poor African American culture (such as when I played basketball in inner city parks or when I went to a local supermarket), meant that I found most of my white classmates culturally distant. This may seem an odd way to describe matters given that I was middle class and I was white, but it is how I remember feeling at the time. Indeed, so great was my rejection of this predominantly white and middle class environment, that after one year in Austin, I decided to return to Houston, and the familiarity of the inner city life I had grown up with, to finish my studies.

In Houston for what were to be the last three years of my life as a full-time resident in the US, I continued to see day-to-day existence through the prism of race, ethnicity and gender and I questioned neither my own middle class existence nor indeed the social class positions – middle class, working class, poor – of my fellow students at the University of Houston. However, I was restless, and I had a sense that I wanted a change in my life, although I do not recall ever formulating any kind of plan to address my restlessness. When I finished a BA in history in August 1978, I left the US for Europe on an unplanned sojourn that was supposed to last a few months, up to one year at the most, but which has not ended to this day. At the time, I was like so many other white middle class liberal Americans, strongly against racism and sexism but oblivious to my own passive class prejudice which mostly manifested itself in my embrace of the invisibility of my middle class habitus and class position in American society. I did not even consider how being middle class afforded me the disposition to travel and the mobility which made it possible for me to move across an ocean to foreign lands where people behaved in very different (and un-American) ways and spoke a lot of different languages.

After having lived a few months in Paris in autumn 1978, I moved to Barcelona and soon after began to work as an English teacher.[7] Over the years I moved up the professional ladder of English language teaching and settled into a middle class existence that was fairly firmly embedded in Catalan society and culture. My world became deracialised to a great extent, given that I was surrounded almost exclusively by white (European) people. Most of the people I associated with were politically on the left, a good proportion having been members of the Catalan Communist party, the *Partit Socialista Unificat de Catalunya* (or PSUC). And I developed over the years a keen sense of how certain parts of the city were associated with particular types of people and corresponding class-inflected behaviour and ways of life. Thus if one mentioned *Pedralbes* or *Bonanova*, two areas in the more elevated, western part of the city, one immediately thought of the upper middle classes of the city. If one mentioned *Clot* or *Sants*, in the lower parts of the city, the connotations were distinctly working class. And the *Eixample*, that vast area of square blocks that serves as the central axis of the city, meant, for the most part, a mix of working class and middle class people, with the latter being dominant. However, despite these realities and common sense constructions of them, I seldom if ever found myself in conversations in which social class was cited explicitly.[8]

Indeed, my awakening as regards social class came during the 16 years that I lived in London, from 1996 to 2012. It is often said that the British are obsessed with social class, the implication being (1) that other nations and their peoples do not share such an obsession with social class and (2) that social class is perhaps no longer useful as a construct with which we can understand increasingly globalised twenty-first-century societies. While I might be persuaded to accept the first of these two notions, one of the main aims of this book is to argue that the second one is highly problematic and I shall suggest that social class should be reconfigured and not abandoned as a construct with which we can understand societies and by extension language practices. Nevertheless, I would say that until fairly recently (up until the end of the last century), social class appeared to be in decline as a validated construct in much social sciences and educational research in Britain, the Anglophone countries in general and indeed, around the world. The embrace of so-called 'identity politics' in contemporary society, the rise of neoliberalism and the individualistic culture that it engendered, and the move in the social sciences and education to poststructuralist epistemological stances, have all been factors which have helped to precipitate a general loss of interest in social class. This trend, however, shows signs of reversal if one is to judge by recent books published in Britain by journalists (e.g. Collins, 2004; Jones, 2012; Mount, 2004; Toynbee, 2003) as well as academics in a wide range of disciplines (e.g. Bennett *et al.*, 2009; Bottero, 2005; Crompton, 2008; Dorling, 2011; Sayer, 2005; Skeggs, 2004; Vincent and Ball, 2006). Matters are not too different on the other side of the Atlantic, in the US, with journalists (e.g. Brooks, 2001; Ehrenreich, 2001; Ehrenreich and Hochschild, 2003) adding their voices to those of academics from a wide range of disciplines (e.g. Benn Michaels, 2006; Ebert and Zavarzadeh, 2008; hooks, 2000; Lareau, 2011; Murray, 2012; Ortner, 2006). Elsewhere there is an increasing amount of interest in social class, both from an individual country perspective, ranging from Japan (Hashimoto, 2003; Ishida and Slater, 2010) to Spain (Navarro, 2006; Subirats, 2012) and France (Bosc, 2008; Bouzou, 2011), and from a regional perspective, ranging from Latin America (Gootenberg and Reygadas, 2010; Parker and Walker, 2013) to the Middle East (Peterson, 2011).

Of course, we might ask ourselves why there has been this renewed interest in social class. However, it is always difficult to answer such questions, especially because trends in what interests groups like journalists and academics are never uniform as regards depth and intensity (different people become part of trends with varying degrees of commitment), extension (it will never be the case that everyone in a particular sector or domain follows the trend) and time (different people and groups may come on board at different times.). Still, it is worth examining in detail some factors that help to explain why social class is once again present in discussions and debates taking place in the social sciences.

The rise of neoliberalism and its consequences

The main reason why many social scientists are returning to social class as a useful contract is the collective realisation that we are living in times – neoliberal times – in which societies are becoming more socioeconomically stratified instead of less so. No one who reads a newspaper, or goes online or watches television on a day-to-day basis can escape the seemingly endless flow of bad news about debt, bailouts and, of course, the ubiquitous 'markets', which seem to have the magical capacity to make us feel terrified about what lies ahead tomorrow, next week or next month. In short, we have moved from the heady times of celebratory globalisation of the 1990s and the early part of this century, to the hard-core realities which that globalisation has bequeathed. In his timely and oft-cited book, *A Brief History of Neoliberalism*, David Harvey defines neoliberalism as follows:

> Neoliberalism is in the first instance a theory of political economic practices that proposes that human well-being can best be advanced by liberating individual entrepreneurial freedoms and skills within an institutional framework characterized by strong private property rights, free markets and free trade. The role of the state is to create and preserve an institutional framework appropriate to such practices. The state has to guarantee, for example, the quality and integrity of money. It must also set up those military, defence, police and legal structures and functions required to secure private property rights and to guarantee, by force if need be, the proper functioning of markets. Furthermore, if markets do not exist (in areas such as land, water, education, health care, social security, or environmental pollution) then they must be created, by state action if necessary. But beyond these tasks the state should not venture. State interventions in markets (once created) must be kept to a bare minimum because, according to the theory, the state cannot possibly possess enough information to second-guess market signals (prices) and because powerful interest groups will inevitably distort and bias state interventions (particularly in democracies) for their own benefit.
>
> *(Harvey, 2005: 2)*

There is a lot going on in this definition that is worthy of mention. First, Harvey makes the connection between neoliberalism as economic doxa[9] and the rise of discourses around the individual that have become so pervasive around the world. As Anthony Elliott and Charles Lemert (2006: 15) put it: '[f]rom Singapore to Tokyo, from Seoul to Sydney, the individualist creed of the new individualism features significantly in the private and public lives of its citizens.' Margaret Thatcher's infamous words – ' … who is society? There is no such thing! There are individual men and women and there are families. … ' – produced during an interview published in *Women's Own* (no. 987, September 23) in 1987 are often cited in the UK as marking a before and after in British society. Thatcher's brief foray into sociology[10] occurred against the backdrop of the liberalisation of the British economy from the mid-1980s onwards and they index the decline of social class (or better said, the decline of class thinking) in public discourses in Britain. Her comment represents the move away from talk about collectivist principles, a full and head-on rejection of Marx's statement in *Die Grundrisse* that '[s]ociety does not consist of individuals, but expresses the sum of interrelations, the relations within which these individuals stand' (Marx, 1973: 265). In her contradiction of

Marx, Thatcher fully embraces individualisation, as a process through which individualism and an individualistic culture arise. Individualisation is defined by Ulrich Beck as follows:

> Individualization … means that each person's biography is removed from given determinations and placed in his or her own hands, open and dependent on decisions. The proportion of life opportunities which are fundamentally closed to decision-making is decreasing and the proportion of biography which is open and must be constructed personally is increasing.
>
> *(Beck, 1992: 135)*

The second noteworthy feature of Harvey's definition is the way that it treats the role of the state in a neoliberal regime in a way that is entirely in conflict with right-wing political discourses (also emanating far too often from supposedly left-wing parties in Europe and North America), which tend to deride the state as parasitic on individual activity and detrimental to the development of individual freedom. For the political right, '[s]tate interventions in markets … must be kept to a bare minimum' (Harvey 2005: 2), but the expectation is that the state will 'guarantee … the quality and integrity of money' and therefore will 'set up those military, defence, police and legal structures and functions required to secure private property rights and to guarantee, by force if need be, the proper functioning of markets' (Harvey 2005: 2).

Elsewhere, Loïc Wacquant adopts a 'thick conception of neoliberalism', writing the following about the state in neoliberal regimes:

> [T]he state actively *re-regulates* – rather than 'deregulates' – the economy in favour of corporations … and engages in extensive 'corrective' and 'constructive' measures to support and extend markets … for firms, products and workers alike. On the social front, government programmes thrust onerous obligations onto welfare recipients and aggressively seek to redress their behaviour, reform their morals, and orient their life choices through a mix of cultural indoctrination, bureaucratic oversight and material suasion … , turning social support into a vector of discipline and the right to personal development into an obligation to work at precarious jobs.
>
> *(Wacquant, 2012: 72)*

Other critics of neoliberalism (e.g. Callinicos, 2010; Crouch, 2011; Žižek, 2009) have made a similar point about the way in which the state generally sides with the interests of big capital. Of course Marx and Engels arrived at this conclusion long ago, writing in *The German Ideology* about how the accumulation of private property by the bourgeoisie in capitalist societies means that 'the state has become a separate entity, beside and outside civil society' and that it is 'nothing more than the form of organisation which the bourgeoisie necessarily adopt both for internal and external purposes, for the mutual guarantee of their property and interests'

(Marx and Engels, 1998: 99). This means, in short, that 'the state is the form in which individuals of a ruling class assert their common interests, and in which the whole civil society of an epoch is epitomised' (Marx and Engels, 1998: 99). The last clause about how a society is 'epitomised' may be linked to what Marx and Engels wrote earlier in the same treatise about how material dominance (possession of property and control over the means of production) is inextricably linked to, and indeed generates, ideational and ideological dominance, that is the power to create and to impose what is right and what is wrong, what is legitimate and what is not, and ultimately how history is told:

> The ideas of the ruling class are in every epoch the ruling ideas, i.e., the class which is the ruling *material* force of society, is at the same time the ruling *intellectual* force. The class which has the means of material production at its disposal, has control at the same time over the means of mental production, so that thereby, generally speaking, the ideas of those who lack the means of mental production are subject to it. The ruling ideas are nothing more than the ideal expression of the dominant material relationships, the dominant material relationships grasped as ideas; hence of the relationships which make the one class the ruling one, therefore the ideas of its dominance.
>
> *(Marx and Engels, 1998: 67)*

With the incessant propagation of individualism and the circulation of public discourses in favour of neoliberal policy and practice, it is little wonder that in recent years people around the world have been living their lives according to the acronym TINA (there is no alternative). Indeed, even in the current economic crisis, dating from 2007 to present (mid-2013), one is still constantly told that there is no alternative to economic policies that transfer private and public money and resources to banks that have precipitated the worse worldwide economic crisis since the depression of the 1930s (Crouch, 2011). And while neoliberalism has only become a term of common parlance in the lay/public realms in recent years, it has been around as the focus of attention among many in the social sciences for quite some time now. In one of his later publications, *The Social Structures of the Economy* (2005), Bourdieu sums up matters well:

> Neoliberal economics, the logic of which is tending today to win out throughout the world thanks to international bodies like the World Bank or the International Monetary Fund and the governments to whom they, directly or indirectly, dictate their principles of 'governance', owes a certain number of its allegedly universal characteristics to the fact that it is immersed or embedded in a particular society, that is to say, rooted in a system of beliefs and values, an ethos and a moral view of the world, in short, an *economic common sense*, linked, as such, to the social and cognitive structures of a particular social order.
>
> *(Bourdieu, 2005: 10, emphasis in original)*

More recently, Slavoj Žižek makes a similar point about the imposition of 'economic common sense' and adds that this imposition continues despite the fact that neoliberalism has been now been greatly discredited by recent events, that is, by the current economic crisis:

> [T]o put it in old-fashioned Marxist terms, the main task of the ruling ideology in the present crisis is to impose a narrative that will not put the blame for the meltdown on the global capitalist system as such, but on its deviations (overly lax legal regulations, the corruption of financial institutions, and so on).
>
> *(Žižek, 2009: 19)*[11]

Indeed, not only do the ruling classes put the blame for the current economic crisis on policies that did not go far enough in the liberalisation of the economy or on a lack of vigilance on the part of institutions (which through their polices they made possible), they also refuse to address their responsibility for the rise in inequality and disadvantage, both internationally and intranationally. And while the general public, and indeed most academics as well, do not understand everything that is going on at the highest levels of the world economy, they do know what they see and live in their homes and their neighbourhoods. And it is the observation of rising inequality and disadvantage that has led many social scientists back to social class as an important lens through which to view contemporary societies and their ongoing evolution.

Globalisation and social class

In a chapter in Block, Gray and Holborow (2012), I chart how my personal engagement with neoliberalism as a phenomenon in need of analysis has led me to grant more space and emphasis to economic matters when thinking about globalisation and how it has also led me to situate social class at the centre of any discussion about identity in which I participate. Changing my way of thinking about globalisation goes somewhat against dominant trends in applied linguistics, where researchers and theorists have tended to frame language-related phenomena associated with globalisation almost exclusively in terms of the social and the cultural. According to this view, globalisation is a diverse, ongoing and ever evolving process, and therefore it cannot be discussed as if it were a well-defined epoch in history. It is a process that involves the ever increasing extension and intensification of the interconnectedness of socially, culturally and historically situated language-related phenomena taking place across a range of time- and space-related scales. In applied linguistics, there has been a near wholesale adoption of the notion of time–space compression: on the one hand, time–space compression is about how activities and events that previously took long periods to carry out and unfold now occur in shorter periods of time, often in seconds or even a fraction of a second (Castells, 1996; Giddens, 2000; Harvey, 1989); on the other hand, it is about how spatial scales, ranging from the household up to the global, are today interrelated to a degree that is unprecedented in history. Ultimately, what happens on a global scale both shapes and is shaped by what happens at more local levels and this recursive shaping can occur within very small timescales (Held *et al.*, 1999).

Some globalisation theorists and researchers (e.g. Held and McGrew, 2007) have framed their discussions of globalisation around three general, differentiable positions: globalists, sceptics and transformationalists. For globalists, we are without a doubt living in an age like no other in the past. On the back of (or simply via) advances in information technology, which have led to an increasingly interconnected world, global capitalism, governance and culture have replaced nation-state-based and more local institutions as those entities that have the most impact on the lives of individuals and collectives. Globalisation has, in short, upset structures, hierarchies and ways of life that only a few decades ago seemed relatively stable.

A contrasting view is held by sceptics, who believe that we are simply living in an age of capitalism by updated and more efficient means (above all, recent developments in information technology), which in general is understood to mean that the accumulation and concentration of financial, political and cultural capital in the hands of nation-states and elites within them continues. Nevertheless, sceptics would also recognise something of Marx's logic of capitalism, whereby larger and larger corporations and conglomerates form and ultimately have a great deal of influence over how political and other forms of social activity are carried out (Baran and Sweezy, 1966).

Held and McGrew's third and final position towards globalisation is called transformationalist. For those subscribing to this view (e.g. Castells, 1996; Giddens, 2000), we are living in an age of great upheaval and change with unprecedented levels of interconnectedness among nation-states, local economies and cultures, wrought to a great extent – although not exclusively – by technological developments. The increasing interconnectedness has led to great transformations across different aspects of our day-to-day lives (e.g. at the political, financial, cultural and environmental levels) and a balance between fragmentation and centrifugal development, on the one hand, and integration and centripetal development, on the other.

In my work over the years, I have generally identified myself with the transformationalist view. Who would not, given its apparent moderation and balance in comparison to the more extremist globalist and sceptic views? However, in recent years I have come round to a more sceptical view, one based more in political economy than in cultural studies. Proponents of such a view include Giovanni Arrighi (2010) and Immanuel Wallerstein (2004), working within a World Systems Theory framework,[12] and David Harvey and Alex Callincos (the first a geographer, the second a philosopher, but both Marxists), who have written critical accounts of the state of global economics in recent years. What all of these authors have in common is that they tend to frame globalisation as part of the rise and spread of capitalism in industrialised and post-industrial societies.[13] This view is summed up well by Wallerstein as follows:

> This term [globalisation] was invented in the 1980s. It is usually thought to refer to a reconfiguration of the world-economy that has only recently come into existence, in which pressures on all governments to open their frontiers to the free movement of goods and capital is unusually strong. This is the result, it is argued, of technological advances, especially in the field of informatics. The term is as much a prescription as a description. For world systems analysts, what is described as something new (relatively open frontiers) has in fact been a cyclical occurrence throughout the history of the modern world system.
>
> *(Wallerstein, 2004: 9)*

Wallerstein's 'harder' view of the world is better able to take on the unevenness in globalisation, both in terms of the relative globalisation or lack of globalisation in different parts of the world and the kind of economic stratification that exists in the world today, both internationally and intranationally. Such phenomena are often glossed over in applied linguistics via class erasure (i.e. negligible or no mention of social class in contemporary societies) coupled with a certain infatuation with new technologies and pop culture to which global élites have the most ready access. As argued in Block *et al.* (2012), the neoliberal times in which we live require a rethink as regards the kinds of phenomenon that we research and above all the kinds of reading that we do in preparation for our research. And this thought serves as a transition to the discussion of political economy and critical realism, which follows.

Political economy and critical realism

Political economy is understood here as an area of inquiry and thought with roots in a Marxist critique of classical economics and society in general. It focuses on and analyses the relationship between the individual and society and between the market and the state, and it seeks to understand how social institutions, their activities and capitalism interrelate. Thinking and writing within a political economy frame means working in an interdisciplinary manner, drawing on work in human geography, sociology, political theory, anthropology and cultural studies. The focus is on the interrelatedness of political and economic processes and phenomena such as aggregate economic activity, resource allocation, capital accumulation, income inequality, globalisation and imperial power (Block *et al.*, 2012).

Part and parcel of any move to adopt political economy as a frame for research and discussion in applied linguists is the belief that the latter should be situated more firmly within the social sciences and that the social sciences should be at the centre of discussions of issues in applied linguistics. Thus if a decade ago, I called for a 'social turn in second language acquisition' (Block, 2003), which in effect meant taking a more sociolinguistically informed and grounded approach to the study of second language acquisition, I would now call for a social turn in applied linguistics as a whole, which means taking a social sciences perspective in '[t]he theoretical and empirical investigation of real-world problems in which language is the central issue' (Brumfit, 1991: 46). Such an approach means including in one's work substantial and sustained discussions of key constructs and frameworks based on readings in the social sciences. This, as opposed to just a passing mention and/or a brief gloss of these key constructs and frameworks before moving onto research (which is generally what happens in applied linguistics books that purport to be based on work in the social sciences and political economy specifically). So, while high-powered edited collections such as *Words, Worlds and Material Girls* (McElhinny, 2007), *Language and Late Capitalism* (Duchêne and Heller, 2013) and *Multilingualism and the Periphery* (Pietikainen and Kelly-Holmes, 2013) certainly situate economic issues at the centre of sociolinguistics, there is often little in the way of in-depth discussion of terms such as 'neoliberalism', 'late capitalism', 'stratification' and 'social class'. However, there are exceptions, as shown by Monica Heller's contribution to Pietikainen and Kelly-Holmes (2013), in which she explains how neoliberalism is not a new phenomenon and how it shapes current realities:

> [O]ur contemporary era is characterized more by continuity than by rupture, albeit in ways which destabilise our taken for granted assumptions about language, identity, culture, nation, and state. The expansion of capitalism set in motion around the sixteenth century is still the central feature of our political economy; however, the late twentieth century and the early twenty-first constitute a moment of reorganisation of the relationship between capital and governance, between the economic and the political. National markets and industrial products are insufficient to allow for continued expansion, and for the increasing saturation of markets. The result has been a re-positioning of the state, from what we have known as the welfare to what we call the neoliberal one, that is, one in which the state is clearer about its role in the support of global expansion of capitalism, and in which, as a result, political discourses are subordinated to economic ones.
>
> *(Heller, 2013: 21)*

Of course one could argue that to do what I propose here – that is, engage in substantial and sustained discussions of key constructs and frameworks – is to get bogged down in theoretical discussions that would distract readers from the main topics of such books, which are issues in language policy and practices. However, I would argue that the kind of macro-level phenomena that make their way into theoretical discussions are integral to discussions of language policy and practices and therefore deserve and need to be explicitly and fully developed in what is written about these issues.

If we are going to base our thinking in political economy and take on neoliberalism as the dominant discourse and set of practices of our times and we are also as a result going to try to bring economics back onto our understanding of globalisation, then we might also have to rethink how we position ourselves according to two key metaphysical dimensions at the heart of our existence as scholars and researchers. I refer to ontology – the nature of being and existence (our 'actual reality', what it is we are studying, what it is we are writing about) – and epistemology – which is about the origin, the nature, and limits of human knowledge and the methods we adopt to obtain this knowledge (how do we know what we know and how do we come to know what we know?).

In my work over the years, I have explained what I mean by 'I am a poststructuralist' or 'I am taking a poststructuralist position' by saying that a poststructuralist is someone who engages with the researched world not with the intention of discovering universal, invariant covering laws that determine and govern all levels of human life, but as someone who is concerned with issues such as:

1 the crisis of representation and associated instability of meaning;
2 the absence of secure foundations for knowledge;
3 the analytic centrality of language, discourses and texts; and
4 the inappropriateness of the Enlightenment assumption of the rational autonomous subject and a counter, contrasting concentration on the ways in which individuals are constituted as subjects.

(Smart, 1999: 38)

In his discussions of epistemology in the social sciences, Roy Bhaskar (2002: 205–6) has identified such thinking as 'postmodern' and he has elaborated a list of issues of concern longer than Smart's, making clear that he finds such thinking highly problematic. Bhaskar's list of postmodern issues includes:

- An emphasis on difference, relativity and pluralism.
- An accentuation on the emphasis of language characteristic to twentieth-century philosophy.
- Scepticism about or denial of the need to say anything about the world.
- The impossibility of giving better or worse grounds for a belief, action (including speech action) or practice.
- Life is viewed as a pastiche, not a totality; an assemblage not a whole.
- The incapacity to sustain an account of change as rational; and hence to topicalise the phenomenon of (individual; collective; global) self-emancipation.
- Heightened reflexivity, without, however, a clear conception of self – hence no self-reflexivity or capacity to situate itself.
- The genesis of a politics or more generally culture, of identity and difference thematising the specificity of particular group interests, and indeed individual ones too, without however sustaining the idea of essential unity of all human (or more generally just all) beings – that is difference and identity without unity and universality.

I am not sure how or if I have subscribed in the past to every single item in these two lists, which of course overlap considerably. However, I have certainly been a *de facto* poststructuralist/postmodernist, or a poststructuralist/postmodernist by default, in that I have emphasised difference, relativity and pluralism; put identity as pastiche at the centre of what I do; tended to prime individual agency over social structure; portrayed reality as discursively constructed (with language and culture being an integral part of this view); avoided making pronouncements about how the world 'really is'; and so on.

However, Bhaskar raises issues and makes points that I now find interesting and worthy of serious engagement. First, he notes how in discussions of epistemology, there is tendency for those who work according to what he calls a hermeneutic perspective (but I would call an interpretivist or social constructivist perspective) to construct very general and unhelpful dichotomies. Indeed, if I think about debates in which I have participated or which I have witnessed over the years, I see that there is often a simplistic view of the world along the lines of positivists vs. constructivists. The divide looks as shown in Table 1.1.

In his work, Bhaskar has attempted to steer a course through these Manichean positions. About the positivist tradition, he writes that it is 'correct to stress that there are causal laws, generalities, at work in social life ... [and] to insist ... that these laws *may* be opaque to the agents' spontaneous understanding' (Bhaskar, 1998: 21). By contrast, Bhaskar believes that the positivist tradition gets matters wrong when it reduces these laws to empirical regularities, that is, the systematic co-presence of natural and social phenomena and states. For example, high crime rates and city size may be found to coincide, and the assumption may be made that this coincidence is due to a law of nature. However, there may be many other factors at work, such as the relative poverty of a city or the type of policing that takes place and the resultant level of complexity acts against attempts to impose interpretations based on regularities. For this reason, Bhaskar writes that the human sciences (i.e. the social sciences) are about 'the direct study of phenomena that only ever manifest themselves in open systems [in which] invariant empirical regularities do not obtain' (Bhaskar, 1998: 45) and which are 'characterised by both a plurality and multiplicity of causes' (Bhaskar, 1998: 87). And all of this makes prediction in its purest form, a hallmark of positivist research, impossible. In addition, as Bhaskar argues,

TABLE 1.1 Two general (and oversimplified) approaches to epistemology in the social sciences

Positivism	Interpretivism/constructivism
Physical world/nature as model	Social world as model
Quantitative	Qualitative
Cognitive	Social, cultural, historical
Causal explanation	Interpretive understanding
Nomothetic science	Ideographic inquiry
Repeatable	Unique
Deterministic structure	Individual agency
Essentialist	Anti-essentialist

social phenomena 'cannot be empirically identified independently of … [their] effects', that is, they cannot be accessed at the level at which they are generated, in isolation from the effects which they have, as is the case with some physical phenomena. Thus, if we conduct an ethnography of English language teaching and learning in a given national context, we might begin with teaching and learning effects, that is phenomena occurring in our presence, which we can capture via observation, interviews, conversation recording and so on. We then move to posit, as causants, social structures which we can imagine and argue for, but which we cannot 'really' access.

As regards what he calls the hermeneutic tradition (the interpretivist/constructivist perspective), Bhaskar writes that it:

> is correct to point out that the social sciences deal with pre-interpreted reality, a reality already brought under concepts by social actors, that is, a reality *already brought under the same kind of material in terms of which it is to be grasped.*
>
> *(Bhaskar, 1998: 21)*

This means that the kind of reality grasped and studied by social scientists, such as the English language teaching and learning context cited earlier, has already been grasped by human beings and has passed through their hands, so to speak. And this is the case because social phenomena are, after all, the outcome of the activity of human beings. By contrast, where the hermeneutic tradition goes somewhat wrong is 'in a reduction of social science to the modalities of this relationship' (Bhaskar, 1998: 21), that is, the conflation of the inability to *show* that social reality exists with social reality itself. Or, to put it another way, in the hermeneutic tradition, there is a tendency to reduce ontology (actual reality) to epistemology (human knowledge). This conflation is known as the 'epistemic fallacy', which, for Bhaskar, is an error because 'statements about being cannot be reduced to or analysed in terms of statements about knowledge, that ontological questions cannot always be transposed into epistemological terms' (Bhaskar, 1989: 17–18).

Bhaskar's search for a third way through this simple divide between two general ways to posit a world to research (ontology) and a way to examine and understand it (epistemology) leads him to critical realism, a position he describes as follows:

> What critical realism says is that there is no inconsistency between being an ontological realist … believing that there is a real world which consists in structures, generative mechanisms, all sorts of complex things and totalities which exist and act independently of the scientist, which the scientist can come to have knowledge of … [and] saying that that knowledge is itself socially produced; it is a geo-historically specific social process, so it is continually in transformation in what I call the epistemological, transitive or social dimension for our understanding of science. Science … is characterised by relativism, … pluralism, diversity, difference and change …
>
> *(Bhaskar, 2002: 211)*

If one adopts the critical realist stance that Bhaskar proposes, society, as the general backdrop to research in applied linguistics, must be understood not only as a product of human activity, but also as having an integrity of its own – and indeed causal powers – independent of human activity. As he explains matters:

> [S]ociety must be regarded as an ensemble of structures, practices and conventions which individuals reproduce or transform, but which would not exist unless they did so. Society does not exist independently of human activity (the error of reification). But it is not the product of it (the error of voluntarism). … Society, then, provides necessary conditions for intentional human action, and intentional human action is a necessary condition for it. Society is only present in human action, but human action always expresses and utilizes some or other social form. Neither can, however, be identified with, reduced to, explained in terms of, or reconstructed from the other. There is an ontological hiatus between society and people, as well as a model of connection (viz transformation).
>
> *(Bhaskar, 1998: 36–37)*

Being a critical realist means being a realist with regard to ontology (it is intransitive, existing independently of the activity of individuals) and a relativist with regard to epistemology (theoretical work is transitive, in that scientific experience changes, as do conceptions of the studied world). It also entails a third shift in thinking, to 'judgmental rationalism', which means embracing the notion that 'even though science is a social process and that we know views and opinions change through time, at any one moment of time there will be better or worse grounds for preferring one rather than another theory' (Bhaskar, 2002: 211–12). Judgmental rationalism allows us to take action, precisely at a time when action is needed to combat various forms of regressive and reactionary politics going on around us – neoliberalism and its various economic, social and psychological permutations being a good example. By contrast, judgmental relativism, which means the inability to take sides because there are no better or worse grounds for preferring one theory to another, generally leads to inaction in the face of injustice. And it is just such inaction which the authors cited at the beginning of this chapter allude to in their critique of the lack of class thinking in applied linguistics, educational research and society in general.

Conclusion

I began this chapter with three quotations lamenting the absence of social class as a key construct in discussions of inequality. I then took the reader through a personal autobiography, the point of which was to argue that Ellen Meiksins Wood is perhaps right when she argues that '[t]he absence of explicit class "discourses" does not betoken the absence of class realities and their effects in shaping the life-conditions and consciousness of the people who come within their field of force' (Wood,

1998: 97). This done, I moved to the topic of why class once again needs to be – and what Halliday, hooks and McLaren and Scatamburlo-D'Annibale have to say notwithstanding, is becoming – present in discussions and debates taking place in the social sciences. To this end, I discussed the rise of neoliberalism and its consequences; globalization and social class; and political economy and critical realism as fundamental bases for the thinking I will present in this book. The remainder of the book is organised in the following way.

In Chapter 2, I will attempt to answer the key question of what social class is. I will do so by taking the reader through my own personal journey on the way to finding an answer to this question. This process will entail going through key sources of my ideas about social class in some detail. The point of all this not to be self-indulgent, but to deal with social class as a construct more profoundly than has previously been the case in applied linguistics.

Following this detailed exploration of the meaning of social class, in Chapters 3, 4 and 5, I look at social class in action in applied linguistics. I begin with the review of the one area of applied linguistics in which social class has historically been the focus of attention, sociolinguistics. I trace the history of social class in this area of inquiry, from the early variationist work of William Labov to the more recent linguistic ethnography of Ben Rampton, including some critical comments along the way. In Chapter 4, I look at another area of applied linguistics, bi/multilingualism research, this time exploring how social class has had a very minor presence. In Chapter 5, I take on second language acquisition and learning, again with a view to exploring how social class has been absent in most discussions, and how it might be inserted into research in this area of applied linguistics. I then move to the final chapter, in which I attempt to tie together strands and look to the future of social class in applied linguistics.

Notes

1 See Rachael Woldoff (2011) for a recent account of the dynamics and effects of white flight in a neighbourhood of a large American city.

2 Homeroom was the first period of the school day. Students were assigned to their homeroom groups by alphabetisation of their surnames. The period lasted some 20 minutes, during which time attendance was taken, announcements were made and the pledge of allegiance (the expression of loyalty to the flag and government of the United States) was said by all students in unison.

3 On reading an earlier draft of this chapter, one colleague noted that the reader might well wonder at this point why my parents would send me to this school and if it was because they were 'paid up' liberals who believed that this kind of experience would be good for me. I think there was an element of the latter line of reasoning at work, although, as I explain here, I never actually felt real, immediate danger or anxiety about going to school every day. And had this been the case, I am sure that my parents would have taken action to find an alternative school. One thing I always found interesting during my high school years, and indeed later when I went to university, was the way that my white middle class peers who had grown up in the predominantly white middle class suburbs of Houston reacted when I told them where I had graduated from high school. Quite often they would make comments like 'I bet you got beaten up every day' or 'How could you stand being the only white kid in your class?' I always found the

thinly veiled racism behind these comments of interest, especially when they were made by individuals who saw themselves as 'liberal'. My response was generally to ask why I would go to a school where I was getting beaten up every day. And of course, I had to ask my interlocutors if they thought that my African American classmates had nothing better to do than beat me up every day and if this was what they had done with the minority of African American students in the high schools that they had attended. Interestingly enough, when my high school came up in conversations with African Americans of all backgrounds – middle class and working class, and those who had attended pre-dominately white schools and those who had attended predominately African American schools – there was generally a kind of knowing nod, often followed by a comment like 'Interesting ... '.

4 Redneck is a derogatory term for white people (generally poor white people from the southern and southwest US) deemed to have reactionary and bigoted values. The 'red neck' is in reference to the sunburned neck of a poor white farmer.

5 I do not wish to imply here that in the late 1960s and early 1970s listening to country music, wearing cowboy-style dress, having short hair and having reactionary political views all *necessarily* went together, although they did often seem to cluster together. I also do not wish to say that only working class people embodied these characteristics as for those of us making such judgments, many middle class people at the time also fell into the category of 'redneck'. However, when I came into contact with this particular life-style, it was generally with people who would have been classified as coming from working class households, as regards their family income, education, behaviour and so on.

6 By contrast, we never saw my mother's extended family as she was from the Midwest state of Iowa and that was too far away to make yearly visits for holidays like Thanks-giving and Christmas feasible. Indeed, I remember making just one trip to Iowa during the time I was growing up.

7 An anecdote. On my second or third day in Barcelona, someone I had met told me that as a native speaker of English, I could easily find a job as an English teacher. As I had an interest in staying in Barcelona for a while, I explored this prospect. Within a week, I was 'teaching' English at Berlitz and making enough money to live on.

8 Actually, class was invoked sometimes in conversations if we count the offhand refer-ences to 'bourgeois values and practices', which were eschewed and to be avoided at all costs, despite the fact that most of my friends and associates were themselves from households which were arguably middle class or clearly middle class. However, I do not recall conversations in which the construct was problematised to a significant degree and there were certainly no occasions in which it was defined! Still, as I was a newly arrived foreigner with limited competence in local languages, it is quite possible that I simply did not follow conversations that were about class or that class was not broached in my presence because it was assumed that I would not understand or be interested.

9 That is, as 'an established order ... producing the naturalisation of its own arbitrariness' (Bourdieu, 1977a: 164). Further to this, Bourdieu describes the power of doxa as follows:

> Schemes of thought and perception can produce the objectivity that they do pro-duce only by producing misrecognition of the limits of the cognition that they make possible, thereby founding immediate adherence, in the doxic mode, to the world of tradition experienced as a 'natural world' and taken for granted.
>
> *(Bourdieu, 1977a: 164)*

10 Unfortunately for Britain and the world at large, Thatcher was a disciple of the work of Friedrich Hayek, for whom collectivism and socialism were incompatible with individual freedom. If instead of reading Hayek's (1960) *The Constitution of Liberty*, she had read *The Great Transformation* by Hayek's contemporary Karl Polanyi (2001) – and crucially, embraced the contents of this book – she might have seen the world in a different way. On the links between economic liberalism and individualism, Polanyi wrote:

Liberal economy gave a false direction to our ideals. It seemed to approximate the fulfilment of intrinsically utopian expectations. It was an illusion to assume a society shaped by man's will and wish alone. Yet this was the result of a market-view of society which equated economics with contractual relationships, and contractual relations with freedom. The radical illusion was fostered that there is nothing in human society that is not derived from the volition of individuals and that could not, therefore, be removed again by their volition.

(Polanyi, 2001: 257–58)

It is interesting to note how in the early 1940s, Polanyi wrote in the past tense about the flawed philosophy of human nature underlying economic liberalism, which he portrayed as a bankrupt ideology. This, especially in the light of how the mantra of capitalism as the natural state of human beings has been repeated incessantly by the global capitalist class since the late 1970s.

11 A good example of the imposition of narrative that suits the interests of the ruling ideology can be found in the way in which so many people have accepted the official narrative of neoliberalism. This narrative maintains that up to and until the beginning of the current crisis in 2007, the world had experienced some 20 years of good economic times and above all sustained high economic growth. This period, so we have been told, was far better in growth terms than the post–World War 2 period (1945–73). However, the story of the 1990s and 2000s as the best times ever does not hold up under the close scrutiny of contrasted economic growth figures. For example, Angus Maddison (2007; cited in Harvey, 2010a) presents generally accepted GDP growth statistics for the past 65 years and projected economic growth up to 2030, which together suggest that the official neoliberal success story cited above is a fabrication.

In a capitalist system, 3 per cent growth is considered the minimum for a 'healthy' capitalist economy, while less than 3 per cent is deemed 'sluggish' and under 1 per cent means that an economy is moving towards recession. If we examine growth over two distinct periods in the recent past, we see that from the end of World War 2 (1945) until 1973, worldwide GDP grew at a rate of 5 per cent and that from 1990 to 2003, it grew by 3.21 per cent. Projections for the period of 2003 to 2030 show 3.23 per cent growth in worldwide GDP. But of course, these projections do not take into account the current economic crisis and how economies of Greece, Ireland, Italy, Portugal and Spain have been experiencing substantial 'negative growth' (now there is an interesting term!) since 2008. Table 1.2 shows past (1990–2003) and predicted (2003–30) GDP growth figures across national states, regions and continents.

TABLE 1.2 Past (1990–2003) and predicted (2003–2030) GDP growth figures across national states, regions and continents

Nation-state/region/continent	GDP growth 1990–2003	GDP growth 2003–2030
Western European	2.05	1.75
Eastern Europe	1.33	1.79
United States	2.91	2.56
Japan	1.17	0.95
China	8.56	4.98
India	5.73	5.68
Latin America	2.61	2.48
Africa	2.96	3.00

My point in citing this example is that the superior figures for the period of 1945–73 need to be explained by those in power as there is a tendency to attack the very economic model which so dominated during this time (for lack of a better term: western European social democracy), even now when it has been dismantled to a great extent in many nation-states where it was a given and was accepted by political parties of the right and left. However, those in power never seem to take up this challenge and defenders of neoliberal doctrine and policies rely on their control over the state as well as official discourses emanating from the state about how the capitalist system in which we live is the best of all possible systems (see Callinicos, 2010, who makes a similar point).

12 WSA takes a long-term look at the history and development of the modern world, contemplating centuries, epochs and cycles rather than limiting itself to timeframes defined in decades or years. It is based on earlier work by the French historian Fernand Braudel (1972), a proponent of 'total history', that is, the belief that history must be studied in a multidisciplinary manner, including dimensions such as geography, climate, religion and literature. Braudel is famous for having introduced a new way to conceptualise time, which takes into account how events and episodes are embedded in processes unfolding over long periods of time, the *longue durée* – the long term. Drawing on Braudel, Wallerstein suggests that in addition to focusing on events, such as wars and natural disasters, historians need to a focus on what he termed 'structural time', that is, timeframes generally spanning several decades or even centuries. In addition, they need to be attentive to large-scale trends, such as economic cycles, political cycles and cultural cycles.

13 Marx and Engels wrote very presciently about globalisation in the *Communist Manifesto*:

> The bourgeoisie has through its exploitation of the world market given a cosmopolitan character to production and consumption in every country … it has drawn from under the feet of industry the national ground on which it stood. All old-established national industries have been destroyed or are daily being destroyed. They are dislodged by new industries, whose introduction becomes a life and death question for all civilised nations, by industries that no longer work up indigenous raw material, but raw material drawn from the remotest zones; industries whose products are consumed, not only at home, but in every quarter of the globe. In place of the old wants, satisfied by the production of the country, we find new wants, requiring for their satisfaction the products of distant lands and climes. In place of the old local and national seclusion and self-sufficiency, we have intercourse in every direction, universal inter-dependence of nations.
>
> *(Marx and Engels, 1948: 12–13)*

2

WHAT IS SOCIAL CLASS?

Introduction

As I explained in Chapter 1, my interest in social class arose from a combination of two major factors. First, from 1996 I was living in the UK, where social class was a concept on the radar in society at large and in the academic circles in which I was immersed at the Institute of Education, University of London. In British society in general, the term was often invoked to deny that it had relevance, from Margaret Thatcher's 1987 radio interview (see Chapter 1) to Tony Blair's call for a merito-cracy in Britain from the mid-1990s onwards. The latter would mean, in Blair's words, 'opening up economy and society to merit and talent', with the intention to 'recognise talent in all its forms, not just intelligence … [,] with a platform that recognises the equal worth … , allowing people's innate ability to shine through' (Blair, 2001; cited in Platt, 2011: 37). However, despite such class denials, coming from two of the most powerful British prime ministers in history, social class at least was acknowledged as a historical reference point, as having been important at some time in the past.

Meanwhile, in recent years there have been rumblings about a 'return' to social class in the social sciences, although one could argue that social class never went away in the sense that it has been a central construct for some scholars in a rela-tively uninterrupted manner over the past several decades (Fiona Devine, Mike Savage and Erik Olin Wright come to mind). One issue arising when one reflects on how academic areas of inquiry (and the academics acting within them) evolve over time is whether or not changes in them are always only theoretical and epis-temological in nature, that is, whether or not they are exclusively about how scholars in a field change their views about what is important and worthy of attention. In this case, the object of inquiry – its ontology – is framed as a reality that exists independently of what researchers might or might not do (see the discussion of Bhaskar's critical realism in Chapter 1) *and* it is deemed to remain relatively stable. However, the latter notion, that the world stands still (or stands relatively still) while researchers decide how to research it, is obviously problematic (and, it should be added, is a view that Bhaskar would reject).

Writing about the history of language and gender studies in applied linguistics, Deborah Cameron (2005) documents shifts in epistemological stances and how gender has been framed in different ways over the years. Specifically, she notes how a generally 'postmodernist' approach has become dominant in recent years. This approach has arisen as a challenge to previous approaches, among which is the *cultural difference* model (Tannen, 1990), which adopts the socially liberal position that men and women are different because they are socialised into different cultures and that relationships between men and women (presumably heterosexual) are often problematic due to the clashing of the different cultures. Crucially here, there is no suggestion that one culture is better than the other; rather they are just different. One point that Cameron makes is that a postmodernist approach is more in keeping with the shifting ontology of gender in late modern societies, that is, the way that in recent decades societies have changed and gendered social structures have changed with them. All of this makes the positing of separate but equal cultures for men and women a highly contentious notion. As she puts it: '[t]he adoption of new theoretical approaches has been motivated, at least in part, by researchers' awareness that they are now dealing with a different configuration of social forces from the ones that prevailed when language and gender studies first emerged as a coherent field of inquiry in the early 1970s' (Cameron, 2005: 490). Thus, in ever more complex societies, and in the response to the ever more complex workings of gender, language and gender scholars have needed to make certain adjustments in how they think about and research the topic.

A similar case can be made if we examine how some scholars in applied linguistics have moved towards political economy as a source discipline (Block *et al.*, 2012; Duchene and Heller, 2013; Heller, 2011; Park and Wee, 2012) in recent years in the face of an increasingly difficult and complex socioeconomic situation. Neoliberalism has been accompanied by 'a different configuration of social forces', which is easily differentiable from that which was in place through the 1950s, 60s and 70s, even if, it should be noted, it is also the continuation of capitalist logic and development (or capitalism by more sophisticated and variegated means). As we observed in Chapter 1, neoliberalism is not just a set of economic policies; rather, it is the real and tangible advance and further implantation of capitalism worldwide, which is accompanied by changes in the way that societies are organised. Among other things, neoliberalism has arisen hand in hand with individualisation in late twentieth and early twenty-first-century societies and this individualisation has engendered new ways of being and doing in societies, to say nothing of new moralities and value systems. No doubt the economic crisis which has been with us since 2007 has been a wakeup call for many in the world, albeit for very different reasons and with very different responses. In my case, it has made me realise that if I wish to understand phenomena such as globalisation and migration, and if I wish to deepen my understanding of identity, I need to adapt my theoretical frames so that they are more aligned with how societies are evolving and what my reading informs me about this evolution. In this context, I have come to see political economy as a broad church from which to establish a base as I endeavour to understand events taking place around me.

It is in this spirit that this chapter will take on the big question in the chapter title: What is class? I begin by moving somewhat methodically through the work and thinking of early authors who wrote about social class and class issues from the mid-nineteenth century onwards. My starting point is one adopted by many for whom social class is a central construct, that is, the foundational work of the holy trinity of European sociology: Karl Marx, Emile Durkheim and Max Weber. I then consider later work which emerged as the twentieth century unfolded, from Lenin to Bourdieu, with the latter scholar receiving more detailed treatment given his current influence in thinking about social class across the social sciences. The chapter ends with my attempt to synthesise and to derive an understanding of social class that will serve subsequent chapters. These chapters will focus on how and to what extent social class has and has not been a key construct in different subfields of applied linguistics.

Marx (and Engels) as a starting point

As a starting point in the elaboration of an answer to the question, 'What is social class?', we might go to the opening section of the *Communist Manifesto* (co-authored with Friedrich Engels), in which the following statement is made:

> The history of all hitherto existing society is the history of class struggles. Freeman and slave, patrician and plebeian, lord and serf, guild-master and journeyman, in a word, oppressor and oppressed, stood in constant opposition to one another, carried on an uninterrupted, now hidden, now open fight, a fight that each time ended, either in a revolutionary reconstitution of society at large, or in the common ruin of the contending classes. In the earlier epochs of history, we find almost everywhere a complicated arrangement of society into various orders, a manifold gradation of social rank. In ancient Rome we have patricians, knights, plebeians, slaves; in the Middle Ages, feudal lords, vassals, guild-masters, journeymen, apprentices, serfs; in almost all of these classes, again, subordinate gradations. The modern bourgeois society that has sprouted from the ruins of feudal society has not done away with class antagonisms. It has but established new classes, new conditions of oppression, new forms of struggle in place of the old ones. Our epoch, the epoch of the bourgeoisie, possesses, however, this distinct feature: it has simplified class antagonisms. Society as a whole is more and more splitting up into two great hostile camps, into two great classes directly facing each other – Bourgeoisie and Proletariat.
>
> *(Marx and Engels, 1948: 9)*

Here the authors make the oft-cited and bold assertion that any historical analysis of a society will have to deal at some point with class struggle. This assertion is followed by a long list of class positions situated historically from ancient Rome to the feudal Middle Ages to the advent of industrialisation. The endpoint is the two great classes which ultimately are the protagonists of a class struggle leading eventually to the triumph of socialism over capitalism. However, there is no definition of social class here, just a list of class positions. And one can go through the entirety of Marx and Engels scholarship and never find a clear and direct answer to the question 'What is social class?'. This has led observers such as Anthony Giddens to comment on Marx's work as follows:

> In most of Marx's writings, ... the concept of class is freely employed without the provision of a formal definition. Not until near the end of his life did Marx feel it necessary to offer a formal discussion of the attributes of class; and the famous fragment of 'the classes', which appears at the end of the third volume of *Capital*, breaks off at just that point at which it would appear that he was about to offer a concise statement of the nature of the concept. It is evident that this is one of the factors which has helped to further complicate the already difficult issues involved in the debate over 'interpretations' of Marx's works in this respect: the formal characteristics of Marx's concept of class have to be inferred from the writings in which he analysed class relationships in specific contexts.
>
> *(Giddens, 1973: 24)*

In this way, Giddens criticises what might be considered one of the great omissions in classical social theory, sociology and political economy. The story is a tragic one: Marx dies just as he is about to write a section defining class in *Capital 3*. But it is also a story that shows how an author can use a term without ever explaining exactly what it means in an explicit manner (the meaning *emerges* from the ways that the term is used) and perhaps more importantly, how the same author can, despite this lack of precision, become intimately associated with the term in question by generations of scholars. For while Marx is known for his detailed analyses of the logic of capitalism, he is also known as a (the?) foundational figure when it comes to discussions of social class in modem societies.

Nevertheless, Marx's failure to provide a direct answer to the question 'What is class?' is perhaps not such a big problem. As Eric Olin Wright notes: '[w]hile Marx never systematically answered the question his work is filled with class analysis' (Wright, 1985: 6). In this writing, we find detailed discussions about individuals and collectives' relations to the means of production, how the ways of life of individuals and collectives emerge from these relations and how different relations to the means of production leading to different ways of life ultimately lead to class conflict between and among individuals and collectives. For example, in *The Eighteenth Brumaire of Louis Bonaparte*, Marx writes that:

> [i]n so far as millions of families live under economic conditions of existence that separate their mode of life, their interests and their culture from those of other classes, and put them in hostile opposition to the latter, they form a class.
>
> *(Marx, 1972: 515)*

This not a definition of social class but it uses class in such a way that the reader understands what is meant, that is, that societies are divided in such a way that individuals live under different economic conditions, which in turn give rise to different ways of behaviour and thought, and ultimately lifestyles in different cultures. And the latter differentiating factors may be seen to constitute class positions in society.

I would add here that the same approach to class, not defining it overtly but subtly inserting an understanding of it through class analysis, applies to Marx's writings with his faithful friend Friedrich Engels, as well as to Engels's single authored pieces. In effect, with Marx and Engels, the reader must construct an understanding of social class and class relations, including how individuals live and experience their class positions, from the authors' detailed descriptions and analyses of the organisation of production in industrialised societies. A good starting point in doing so is the particular Marxist understanding of society, which is presented in the preface of *A Contribution to the Critique of Political Economy*:

> In the social production of their existence, men inevitably enter into definite relations, which are independent of their will, namely relations of production appropriate to a given stage in the development of their material forces of production. The totality of these relations of production constitutes the economic structure of society, the real foundation, on which arises a legal and political superstructure and to which correspond definite forms of social consciousness. The mode of production of material life conditions the general process of social, political and intellectual life. It is not the consciousness of men that determines their existence, but their social existence that determines their consciousness.
>
> *(Marx, 1904: 11–12)*

Here we have Marx's well-known distinction between base and superstructure. The economic base of a society is constituted by the organisation of production in that society, that is, the activity engaged in to satisfy basic needs (food cultivation, cattle raising, factory-based commodity production, etc.). Crucially, production engenders particular social relations, that is, modes of interaction among individuals. We can imagine, therefore, that in a feudal, rural, agrarian economy, production would be organised in a particular way leading to particular social relations, and that these social relations would be very different from those emerging in a capitalist, urban, factory-based economy.

These social relations arising from production serve as the foundation for the superstructure, that is, the 'social, political and intellectual life' of a society. And, ultimately, they condition and shape the legal and political structures that constitute the state. The state therefore emerges as a contingent structure that both depends on and reflects how production is organised. Importantly, at any given point in history, the state is the legal and political superstructure of a society which serves as a guarantor of the class-based status quo which emerges from the organisation of production. The state also embodies and is based on the dominant ideologies, the ruling ideas, of a given time. As we observed in Chapter 1, '[t]he ideas of the ruling class are in every epoch the ruling ideas, i.e., the class which is the ruling *material* force of society, is at the same time the ruling *intellectual* force' (Marx and Engels, 1998: 67).

Marx's discussion of the base and superstructure is the essential groundwork for his theory of class. However, because of its deterministic overtones, it is where many readers part company with Marxist thought. Statements such as 'It is not the consciousness of men that determines their existence, but their social existence that determines their consciousness' (Marx, 1904: 11–12) seem to shut the door on the prospect of individual agency, even if Marx's work is replete with humanistic discussions of the individual as a social being with a conscience, as we shall see later. However, it is worth noting that previous to the line about determined consciousness, Marx writes that 'the mode of production of material life *conditions*' (NB not *determines*) 'the general process of social, political and intellectual life'. As Marnie Holborow (1999: 22) notes, 'conditioning something is not the same as determining something in a mechanical fashion'. Still, here and elsewhere, Marx is understood by many to argue for an overly simplistic and deterministic model of society that affords far too much to the economic realm of human existence. I have two things to say about this. First, as scholars like Alex Callinicos have done, we can argue that Marx was not as crudely deterministic as so many have willfully made him out to be:

> The picture of society outlined here is not one in which the superstructure – politics and ideology – merely passively reflects what happens in the economy. ... Rather, what happens is that the forces and relations of production set limits to developments in the superstructure. Now if this is so, there is considerable scope for political and dialogical factors to develop according to their own rhythms, and to react back onto the economy.
>
> (Callinicos, 1995: 125)

For Callinicos, support for this more nuanced view of Marx's supposed determinism can be found in a letter written by Engels several years after Marx's death:

> According to the materialist conception of history the *ultimately* determining element in history is the production and reproduction of real life. More than this neither Marx nor I have ever asserted. Hence, if somebody twists this into saying that the economic element is the *only* determining one, he transforms that preposition into a meaningless, abstract, senseless phrase. The

> economic situation is the basis, but the various elements of the super-
> structure – political forms of the class struggle and its results ... also exercise
> their influence upon the course of historical struggles and in many
> cases preponderate in determining their *form*. There is an interaction of all of
> these elements, in which ... the economic movement finally asserts itself as
> necessary.
>
> *(Engels, 1965: 417; cited in Callinicos, 1995: 126)*

Of course a single letter written by Engels, several years after Marx's death, does
not absolve the latter of being overly deterministic. However, given Engels close
relationship with Marx, both personal and intellectual, it may be taken as a significant interpretation of how Marx might have understood the dynamics of
structure and agency in human activity late in his life. In any case, this quote leads
me to a second possible response to the view that Marx is overly deterministic and
economics bound, and that is to take to heart Engels's statement that '[t]he economic situation is the basis, but the various elements of the superstructure – political forms of the class struggle and its results ... also exercise their influence'. In
other words, one can appropriate the idea that economic activity is the base for all
social activity and development while arguing for a more dialectical approach to
how the economic base interacts with Marx's 'social, political and intellectual life'.

Moving from this slight digression back to the matter at hand – class in Marxist
scholarship – it is worthwhile not to lose sight of how Marx himself was interested
in social change and therefore saw his theorising and writing as the way to an
understanding of the logic of capitalism that would inform its eventual overthrow.
In addition, he always wrote about class, not as an attribute of people or as a static
position in societies, but as a social relation, as emergent in the social world of
interactions with others and the collective associations that people engaged with, all
produced by the economic order in societies. Wright (2005) identifies five key
concepts in Marxist class analysis, which are relevant to his understanding of class
and Marx's sense of purpose.

- Class *interests*: these are the material interests of people derived from their location-
  within-class-relations. 'Material interests' include a range of issues – standard of
  living, working conditions, level of toil, leisure, material security, and other
  things. ... [T]he opportunities and trade-offs people face in pursuing these
  interests are structured by their class locations. ...
- Class *consciousness*: the subjective awareness people have of their class interests
  and conditions for advancing them.
- Class *practices*: The activities engaged in by individuals, both as separate persons
  and as members of collectives, in pursuit of class interests.
- Class *formations*: The collectivities people form in order to facilitate the pursuit
  of class interests. These range from highly self-conscious organizations for the
  advance of interests such as unions, political parties, and employers' associations,
  to much looser forms of collectivity such as social networks and communities.

- Class *struggle*: Conflicts between the practices of individuals and collectives in pursuit of opposing class interests. These conflicts range from the strategies of individual workers within the labor process to reduce their level of toil, to conflicts between highly organized collectivities of workers and capitalists over the distribution of rights and powers within production.

(Wright, 2005: 20–21)

This a helpful breakdown of the key elements of Marxist class analysis, wherein there is a kind of cascade effect represented. The material conditions and interests shape the consciousness of people, the social relations emergent in the practices of individuals and collectives and, ultimately, the conflicts around class interests which arise when interests, consciousness, practices and social formations come together. And with this understanding of class relations in mind, I think it is worthwhile to consider how social class is portrayed in Marx and Engels's publications as explicit lived experience. However, I start with a more technical point, one foundational to understanding the economic base of capitalism – Marx's labour theory of value – before moving to the experiential notion of alienation.[1]

The labour theory of value derives directly from the work of Smith (1982) and Ricardo (2004) and at its simplest level, it means that value of a commodity derives from the labour expended in its manufacture. However, Marx added two further dimensions. First, he addressed how manufacturing has always existed, as there has always been the need to make tools, to make things of day-to-day utility using these tools, to make clothing and so on. What is different in capitalism is that individuals as workers begin to make things that have no direct use value for them, but have exchange value in a market where the products of labour can be bought and sold. The latter process, of course, is controlled not by the worker producing the products, but the capitalist who has control over the means of production and ultimately the means of distribution of finished products. Marx noted that in the political economy of Adam Smith and David Ricardo, this transformation in the way that economies are organised is never sufficiently explored, and therefore, an opportunity for a more profound understanding of capitalism is lost. The second dimension that Marx added to the basic understanding of the labour theory of value relates to values in the market. Marx argued against the notion that commodities have exact and fixed exchange values, that, for example, a bundle of linen will always obtain the same price on the open market. Rather, Marx noted how commodity values are relative to the values of other commodities. Thus, the bundle of linen will vary in price depending on the value of other commodities like a linen coat.

According to Marx, in the process described above, capitalists, as 'unproductive' individuals, extract surplus value from the labour power of 'productive' workers who make commodities, by paying these workers significantly less money for their expended labour power than what the capitalist will eventually collect for the produced commodities in the market. This system of exploitation leads Marx to consider the life conditions of workers and what he termed the 'alienation of labour', which he defined as follows:

> What constitutes the alienation of labor? First, the fact that labor is *external* to the worker, i.e., it does not belong to his essential being; that in his work, therefore, he does not affirm himself but denies himself, does not feel content but unhappy, does not develop freely his physical and mental energy but mortifies his body and ruins his mind. The worker therefore only feels himself outside his work, and in his work feels outside himself. ... his labor is ... not voluntary but coerced; it is *forced labor*. It is therefore not the satisfaction of a need; it is merely a *means* to satisfy needs external to it.
>
> *(Marx, 1988: 74)*

Alienation from labour unfolds in four interrelated dimensions. First, the worker comes to feel alienated from the product of his labour, because through the division of labour the thing that he makes becomes 'an alien object exercising power over him' (Marx 1988: 75). The worker also feels alienated from the process of labour, the act of production, living it 'as an alien activity not belonging to him' as he tires of 'suffering strength as weakness ... [and] begetting as emasculating'. Third, the worker feels alienated from himself as a human being as 'estranged labor turns ... [m]an's species being, both nature and his spiritual property, into a being *alien* to him' (Marx, 1988: 77). In other words, alienation from labour takes away that which distinguishes human beings from animals, the capacity not only to eat, sleep and procreate, but also the ability to create and to reflect and to 'make ... life activity the object of ... [one's] will and of ... [one's] consciousness' (Marx, 1988: 76). Ultimately, this estrangement from one's self as a human being becomes the fourth dimension of the alienation from labour, what Marx calls '*estrangement of man* from *man*' and which he explains as follows:

> If a man is confronted by himself, he is confronted by the other man. What applies to a man's relation to his work, to the product of his labor and to himself, also holds of a man's relation to the other man, and the other man's labor and object of labor.
>
> *(Marx, 1988: 78)*

In his description of the feelings of alienation experienced by workers in mid-nineteenth century England, Engels may be credited with having influenced Marx. According to Tristram Hunt (2009), Engels's *The Condition of the Working Class in England*, published in 1845, had a profound effect on Marx when he first read it. Indeed, in *Capital 1*, he writes of 'how well Engels understood the spirit of the capitalist mode of production ... and how wonderfully he painted the circumstances [of workers] in detail' (Marx, 1976: 349). The publication of Engels's book coincided with a period of time in which Marx's reading and thinking were shifting from philosophy (with an attendant detailed concern with the work of Hegel and Feuerbach) to political economy (as he grappled with the foundational work of Smith and Ricardo). In it, Engels charts large-scale population growth and movement to industrialising cities during the period 1780–1840, adopting at times an almost celebratory tone as regards England's status as the most industrialised society on earth at this time in history.[2] The book is, in part, directed at 'the English middle class, especially the manufacturing class, which is enriched directly by the poverty of the workers' (Engels, 2009: 63) in these emerging industrial centres. For Engels this is a class of people who ignore the misery which is growing around them as industrialisation, as part of the rise of capitalism, continues inexorably:

> Everywhere barbarous indifference, hard egotism on one hand, and nameless misery on the other, everywhere social warfare, every man's house in a state of siege, everywhere reciprocal plundering under the protection of the law, and all so shameless, so openly avowed that one shrinks before the consequences of our social state as they manifest themselves here undisguised, and can only wonder that the whole crazy fabric hangs together.
>
> *(Engels, 2009: 69)*

Engels goes into great detail about the life conditions of those working in factories and mines – the filth the disease (e.g. consumption, lockjaw, all manner of lung disease, pneumonia) to say nothing of injustices sustained in the workplace. Regarding children, the situation is presented as particularly serious, with growth stunted due to entry into the workplace at too young an age, with malnutrition, poor air quality and physical confinement taking their toll. He discusses in detail the cities in which the proletariat must live (Engels, 2009: 68–110). And he in turn provides a definition of class, not as exclusively rooted in wealth, property and one's relationship to the means of production; rather, Engels had an eye for other manifestations of class position. This comes across in the following quote, in which he summarises the content of his chapter about cities. He cites a series of variables denoting class, such as neighbourhood, type of dwelling (and the conditions inside in terms of space, ventilation and furnishing); the amount and quality of clothing; and food (quality and amount available for consumption):

> Every working man … is therefore constantly exposed to loss of work and food, that is to death by starvation, and many perish in this way. The dwellings of the workers are everywhere badly planned, badly built, and kept in the worst condition, badly ventilated, damp, and unwholesome. The inhabitants are confined to the smallest possible space, and at least one family usually sleeps in each room. The interior arrangements of the dwellings is poverty-stricken in various degrees, down to the utter absence of even the most necessary furniture. The clothing of the workers, too, is generally scanty, and that of great multitudes is in rags. The food is, in general, bad, often almost unfit for use, and in many cases, death by starvation results.
>
> *(Engels, 2009: 108)*

And further to how the class divide manifests itself, he writes:

> [T]he working class has gradually become a race wholly apart from the English bourgeoisie. The bourgeoisie has more in common with every other nation of the earth than with the workers in whose midst it lives. The workers speak other dialects, have other thoughts and ideals, other customs and moral principles, a different religion and other politics than those of the bourgeoisie.
>
> *(Engels, 2009: 150)*

As Hunt (2009) notes, at the time of writing, this was powerful material and the book became very popular among socialist movements then in existence in Europe. Importantly, it marked the beginning of Engels's relationship with Marx, which was to last until the latter's death and even beyond as Engels kept watch over Marx's legacy, editing *Capital 2* and *Capital 3*.[3] Not in vain, upon Marx's death he wrote in a letter to fellow communist Friedrich Sorge that 'mankind is shorter by a head, and that[,] the greatest head of our time' (Callinicos, 1995: 51).

Nevertheless, Marx and Engels's legacy has been mixed and very much an up-and-down affair over the past century and half, especially in the social sciences. Many scholars attempt to mark their distance from their work for reasons which include:

1 the seemingly deterministic view of workings of societies, embodied in the base and superstructure model
2 the insistence on the dominance of economics over all other social phenomena in the shaping of the lives of individuals
3 the labour theory of value, which, among other things, cannot easily accommodate service sector workers who do not produce material objects with exchange values, and who, therefore, may be deemed 'unproductive'
4 the dualistic view of class struggle, which came down to the capitalist class and the proletariat, leaving to the side acknowledgements elsewhere in Marx and Engels's work that there was a multitude of class positions
5 the apparent static and fixed nature of the class system as there is no clearly outlined model of social mobility in Marx and Engels's work
6 Marx and Engels's lives as a political activists, reflected so well in writing styles which took no prisoners (see especially how Engels wrote about the lives of the English working class in the mid-nineteenth century).

None of these versions of Marxist thought completely stands the test of close scrutiny, as both Marx's and Engels's scholarship is far more nuanced than casual observers might wish to think (see Callinicos, 1995; Harvey, 2010a, 2010b). Nevertheless, against the backdrop of developments since the times when Marx and Engels were writing (among other things, the increasing complexification of modern societies and social stratification within them), many people who situate themselves on the political left 'have pulled back from the grandiose explanatory claims of historical materialism (if not necessarily from all of its explanatory aspirations)' (Wright, 2005: 4). And in making such a move, they have tended to seek ideas for how to understand social stratification and social class elsewhere, either in the older, classic work of the likes of Emile Durkheim and Max Weber, or in the more recent work of scholars such as Pierre Bourdieu. I now turn to the first two scholars to examine some of the ways in which they expanded understandings of class.

Durkheim and Weber: redefining social class

Some have looked to the work of Emile Durkheim, in particular his classic text *The Division of Labour in Society* (1984) for either an alternative to Marxism or for an improvement on Marx's thinking. Durkheim was not primarily concerned with the intricate workings of capitalism and the injustices of the class system which arise from its development. Rather, he was interested in how the division of labour in modern industrial societies (European, and of the late nineteenth century, it should be added) was inextricably linked to a major shift in the type of solidarity that predominated in these societies – the shift from mechanical solidarity to organic solidarity. Mechanical solidary is based on high levels of tradition, social cohesion, obligation and the similarity and conformism of individuals in terms of religious practices, kinship structures and belief systems across a range of social domains. Organic solidarity, by contrast, is based on low levels of all these parameters, that is, a less tradition-bound and more occupationally and legally based society in which the differentiation and autonomy of individuals come to be more and more dominant. Specifically, in *The Division of Labour in Society*, Durkheim focuses on the tensions arising between social cohesion and solidarity, on the one hand, and individual autonomy, on the other:

> [T]he connection between the individual personality and social solidarity ... [and h]ow ... it come[s] about that the individual, whilst becoming more autonomous, depends ever more closely upon society ... [and h]ow ... he become[s] at the same time more of an individual and yet more linked to society.
>
> *(Durkheim, 1984: xxx)*

As he did at times in his other work (e.g. *The Rules of Sociological Method*, published in 1895), Durkheim writes at least to some extent against Marx, questioning whether class struggle must always arise from the development and evolution of capitalism. Durkheim's argument is, in general terms, that while a macro-level understanding of social class (i.e. large class categorisations like capitalists, land-owners and the proletariat) was a blunt instrument for understanding the increasing complexity of people's lives in industrialised European societies in the late nineteenth century, a micro-level conceptualisation of 'small class' formations, related to occupations that were increasing both in type and complexity, provides a more appropriate frame. Indeed, with his focus on the micro level, Durkheim made a twofold contribution to class analysis. He continued the Marxist tradition of understanding the human condition arising from relations to the means of production. However, he took this notion in a different direction from Marx. While the latter always kept the base-level material conditions of capitalism close to his understandings of the political, social and cultural (see his account of factory conditions and the working day in *Capital 1*), Durkheim introduced the notion of occupational groups, which bring individuals together. This is a more cultural notion than a material one, which he formulated as follows:

> Within a political society, as soon as a certain number of individuals find they hold in common ideas, interests, sentiments and occupations, which the rest of the population does not share in, it is inevitable that, under the influence of these similarities, they should be attracted to one another. They will seek one another out, enter into relationships and associate together. Thus a restricted group is gradually formed within society as a whole, with its own special features.
>
> *(Durkheim, 1984: xliii)*

Unlike Marx (and always with the benefit of having lived in the decades which followed Marx's death), Durkheim anticipated how industrialised societies would, with time, adapt to and ultimately absorb (or co-opt) organised labour movements. As Grusky and Galescu (2005) note, this would happen through the state's intervention in production and labour processes, and the creation of regulations to protect workers from poor working conditions and over-long working days. In this way, class struggle would be 'institutionalised', that is, it would be channelled through the state apparatus, the legal system and trade unions.

In addition, Durkheim predicted that individualism would arise from social mobility within established class systems. In other words, 'the rise of achievement-based mobility ... [would] legitimate inequalities of outcome by making them increasingly attributable to differential talent, capacities, and investments rather than differential opportunities (i.e. the rise of "equal opportunity")' (Grusky and Galescu, 2005: 54). In Durkheimian sociology, specialised occupations lead to specialised cultures, that is, cultures differentiated by shared values, worldviews and behaviour and so on, because the same kinds of people tend to go into particular professions and the ongoing interactions among co-workers serve to maintain a collective alignment of values, worldviews and modes of behaviour. In this sense, Durkheim may be seen to have elaborated an early version of what some today would call 'communities of practice'.[4] In such a context, individuals may become highly specialised, but they do not live their specialisation as exploitative or routine, leading to alienation (*pace* Marx); rather, specialisation may give a sense of meaning to workers as they see themselves as part of the same occupational and specialised culture as their fellow workers.

Durkheim, in fact, wrote little directly about class, being more interested in the experiences of individuals in occupational groups as subsets of a larger social structure called society. His semi-contemporary, Max Weber,[5] also wrote little about social class *per se*, although he did write more explicitly about it than Durkheim, defining social class and situating it in a larger view of stratification in modern societies.[6] In this sense, far more than Durkheim, he stands out as the key source of alternative ideas to Marx for class theorists. Weber shared with Durkheim a rejection of Marx's activism, whereby social theory (in fact Marx's revision of political economy) was seen as a means of critiquing capitalist societies and the foundation for political movements established to change them. He proposed instead a more 'value free' social science, which would be based on rigorous observation and theorising. Also in common with Durkheim, Weber was aided in his task of developing his social theory by the fact that he lived and wrote several decades after Marx, producing what certainly was his most expansive work, the two-volume set *Economy and Society*, during the last decade of his life (and published posthumously in 1922).[7] By the second decade of the twentieth century, Europe, North America, East Asia and other parts of the world had become more industrialised than had been the case in Marx's time, and Weber bore witness to and experienced first hand how the socioeconomic stratification of societies around the world had become more nuanced and complex during this process. In particular, he believed that the kind of class antagonisms which Marx documented in his work were no longer relevant in the twentieth century and that, in essence, a new set of concepts and frameworks were necessary if social theorists were to elaborate accurate and comprehensive understandings of how modern societies worked. Indeed, as Richard Breen (2005: 33) notes, 'there is no assumption in Weber that class will be the major source of conflict within capitalist society or that classes will necessarily serve as a source of collective action'.

This leads to the third and final major fundamental discrepancy with Marxism that Weber shared with Durkheim, that is, the belief that it is not just the economic bases of societies and individuals' relationships to the means of production that are determinant in social stratification; rather, there are other forces at work. Indeed, Weber conceived of societies as emergent at the crossroads of four interrelated but independent social structures: the economic, the political, the legal and the religious. As Marx conceived of the legal structures necessarily as part of the social superstructure which were based on economic relations within the capitalist mode of production (the economic status quo), it is perhaps instructive to examine briefly how Weber framed this relationship. On the one hand, Weber (1968: 334) acknowledged the relationship between the economic and other social structures, and even that economic structures could dictate legal structures, when he wrote: 'Obviously, legal guarantees are directly at the service of economic interests'. On the other hand, he immediately added to this claim: 'to a large extent'. And elsewhere in the same discussion, he made clear that the two spheres, the economic and the legal, could exist independently of one another:

> Law … guarantees political, ecclesiastical, familial, and other positions of
> authority as well as situations of social preeminence … which may indeed be

economically conditioned or economically relevant ... but which are neither economic in themselves nor sought for preponderantly economic ends.

(Weber, 1968: 333)

From such fundamental differences with Marxist thought, Weber could not but develop a different view of class. In *Economy and Society*, he begins his discussion of class with the notion of 'class situation', defined as:

the typical probability of (1) procuring goods (2) gaining a position in life and (3) finding inner satisfactions, a probability which derives from the relative control over goods and skills and from their income producing uses within a given economic order.

(Weber, 1968: 302)

'Class' is then defined as 'all persons in the same class situations', and two general classes are identified: '(a) A "property class" ... primarily determined by property differences and (2) A "commercial class" [determined] by the marketability of goods and services' (Weber, 1968: 302). Weber adds that '[a] "social class" makes up the totality of these class situations within which individual and generational mobility is easy and typical' (Weber, 1968: 302). Class situation and class are then said to 'refer only to the same (or similar) interests which an individual shares with others ... [as] the various controls over consumer goods, means of production, assets, resources and skills each constitute a *particular* class situation' (Weber, 1968: 302).

Weber goes on to elaborate on these key basic terms, but he does so in a rather confusing manner. The two classes eventually become four principal classes: a propertied class (probably rentiers), an entrepreneurial class (the bourgeoisie), a credentialised working class (middle class) and a lesser or non-credentialised category of workers (working class). We might see all of this as a basis for what eventually became common in class theorising, the elaboration of long lists of class positions into which individuals can be slotted (more on this later). But perhaps the most significant aspect of this definition and Weber's subsequent discussion is how he sees class as related to the individual's position in a market, which is understood to be a social order regulating the exchange of objects for money. Weber sees class as social (individuals share interests with others) and based in the means of production *and* the consumption of goods. He also inserts the notion of resources and skills that individuals possess, which allow them to participate in the market as relatively powerful or weak players, a precursor of Bourdieu's notion of capital, which we will discuss later. In his way, Weber addresses more levels of social activity within the notion of class than Marx did.

As we have observed, Weber, unlike Marx, did not believe that the mode of production gives rise to certain social and class relations, which then generate social organisation and activity in modern societies. And he discussed the impact of nationalism, religion and ethnicity and race on collective and individual identities

in a way that can only be qualified as prescient, when one considers recent literature on these identity inscriptions. Focussing on race, Weber (1968: 385) wrote that it
'creates a "group" only when it is subjectively perceived as a common trait', thus
recognising the way that race is, in part, socially constructed. And he added that
'this happens only when a neighborhood or the mere proximity of racially different
person is the basis of joint ... action ... ', thus showing his understanding that race
is often as much about who people are not as it is about who people are. But more
importantly, by writing in this way, Weber was developing a way of understanding
how societies are organised and how individuals and collectives fit into them,
which would complement his understanding of class and class situation. And this
additional understanding led him to introduce the notion of status, which is meant
to capture the dynamics of stratification based not only on material conditions but
also on abstract notions like honour and social esteem. He defined 'status' as:

> the effective claim to social esteem in terms of positive or negative privi-
> leges ... , [which] is typically founded on (a) style of life ... , (b) formal
> education, which may be ... empirical training or ... rational instruction, and the
> corresponding forms of behavior, ... and (c) hereditary or occupational prestige.
>
> *(Weber, 1968: 305–6)*

As regards the interrelationship between class and status, Weber wrote:

> Status *may* rest on class position of a distinct or an ambiguous kind. How-
> ever, it is not solely determined by it: Money and entrepreneurial position
> are not in themselves status qualifications, although they may lead to them;
> and the lack of property is not in itself a status disqualification, although this
> may be a reason for it.
>
> *(Weber, 1968: 306)*

The distinction made here is between class, based solely in economic activity around
property, entrepreneurial activity and labour, and status as the non-economic cultural realm of personal characteristics, personal relationships, social activities and
ways of thinking and behaving. So, if we return to race as outlined earlier, we see
how it is about all of these dimensions of the social with no *necessary* connection to
the economic sphere of society even if race and class are often inextricably linked
(Cole, 2009; hooks, 2000). Nevertheless, Weber does see interrelationships, and
quite strong ones, between the economic and social realms when he adds:

> Conversely, status may influence, if not completely determine, a class posi-
> tion without being identical with it. The class position of an officer, a civil
> servant or a student may vary greatly according to their wealth and yet not
> lead to a very different status since upbringing and education create a
> common style of life.
>
> *(Weber, 1968: 306)*

This statement seems in some ways to turn Marx's base and superstructure on its head, with superstructural phenomena having to do with status determining class as opposed to more base, material phenomena, such as income. And in this way, Weber makes his break with Marxism clear with regard to the directionality of influence between the economic and the social foundations of societies. Here also Weber mentions upbringing, education and lifestyle, which brings us to another noteworthy aspect of Weber's thinking, one which is extremely relevant to discussions of identity (and class) today. I refer here to Weber's introduction of the terms 'style of life' and 'stylization', understood to be an amalgam of positions and activities: ranging from bloodline and heritage, to neighbourhood and type of dwelling, to imposed norms of social interaction (both how it is done and whom it is done with). Weber makes the point that 'status groups are the specific bearers of all conventions ... [and] all stylization of life either originates in status groups or is at least conserved by them' (Weber, 1968: 935–36). Weber was quite prescient in his use of these terms and indeed in his overall conceptualisation of status, which has certainly been taken forward by sociologists like Bourdieu and in sociolinguistics where 'style', and derivative terms such as 'styling' and 'stylisation', have become well-established constructs (Coupland, 2007; Rampton, 2011). I will have more to say about Bourdieu later in this chapter and more about style in sociolinguistics in Chapter 3.

Weber concludes his discussion of class and status with a very clear distinction between the two (which, it might be added, contrasts stylistically with his earlier discussion, which is often difficult to decipher):

> With some over-simplification, one might thus say that classes are stratified according to their relations to the production and acquisition of goods; whereas, status groups are stratified according to the principles of their *consumption* of goods as represented by special styles of life.
>
> *(Weber, 1968: 937)*

Much has been written over the years about the great differences between Marxist and Weberian approaches to class. While Weber is seen to be in fundamental agreement with Marx about the material base for class, he is also seen to downgrade class, and indeed the economic/material base of society, in favour of a more cultural explanation of societal organisation and individual and collective behaviour. Nevertheless, as observers such as Giddens (1973) and Wright (1985) have noted, these differences might be seen as more complementary rather than contradictory and mutually disqualifying, especially when one sets out to understand class in the present. This more conciliatory approach is in evidence in Mike Savage's contrastive statement:

> Because Weber defined classes in terms of the labour market position of different groups of workers, writers within the Weberian tradition define classes in part through the kinds of income levels they can command.

Marxists, by contrast, focus on employment relationships (notably the division between capital and labour) as being the crucial defining feature of class, and the *source* of income, rather than its *amount*, is held to be crucial. ... However, like Weberians, Marxists also see class as ultimately tied up with social inequality, and would normally anticipate a clear relationship between ... [amount of income and class].

(Savage, 2000: 58)

This kind of synthetic thinking among sociologists interested in class has led Wright to sum up the differences between Marx and Weber as follows:

The typical characterization is that Weber adopts a definition of classes based on *market* or *exchange* relations, whereas Marx adopts a *production* relations definition. The real difference is subtler. Both Marx and Weber adopt production-based definitions in that they define classes with respect to the effective ownership of production assets: capital, raw labour power and skills in Weber; capital and labour power (for the analysis of capitalism) in Marx. The difference between them is that Weber views production from the vantage point of the market exchanges in which those assets are traded, whereas Marx views production from the vantage point of the exploitation it generates, and this in turn ... reflects the fundamental difference between a cultural and materialist theory of society.

(Wright, 1985: 107)

Nevertheless, as Marnie Holborow (personal communication, 29 January 2013) notes, displacing the description of class to the cultural realm – markets – does mean the removal of a fundamental element of Marxist thought in any discussion of class: the centrality of class struggle in the structure of societies and how one class can only be understood relationally, vis-à-via another class (the existence of the proletariat does not make sense without the existence of the capitalist class and vice versa).

Post-Marxist/Durkheimian/Weberian thinking on class

In the wake of Marx, Durkheim and Weber, and as the twentieth century advanced, a long list of prominent western scholars took on the notion of class in modern societies, albeit in some cases somewhat indirectly. Writing at the turn of the nineteenth century, American economist Thorsten Veblen adopted a distinctly culturalist position in his perceptive portrayals of the lifestyle and consumption patterns of the wealthy, charting how these related to power, status and esteem in late nineteenth century American society. Influenced by theories of evolution in circulation at the time, Veblen wrote about a capitalist society in which class relations played out in what Weber would have called a market. In this market, 'predatory' individuals won out over less predatory individuals and self-complacency, conspicuous consumption and conspicuous leisure became the superficial markers of the triumphant, the upper classes. Meanwhile, the absence of conspicuous behaviours indexed lower class positions in society; indeed, the lower classes would be far too occupied with making a living to engage in such behaviour. Of the need of the wealthy not only to accumulate wealth but to flaunt it once they had it, and of the need not only to abstain from labour, but also to make of this abstinence an ostentation, he wrote:

> In order to gain and hold the esteem of men it is not sufficient merely to possess wealth and power. The wealth and power must be put in evidence, for esteem is awarded only on evidence. … Conspicuous abstention from labour therefore becomes the conventional mark of superior pecuniary achievement and the conventional index of reputability; and conversely, since application to productive labour is a mark of poverty and subjection, it becomes inconsistent with a reputable standing in the community.
>
> *(Veblen, 2007: 29–30)*

Writing two decades after Veblen, the Russian Bolshevik leader Vladimir Lenin (1947) was less concerned about questions of status and consumption, in retrospect a Weberian orientation, as he situated his discussion of class in a strict Marxist framework. He defined class as follows:

> Classes are large groups of people which differ from each other by the place they occupy in a historically determined system of social production, by their relation (in most cases fixed and formulated in law) to the means of production, by their role in the social organization of labour and, consequently, by the dimensions and method of acquiring the share of social wealth of which they dispose. Classes are groups of people one of which can appropriate the labour of another owing to the different places they occupy in a definitive system of social economy.
>
> *(Lenin, 1982: 57)*

In many ways, this is the definition of class that Marx never provided. Lenin updated Marxism for the circumstances of early twentieth-century Russia, while retaining the basic view of class as rooted and embedded in the material conditions of people's lives. And true to the Marxist tradition, he did this as a political activist, one who was to have considerably more practical success than Marx ever had or even could have dreamed of having.

Some four decades later, in *The Great Transformation*, Karl Polanyi (2001) developed a view of class that was based in economics but which also captured the notion of class as a social and political relationship. Although a socialist himself, and someone who aligned himself with Marxism on the whole, Polanyi was also strongly influenced by the work of Durkheim and Weber (Buruwoy, 2003) and he decried Marxism's 'crude class theory of social development' (Polanyi, 2001: 158). In *The Great Transformation*, he argues, contra Marx, that:

[t]he fate of classes is more frequently determined by the needs of society than the fate of society is determined by the needs of classes [and therefore] neither the birth nor the death of classes, neither their aims nor the degrees to which they attain them, neither their cooperations nor their antagonisms can be understood apart from the interests of society, given by the situation as a whole.

(Polanyi, 2001: 159)

He based this assertion on his observation that events such as the improvement in working conditions in factories and shorter working days (both anticipated in Durkheim's work) came neither exclusively nor even primarily from the interests of the workers and actions they might have taken, although these two phenomena were obviously important. Rather, advancement of this kind was due to the clustering of interests in society at large, which meant that during the early stages of the industrial revolution in continental Europe in the nineteenth century, there was at times a seemingly unnatural alliance of the landed aristocracy and industrial workers, whose mutual enemy was the emerging capitalist, whose rising power and control over economic, social and political affairs was feared. Another example, and one which involves a different temporary alliance, is how many of the measures adopted to control the free market favoured not only workers' interests but also the general progress of industrialisation, while playing to a range of class interests. For example, legislation in favour of cleanliness in food production and safety measures in factories may be seen as beneficial to both capitalists and workers, as it was not in the former's interests if their workers suffered from food poisoning or their factory burned down due to faulty wiring. And measures such as the introduction of customs tariffs likewise favoured both capitalists and workers, as they guaranteed the survival of factories, which was certainly in capitalists' interests, as well as reasonable wages and job security, which was certainly in workers' interests.

Polanyi also wrote against what he termed the 'equally mistaken doctrine of the essentially economic nature of class interests', as '[p]urely economic matters such as affect want-satisfaction are incomparably less relevant to class behaviour than questions of social recognition' and that 'the interests of a class most directly refer to standing and rank, to status and security, that is, they are primarily not economic but social' (Polanyi, 2001: 160). This is clearly a Weberian view on matters even if Polanyi does not cite that author when he presents it. Rather, he bases his view once again on his observations, such as how some of the advances for workers cited above (e.g. job security and better work conditions) were about status and respect as much as they were about economics. Polanyi also argues that other advances such as moves towards universal education and greater safety at work, even the job security that came with customs tariffs, were more about the social standing of workers than their economic interests. This is all debatable from a more Marxist perspective as just about all of these advances very clearly favour the ongoing march of capitalism, albeit a capitalism mitigated by, rather than surrendered totally to, radical free marketism. Thus while major changes in society such as universal education might be seen as social victories for common people, they must also be seen as the establishment of institutions that guarantee the social and political order desired by the dominant classes.

Somewhat more loyal to Marxist thinking, although not immune to the influences of Durkheim and Weber, British scholars such as Raymond Williams and E. P. Thompson took a view of class based on the material conditions of human existence, but which primed both culture and history. Williams, a Cambridge graduate from a working class background, might be seen as the embodiment of a certain social mobility that existed in otherwise class-ridden British society from the mid-twentieth century onwards. However, apart from his discussion of the history of class as a construct in his oft-cited *Keywords* (Williams, 1976), he did not, as a rule, write about class in an explicit manner and in his work he generally grappled with the interrelationship between the material and the cultural at a highly theoretical level (e.g. Williams, 1977, 1980). He therefore did not use the term 'class' analytically, although he did often use 'working class' and 'middle class' as he wrote about culture in families, neighbourhoods and other social/institutional contexts. And in doing so, he showed a keen sensitivity to how class positions are inextricably linked to language use and engagements with cultural artefacts (e.g. films, books, television programmes).

Meanwhile, in his classic volume, *The Making of the English Working Class*, E. P. Thompson (1980) did write explicitly about class. And true to his vocation as a historian, he argued for the historisation of the construct:

> By class I understand a historical phenomenon, unifying a number of disparate and seemingly unconnected events, both in the raw material of experience and in consciousness. I emphasise that it is a *historical* phenomenon. I do not see class as a 'structure', nor even as a 'category', but as something which in fact happens (and can be shown to have happened) in human relationships.
>
> *(Thompson, 1980: 8, emphasis in original)*

For Thompson, then, the study of class was not a question of putting individuals into static categories but one of documenting their experiences in the material world – their relationships to the means of production – and then examining how these experiences contributed to the construction of class positions in societies. In this sense, his work parallels that of Polanyi, who focused on how human beings fashion history via the social circumstances in which they live. Thompson was interested in what Marx understood by 'class in itself', that is class as an objective reality independent of the actions or thoughts of individuals. However, Thompson's realism did not remain at the level of the objective and material, as he was also interested in the other half of Marx's distinction, 'class for itself'.[8] As he explained:

> And class happens when some men, as a result of common experiences (inherited or shared), feel and articulate the identity of their interests as

between themselves, and as against other men whose interests are different from (and generally opposed to) theirs. ... Class-consciousness is the way in which these experiences are handled in cultural terms; embodied in traditions, value systems, ideas, and institutional forms. If the experience appears as determined, class consciousness does not.

(Thompson, 1980: 8–9)

Elsewhere, in *Class and Class Conflict in Industrial Society*, Ralph A. Dahrendorf (1959) engaged in far more direct and detailed critique of Marxist thinking about class than any of the authors cited thus far. He first of all noted changes that had taken place in industrial societies after Marx's death, arguing that these changes invalidated most of Marx's materialist theory of class. One such change occurred in the way that capitalism worked, as from the late nineteenth century onwards, ownership of companies moved from the prototypical model of single ownership to joint ownership. This meant that the notion of 'a capitalist' was changing, as was the notion of a two-class system attributed to Marx, even though Dahrendorf does acknowledge that in his work Marx often made reference to a multitude of classes and that the issue of the capitalist/labour class divisions was more of an heuristic that allowed him to take on the bigger prize, the in-depth analysis of capitalism. Nevertheless, Dahrendorf goes on to discuss in detail how class systems had evolved by the time he was writing in the 1950s, noting how there were by then three distinguishable types of capitalist: (1) the traditional capitalists as those who own and manage a company which they themselves founded; (2) the heirs as those who were born into the ownership of a company, but who did not necessarily have experience in management; and (3) the bureaucrat/manager, in the old days someone who had worked their way up to the position of manager through hard work for the company, but more recently, someone who accedes to the station of manager via the acquisition of credentials, such as a business degree. Further down the class system, Dahrendorf noted a multitude of class positions based on occupations which had emerged:

> [W]ithin the labor force of advanced industry we have to distinguish at least three skill groups: a growing stratum of highly skilled workmen who increasingly merge with both engineers and white collar employees, a relatively stable stratum of semi-skilled workers with a high degree of diffuse as well as specific industrial experience, and a dwindling stratum of totally unskilled laborers who are characteristically either newcomers to industry (beginners, former agricultural laborers, immigrants) or semi-employables.
>
> *(Dahrendorf, 1959: 50)*

Further to this, the 'new middle class' is discussed, as 'the salaried employees in the tertiary industries, in shops and restaurants, in cinemas, and in commercial firms, as well as those highly skilled workers and foremen who have acquired salaried status' (Dahrendorf, 1959: 55). This new middle class experiences this salaried status along with certain levels of social status and prestige in society at large. And its ascent is related to another development arising between the death of Marx in 1883 and the 1950s, when Dahrendorf was writing – social mobility. The latter comes about via the diversification of capitalist economies and the concomitant diversification of the class system. Put simply, a broader range of jobs emerges, which in turn necessarily means that large parts of the population move up in terms of income, status, prestige and ultimately power.

Much of what Dahrendorf put forward as a critique of Marx was to be taken up in British sociology from the 1960s onwards under the heading of the 'embourgeoisement thesis'. In an early discussion of this thesis, Goldthorpe and Lockwood (1963: 124) suggested that 'a picture has been built up – and it is one which would be generally accepted – of a system of stratification becoming increasingly fine in its gradations and at the same time somewhat less extreme and less rigid'. In later work, they described developments in the 1950s as follows:

> [I]t was estimated that the average real earnings of industrial workers had risen by more than 20% between 1951 and 1958. ... It was revealed further ... that by 1959 among ... [the] more prosperous half of the working class 85% of all households had a television set, 44% a washing machine, 44% a lawnmower, 32% a car and 16% a refrigerator. In addition, 35% ... owned, or were buying, their own house. ... Given such circumstances, it was obviously a tempting idea to place the outstanding economic and political trends of the period in relationship of cause and effect, and to see ... a shift among certain sections at least of the British working class towards middle class life-styles and social attitudes.
>
> *(Goldthorpe et al., 1969: 22)*

According to this thesis, from the early 1950s onwards British society experienced great change on several fronts. First, the conditions on the shop floor, and indeed conditions across a range of work contexts, had begun to be affected by new technologies. Work itself was becoming less manual and more about the operation of machinery. In addition, there was a general tendency towards the humanisation of the workplace as well as new and different forms of interaction among workers and management in work contexts, namely, more egalitarian ones. Advanced technology also meant that consumer goods were available in increased abundance and at lower prices, which meant that, as noted in the quote above, working class people could *consume up*, buying products that previously were the exclusive domain of the middle classes and the wealthy. Car ownership also increased during this time and this increased mobility went hand in hand with the above-cited increase in home ownership. The latter, in turn, was often linked to moves to new suburban housing developments away from more inner city neighbourhoods traditionally identified as working class. All these changes and developments were documented in the work of Goldthorpe and Lockwood and there is no question that they took place. However, the issue is whether in and of themselves they constituted or caused an *embourgeoisement* of the British working class.

For many authors, there were always reasons to be careful, if not sceptical, about the embourgeoisement thesis. Chas Critcher writes the following about Goldthorpe and Lockwood's work:

> [There are] four major criticisms of the *Affluent Worker* study: an ill-considered and ahistorical conception of 'traditional' working-class consciousness; an inflexibility of method; the resort to a concept of 'instrumental orientation', the dimensions and sources of which remain unclear; and a prevarication between the language of straight sociology and that of Marxism, when faced with the problem of defining class.
>
> *(Critcher, 1979: 33)*

Nevertheless, the definitive debunking came from the authors most associated with it, Goldthorpe and Lockwood. The findings coming out of their *Affluent Worker* study cast doubt on the thesis or, at the very least, showed a nuanced view of working class culture (see Goldthorpe *et al.*, 1969). On the one hand, their study of 1960s' Luton, a predominantly working class town situated just north of London, did show that there was an increasing privatisation of life among working class people, and how this was a consequence of changing living patterns leading to a lack of the community spirit traditionally associated, often romantically, with the working class (Critcher, 1979; Day, 2006). On the other hand, the researchers found that a diverse range of factors – such as changes in housing, more women working, the increase in home entertainment (music and television) – all came together to make the nuclear family/working class community model seem obsolete. However, there was a problem in the claim that Luton might in any way be typical of working class towns or cities in the 1960s, given that much of the study's focus was on the Vauxhall automobile factory. There, workers were something of an élite when compared to the general working class population due to their greater affluence and the fact that they worked in industrial facilities fitted with advanced technology and, as a result, a different organisation of production. And overall, the discussion of the demise of the working class, then as now, seemed to be based on well-worn stereotypical versions of working class culture. In short, the 'embourgeoisement thesis', as a straightforward statement that 'everyone is now middle class', was deemed by Goldthorpe *et al.* (1969) to be highly problematic.

More recently, in a detailed discussion of the 'embourgeoisement thesis', Ken Roberts acknowledges changes in British society up to 2000, in particular a general rise in living standards that cannot have left people of all class positions unaffected. However, he takes issue with the embourgeoisement thesis, elaborating his objections as follows:

> There are three basic weaknesses in the embourgeoisement thesis. First, whenever the working class has improved income levels and living standards,

the middle class has advanced in line, so there has been no catching up. Over the long term, class-related income inequalities have remained remarkably stable. Second, it is necessary only for something to become common within the working class for it to lose its middle class associations. This has happened to seaside holidays, television sets, washing machines, motor cars and owner occupied dwellings. In the late 1950s manual families who are rehoused from the inner cities to suburban council estates were regarded as upwardly mobile. Nowadays being a tenant on most of the outlying estates has entirely different social connotations. Third, even if manual workers caught up with middle-class income and spending levels, they would simply be affluent workers rather than middle class. Their jobs – their day-on-day and lifelong experiences of earning their livings – would remain very different from those of senior managers.

(Roberts, 2001: 13)

In this critique, there is a mixture of issues ranging from the economic to the social and cultural. First, there is the economic issue of the enduring proportional income differences across class lines, despite a general increase in prosperity in a society as a whole. Second, there is the status-in-society issue in the form of activities and symbolic behaviours becoming devalued once they are no longer the exclusive domain of the middle classes. Third, there is the cultural side of class, that is how increased income and buying power does not, in and of itself, confer on one a higher class position, as there are all kinds of other class markers such as education and taste (see the discussion of Bourdieu's work later in this chapter) that also come into play.

In a sense, the embourgeoisement thesis is part of a larger, and longer, tradition of minimising the importance of class in social analysis in different countries around the world. Thus in the early 1960s, French sociologist Raymond Aron, greatly influenced by Weber, put forth the following view:

A class is not a real ensemble, but a conglomeration of individuals. Individuals are differentiated from each other by multiple criteria and social status or class is only one among several discriminations determined essentially by psychological phenomena. Each is in the class which is imposed by the idea which others have of the position he occupies. Each has a status which is defined by the esteem of others. A definition of this kind regards the psychology of individuals, with all the contradictions it may allow for, as the essence of the phenomenon.

(Aron, 1969: 75)

However, such views seem more about self-positioning as a particular type of scholar than conclusions arrived at empirically: more than anything else, they derive from a rejection of Marxism and the original sin of putting class at the centre of the study of all societies, both historically and sociologically. By contrast, embourgeoisement thesis researchers base their views more on empirical evidence (e.g. statistics on employment, income, housing, consumption habits and so on), while other scholars have written about the demise of class in post-industrial societies based on their informed observations of the evolution of these societies (e.g. Beck, 1992; Castells, 1996; Gorz, 1982; Lash and Urry, 1994; Pakulski and Waters, 1996; Touraine, 2007). In this latter vein, Jan Pakulsi writes about changes in these societies as follows:

> The novel elements include:
>
> - Flexible specialization that erodes consistency of occupational tasks and homogeneity of occupational categories. Proliferation of roles requiring flexibility and adaptability. Increasing scope of flexible employment.
> - Extending scope and diversity of market transactions due to the tendency to extend commodity status to new aspects of human products and activities (e.g. brands, software, genetic materials). Access to information, signs and symbols become [an] important aspect of lifechances.
> - Proliferation of horizontal networks within and across the bureaucratic corporate hierarchies. Declining clarity of hierarchical relations.
> - Growing density of social relations facilitated by widening access to new communication and information technologies.
> - Increasing consumption, especially of symbols and services. Proliferation of lifestyles and social identities related to consumption styles and tastes.
>
> *(Pakulski, 2005: 176)*

Nevertheless, while Pakulski and others who share his views certainly are right to point out how societies have become more complex over the last century, they err in their failure to take on board how such complexification does not, in and of itself, mean that class and class conflict have disappeared in recent decades. In countries that have moved to a service-based economy, inequality has not disappeared and neither has the alienation of the workforce.

The latter was charted all too well in a series of books appearing in the 1950s and 1960s in the United States (e.g. Marcuse, 1964; Mills, 1951; Whyte, 1956), which pinpointed the feelings of emptiness and desolation engendered by the social and psychological conformism of the new middle classes of post-World War 2 capitalism. C. Wright Mills, a scholar greatly influenced by Weber, wrote in his book *White Collar* of 'the new little people, the unwilling vanguard of modern society' and how they were becoming '[e]stranged from community and society in a context of distrust and manipulation; alienated from work and, on the personality market, from self; expropriated of individual rationality, and politically apathetic ... ' (Mills, 1951: xviii–xix). Meanwhile, William Whyte wrote in *The Organization Man* of the post-war generation of Americans who were 'so well equipped, psychologically as well as technologically, to cope with the intricacies of vast organisations; ... to lead a meaningful community life; and ... [who were] so adaptable to the constant shifts in environment that organization life … [was] so increasingly demanding of them' (Whyte, 1956: 363). He noted how along with and despite all of this preparation came a mindset (my term, not his) that made it possible for this generation of Americans to accept their status as 'the interchangeables of … society … with understanding' (Whyte, 1956: 363). Finally, Herbert Marcuse, a Marxist in his foundations, decried in *One-Dimensional Man* how by the 1960s the American people had come to 'recognise themselves in their commodities … [and] find their soul in their automobile, hi-fi set, split-level home, kitchen equipment' (Marcuse, 1964: 9).

With regard to inequality, more recent scholarship has noted how for all of the claims of technological and social progress (and who can doubt that there have been large doses of both over the past seven decades), capitalism has simply not delivered. Indeed, by all reliable estimations (see Dorling, 2011; Duménil and Lévy, 2011), income inequality leading to social inequality has increased in most countries in which diversification of the economy has been most pronounced (e.g. North America, western Europe). And if we move away from the services-based economies to the newly industrialising societies, such as China, we find the kind of working conditions that Engels (2009) denounced in mid-nineteenth century Britain. The following quote from a Shenzhen textile worker, cited in Ching Kwan Lee's (2007) study of twenty-first century Chinese workers, makes this point eloquently:

> There is no fixed work schedule. A twelve-hour day is minimum. With rush orders, we have to work continuously for thirty hours or more. Day and night … the longest shift we had worked non-stop lasted forty hours … It's very exhausting because we have to stand all the time, to straighten the denim cloth by pulling. Our legs are always hurting. There is no place to sit on the shop floor. The machines do not stop during our lunch breaks. Three workers in a group will just take turns eating, one at a time … The shop floor is filled with black dust. Our bodies become black working day and night indoors. When I get off from work and spit, it's all black.
>
> *(Ching Kwan Lee, 2007: 235; cited in Gray and Block, 2013: forthcoming)*

So, on the one hand, we have the increasing complexification of societies around the world, which has seemingly led to an eroding of traditional class divisions, while on the other hand, we have what seem to be nineteenth century class conditions in others. Where does all this leave class as a useful construct? From Marx down to scholars such as Pakulski, we see a multitude of phenomena that index class and class position in societies, all of which create the need for a synthesis of a long list of elements that might be configured into a unified framework for understanding class. I aim to do just this later in this chapter. First, however, I will examine the work of Pierre Bourdieu, to my mind, a social theorist who has acted as a bridge across the various phenomena and class-based dimensions that have been discussed thus far in this chapter.

Bourdieu on class

> The opposition between a mechanics of power relations and the phenomenol-
> ogy ... of sense relations is most visible, and most sterile, in the theory of social
> classes. On the one hand, there are strictly objective definitions which, like the
> economic strand of Marxism, seek the principle of class determination in properties
> that owe nothing to the agents' perceptions or action. ... On the other hand, there
> are subjectivist or nominalist definitions, including Weber's theory of 'status groups'
> which privileges the symbolic properties constituting a life-style ... [and] empirical
> analyses seeking to establish whether and how classes exist in the agents' repre-
> sentations ... [which] conceive the social world 'as will and representation', in
> which respect they are close to political spontaneism, which identifies a social class
> (and especially the proletariat) with a kind of purge of consciousness.
>
> *(Bourdieu, 1990: 136)*

Pierre Bourdieu, anthropologist, sociologist, social theorist and social critic, wrote
extensively about class during an academic career spanning six decades (and well
beyond if one considers that his publications continued to come out after his death
in 2002). A scholar whose work became progressively well known in the Anglophone world from the 1980s onwards, Bourdieu wrote prolifically, publishing over
30 books and numerous articles and book chapters. In his elaborate discourse,
which often includes seemingly endless, labyrinthine sentences, one finds a richness
of layers that makes him unique in contemporary scholarship in the social sciences.
In this quote, he lays out his stall as regards class and above all, the views of Marx
and Weber, or better said the views derived from certain readings of Marx and
Weber. On the one hand, there are those who subscribe to a kind of primitive
economic determinism, according to which classes and individuals' positions within
them are determined by economic conditions, leaving little for the realm of individual agency. On the other hand, there are extreme phenomenological approaches to class, which see it as discursively constructed, as existent only in abstract
conceptualisations in the minds of individuals. These are two extreme positions
(indeed, quasi-caricatures) which are rather easy to reject, but they work rhetori-
cally to allow Bourdieu to elaborate on two key themes in this work, class and the
interrelationship between structure and agency. While these two themes are inextricably linked, we are concerned here far more with Bourdieu's conceptualisation
of class.[9] But, what does this conceptualisation look like?

> [C]lass or class fraction is defined not only by its position in the relations of
> production, as identified through indices such as occupation, income, or
> even educational level, but also by a certain sex-ratio, a certain distribution in
> geographical space (which is never socially neutral) and by a whole set of
> subsidiary characteristics which may function, in the form of tacit require-
> ments, as real principles of selection or exclusion without ever being formally
> stated (this is the case with ethnic origin and sex). A number of official

criteria: for example, the requiring of a given diploma can be a way of demanding a particular social origin.

(Bourdieu, 1984: 102)

This definition is taken from *Distinction,* Bourdieu's oft-cited examination of class in 1960s' and 1970s' France. In it, he makes the very good and by now generally accepted point that class must be conceptualised not only in terms of traditional indexes of income, occupation and education, but also in terms of status and a range of social practices. Drawing on Marxism to an extent, but far more influenced by Weber, Bourdieu is perhaps the social theorist who best captured what class had become in the wealthy west by the end of the twentieth century. Like Marx, Bourdieu saw class as based in material states and processes, but like Weber, he was conscious of status emergent in cultural activity and markets.

Fundamental to Bourdieu's work is a series of interrelated constructs – 'capital', 'habitus' and 'field' – all understood in terms of a contrast between the objective world of social structures and the subjective world of individual agency. Capital is a term that, on the surface at least, would appear to have been borrowed from Marx but in Bourdieu's work it has always meant something different from what Marx had in mind.[10] Indeed, Bourdieu used the notions of economy and market so that they covered not only material production, exchange and the social intercourse necessary in the move from one to the other, but also metaphorically, as ways of understanding how symbolic practices constitute social structure and are themselves constituted by social structure. He therefore argued that in the social sciences, there is a need to 'abandon the dichotomy of the economic and the non-economic which stands in the way of seeing the science of economic practices as a particular case of a *general science of the economy of practices,* capable of treating all practices, including those purporting to be disinterested or gratuitous, and hence non-economic, as economic practices directed towards the maximizing of material or symbolic profit' (Bourdieu, 1977a: 183). In this way, Bourdieu understood that there is economic capital, that is, capital as personal material wealth – income, property and assets – which allows one greater or lesser power in contexts in which such capital is validated and legitimised. And with this one dimension of capital, one can devise a system of putting individuals and families into class positions (more on this later). However, such a view of how societies are stratified, one which works exclusively in material terms, is no doubt limited, and Bourdieu dedicated much of his writing to making this point. He drew on much of the work cited thus far in this chapter to elaborate a *'general science of the economy of practices',* which requires additional socially and symbolically inflected capitals that serve as resources for individuals to invoke or deploy in a range of fields of social activity and practices. It is in *Distinction* where he most fully developed this view, taking into account not only the material, but also the symbolic, as the following comment about playing sports shows:

[E]conomic barriers – however great they may be in the case of golf, skiing, sailing or even riding and tennis – are not sufficient to explain the class distribution of these activities. There are more hidden entry requirements, such as family tradition and early training, or obligatory manner (of dress and behaviour), and socializing techniques, which keep these sports closed to the working class.

(Bourdieu, 1984: 217)

The two most common capitals to appear in Bourdieu's work spanning decades and the two which relate directly to 'family tradition and early training, or obligatory manner (of dress and behaviour)' and 'socialising techniques', are cultural capital and social capital respectively. In 'The forms of capital', a much cited piece published in 1986, Bourdieu defined these two capitals as follows:

> Cultural capital can exist in three forms: in the *embodied* state, i.e., in the form of long-lasting dispositions of the mind and body; in the *objectified* state, in the form of cultural goods (pictures, books, dictionaries, instruments, machines, etc.), which are the trace or realization of theories or critiques of these theories, problematics, etc.; and in the *institutionalized* state, a form of objectification which … , … in the case of educational qualifications … is what makes the difference between the capital of the autodidact, which may be called into question at any time, … and the cultural capital academically sanctioned by legally guaranteed qualifications, formally independent of … the bearer.
>
> *(Bourdieu, 1986: 47, 50)*

> Social capital is the aggregate of the actual or potential resources which are linked to possession of a durable network of more or less institutionalized relationships of mutual acquaintance and recognition – or in other words, to membership in a group – which provides each of its members with the backing of the collectivity-owned capital, a 'credential' which entitles them to credit, in the various senses of the word.
>
> *(Bourdieu, 1986: 51)*

The important distinction made by Bourdieu about cultural capital is that it can be subjective and objective. It is subjective because it is 'embodied', as one's ever evolving psychomotricity and the 'feel for the game' required to interact with conspecifics in social activities. It is objective: first, as existent in material artefacts (cultural goods like books and gadgets), which come to index distinction and taste; and second, as the congealed social validation, legitimation and recognition conferred onto those who have the right educational qualifications or taste in art or other forms of cultural expression. Meanwhile, social capital is about networking and recognition from others. It is about belonging to a range of groups, where membership is directly dependent on the relative possession of the right economic and cultural capitals in different fields of social activity.

David Cameron, British Prime Minister at the time of writing, fully embodies a particular class position, wealthy and élitist, which can be analysed according to Bourdieu's capitals. First, Cameron is no doubt from a wealthy family and is wealthy himself; he therefore possesses relatively high economic capital in comparison to the majority of British people. The fact that he comes from a wealthy family means that from an early age he had access to the best education that money can buy, studying first at Heatherdown Preparatory School and then later at Eton, before attending university at Oxford. Studying at public schools and Oxford University provided him with the opportunity to acquire the knowledge, taste and distinction most valued in the upper realms of British society. But most importantly, attending the right schools put him in a milieu with the right people, the kind of people who are good contacts to have as one gets on with one's life, and the kind of people who would eventually smooth Cameron's path into 10 Downing Street, the official residence of the British prime minister. It is therefore not in the least surprising that David Cameron has been able to go as far as he has gone in life, given the economic, cultural and social capital he has had easy and full access to during his lifetime.

The second key construct in Bourdieu's understanding of class is *habitus*. Habitus is one of the most defined constructs ever used in sociology as Bourdieu elaborated on what he meant by it in most of what he wrote, often doing so more than once in the same work. For example, in one his first books to be published in English, *Outline of a Theory of Practice*, he defined habitus at one point as 'systems of durable, transposable *dispositions*, structured structures predisposed to function as structuring structures, that is, as principles of generation and structuring of practices and representations' (Bourdieu, 1977a: 72; emphasis in original), and then later as an 'acquired system of generative schemas objectively adjusted to the particular conditions in which it is constituted' (Bourdieu, 1977a: 95). In *Distinction*, he wrote that '[t]he habitus is both the generative principle of objectively classifiable judgments and the system of classification (*principium divisionis*) of these practices', adding that '[i]t is in the relationship between the two capacities which define the habitus, the capacity to produce classifiable practices and works, and the capacity to differentiate and appreciate these practices and products (taste), that the represented social world, i.e. the space of life-styles, is constituted' (Bourdieu, 1984: 170). A few years later, in *The Logic of Practice*, he wrote that it is 'an infinite capacity for generating products – thoughts, perceptions, expressions and actions – whose limits are set by the historically and socially situated conditions of its productions' (Bourdieu, 1990: 55). Finally, in one of his late works, *Pascalian Meditations*, he wrote of the habitus as 'inscribed in ... bodies by past experience', and as 'systems of schemes of perception, appreciation and action [which] enable [people] to perform acts of practical knowledge based on the identification and recognition of conditional, conventional stimuli to which they are predisposed to react' (Bourdieu, 2000: 138).

Examining all these definitions together, we glean an understanding of habitus as (1) backward looking, based on past experience, and (2) forward looking, as a set of dispositions anticipating and shaping present and future action. In short, habitus is *structured* by past experience and it *structures* activity in the present and future. It is also about the uniqueness of individual histories and trajectories. In addition, habitus is embodied, that is, it is 'a permanent disposition, a durable way of standing, speaking, walking and thereby of feeling and thinking' (Bourdieu, 1990: 69–70) and it is part of a body hexis (*hexis corporel* in French), which 'speaks directly to the motor function, in the form of a pattern of postures that is both individual and systematic', which is 'linked to a whole system of techniques involving the body and tools, and [is] charged with a host of social meanings and values' (Bourdieu, 1977a: 87). These techniques include 'a way of walking, a tilt of the head, facial expressions, ways of sitting and of using implements, always associated with a tone of voice, a style of speech, and … a certain subjective experience' (Bourdieu, 1977a: 87).

Nevertheless, these deeply experiential and bodily associations notwithstanding, we should not lose sight of the *social* embeddedness of habitus and how the 'systems of durable, transposable *dispositions*' (Bourdieu, 1977a: 72) are formulated out of individuals' engagement with and participation in situated social practices and they are formed and later shaped in an ongoing manner by social structures which exist both previous to and independently of individuals' activity (i.e. as Bourdieu puts it, they are 'objective').[11] In this sense, habitus is linked to the *objective* understanding of cultural capital discussed already, as in the example of education, 'the cultural capital academically sanctioned by legally guaranteed qualifications, formally independent of … the bearer' (Bourdieu, 1986: 50). This sanctioning, and indeed all acts of acknowledgement, legitimisation and validation, act as structures shaping individuals' activity taking place in what Bourdieu calls fields, that is 'separate social universe[s] with … [their] own laws of functioning, … relations of force, … its dominants and its dominated, and so forth … with particular institutions and obeying particular laws' (Bourdieu, 1993: 163). Fields may be seen as domains of social practices, such as education or the world of art, within which there are ever evolving and emergent ways of thinking and acting, which participants adopt as they struggle for positions of power, distinction and legitimacy. In fields, and the struggles which unfold within them, social capital, as the 'aggregate of the actual or potential resources which are linked to possession of a durable network of more or less institutionalized relationships of mutual acquaintance and recognition' (Bourdieu, 1986: 51), is invoked. Crucially, fields are the sites of both the reproduction and creation of sociocultural and socioeconomic stratification, as the example of David Cameron just discussed illustrates so well. One important issue which arises in discussions of habitus and fields is the relationship between the two, a relationship which Bourdieu outlines as follows:

> There is nothing mechanical about the relationship between the field and the habitus. The space of available positions does indeed help to determine the properties expected and even demanded of possible candidates, and therefore the categories of agents they can attract and above all *retain*; but the perception of the space of possible positions and trajectories and the appreciation of

the value each of them derives from its location in the space depend on these dispositions.

(Bourdieu, 1993: 65)

Here if we read 'space' as 'field' and 'dispositions' as 'habitus', we see how Bourdieu is interested in reconciling any tension there might be between structure and agency, and by extension theories of reproduction of social orders and theories of generation of social orders.

As I note elsewhere (Block, 2012; Block *et al.*, 2012), a perusal of recent publications in which sociologists research class (e.g. Bennett *et al.*, 2009; Lareau, 2011; Platt, 2011; Subirats, 2011; Vincent and Ball, 2006) reveals how there is a kind of consensus that has arisen, one in which all or some of Bourdieu's ideas are dominant. In the next section, I present my understanding of class, which draws heavily on Bourdieu's work, but in addition has more direct links with some of the work that informed Bourdieu's thinking (e.g. Marx, Durkheim, Weber), as well as other sources that have moved beyond Bourdieu or simply cover terrain Bourdieu did not cover.

What is social class?

First of all, I see social class as fundamentally an economic notion. In this sense, I adopt a Marxist perspective whereby economic phenomena are seen as the bases of much of what goes on in our lives and our interactions with politics, cultural worlds and institutions like the legal system. I say 'much' here with great care as I in no way wish to be the object of accusations of 'economism', which seems to be the fate of anyone who dares to recover Marx as a basis for understanding a range of phenomena assumed to be exclusively in the realm of the social and cultural. The economic base of society, and above all, the individual's relationship to the means of production, therefore does not determine everything that happens at the social and cultural (and indeed political) levels of existence, but it is the driving force in society often in very subtle ways. In Chapter 1, I discussed how neoliberalism works as a dominant discourse in societies today, working from a model of economics up and into social phenomena such as the rise of individualisation and the marketisation of education in an increasing number of societies around the world. Ingrid Piller and Jinhyun Cho (2013) capture the links between neoliberalism and the marketisation of education well in their recent discussion of English in higher education in South Korea. The authors describe how what amounts to a neoliberal economic *doxa* – 'an established order … producing the naturalisation of its own arbitrariness' (Bourdieu, 1977a: 164) – has shaped education policy and, among other things, has driven the spread of English-medium instruction in universities in which neither faculty nor student is ready for such an 'innovation'.

Over the decades, a good number of sociologists have devoted their efforts to the measurement of wealth and income as the salient indicators of class, which, in turn, has led to the development of schemes designed to reflect the class-based stratification of entire societies. In doing so, they have moved on considerably from early breakdowns of class in capitalist societies: from Marx's two-part model (the bourgeoisie and the proletariat) to more generalised lay notions that society is divided up into upper class, middle class and lower class, or upper class, middle class and working class. One of the better known schemes to be developed over the years is one that focused initially on British society, and then later, in an upgraded version, on a range of industrialised nations. I refer to the scheme associated above all with John Goldthorpe, which was first developed for the Oxford Social Mobility Study of England and Wales, carried out in 1972 (see Goldthorpe, Llewellyn and Payne, 1980), and then later used, in adapted form, in the Comparative Study of Social Mobility in Industrial Nations (CASMIN), which involved 12 European countries and three non-European nations (see Erikson and Goldthorpe, 1992). Both studies were based on batteries of questionnaires asking respondents about their income, their occupations, their education and training, their place of residence, their political affiliations and their family and friendship relationships. In its later CASMIN version (see Appendix 1), this scheme contained no fewer than 12 categories, ranging from 'higher grade professionals' down to 'agricultural and other workers in primary production'. A much more recent endeavour, the British NS-SEC (National Statistics Socio-economic Classification) (2010) scheme (see Appendix 2), focuses exclusively on occupations and the employment relations and conditions of occupations. It contains 17 class positions, 14 of which are considered to be 'functional', that is, with a direct relationship to employment, and three which are considered to be 'residual', that is, they are not clearly defined or, in the case of students, only indirectly linked to employment. At the top are 'employers in larger establishments' and 'higher managerial and administrative occupations' and at the bottom are 'never worked and long-term unemployed' and 'full-time students'.

This class categorisation scheme, the ones discussed previously, and the multitude of others that have been used over the years to describe the stratification of societies in terms of class, have the advantage of clarity. In effect, most people can immediately relate to the categories provided and situate themselves in the hierarchy, even if their self-categorisations might be quite different from what their completion of the relevant questionnaires would suggest. However, there has been a good deal of criticism of such schemes, not least because in some of them – and the CASMIN scheme is a good example of this – each individual category can always be broken down further than it has been. This, because there will always be very different working conditions that apply to individuals classified as equal in terms of class position. Thus, in CASMIN, there is a category, 'lower grade professionals', which represents a very broad range of differentiable subcategories, such that there is a big difference between a high-grade technician and a manager in small industrial establishments when it comes to any number of experiential elements such as multitude of tasks, stress levels, status in a local community and so on. The NS-SEC goes some distance towards correcting this problem, providing far more categories, such as (1) the long-term unemployed; (2) those who live their lives in and out of employment, and what has been termed the underclass (e.g. Gans, 1979), but might better be framed as outcasts (Wacquant, 2008); and (3) the growing army of NEETS (not in employment, education or training), a term with UK origins used to refer to 16–18-year-olds but which is now applied around the world to young people in their 20s who have finished university studies but cannot find work and are not currently enrolled in a programme of study. Nevertheless, the NS-SEC suffers from other shortcomings which are endemic to this way of focusing on class, such as how to deal with possible tensions between what Bourdieu would call 'class habitus', that is, the class-related dispositions derived from experience, and the objective position on an employment scale like the NS-SEC. For example, what is to be done with an individual from a L13.4 background, who begins his/her working life in a factory but ends up as a self-employed decorator (an L3.4 position)? Such an individual would likely earn a high income while retaining the same general outlook on life and patterns of behaviour as before. Further to the limitations of focusing exclusively on occupation as a way of slotting individuals into class positions, Rosemary Crompton writes the following:

> Any system of classification is limited by the number of dimensions that can be incorporated into it. ... [If it] is focused solely on employment status and employment relationships ... [i]t does not ... include substantial holders of wealth or capital, arguably one of the most important groups in any class system. More particularly, it does not incorporate cultural dimensions, which many sociologists regard as central to the discourse of 'class analysis'. It would be difficult ... to incorporate a 'cultural' dimension systematically into such a scheme. There might well, for example, be cultural artefacts – such as tastes in music or holidays – that are systematically associated with occupational categories but by their nature are fluid and changing.
>
> *(Crompton, 2008: 68)*

To conclude, there is something to be gained by attributing class to individuals and collectives according to big categories such as income, property and occupation. And schemes that purport to represent entire societies as scales of class positions can be of some use. However, they lack a subjectively experienced cultural side – that is, class as lived experience – which comes through in discussions of class that examine the life conditions of individuals and collectives, drawing on a tradition begun by authors such as Engels (2009) and Mayhew (2008). A move in this direction can be seen in the spate of books appearing in the UK in the late 1950s and early 1960s chronicling the life conditions of working class neighbourhoods and communities. Among these were Dennis, Henriques and Slaughter's (1956) *Coal is Our Life*, Hoggart's (1957) *The Uses of Literacy* and Young and Wilmott's (1957) *Family and Kinship in East London*. In these books and other publications like them, the authors focused on where people lived, the type of dwellings that they lived in and above all how they lived as members of communities. Something of the flavour of these publications is captured in the following quote:

In Bethnal Green people … commonly belong to a close network of personal relationships. They know intimately dozens of other local people living near at hand … They know them well because they have known them over a long period of time. Common family residence since childhood is the matrix of friendship.

(Young and Wilmott, 1957: 161)

As Day (2006) notes, there are quite a few criticisms of this literature on working class cultures. For example, Chas Critcher (1979) offers a rather scathing critique of this body of work on these grounds. Apart from noting the tendency to romanticise, he argues that there are methodological flaws as he situates them more in the realm of armchair sociology than rigorously organised and executed social science. Thus, in these books it is often unclear where, how and from whom the authors obtained the information that they present as factual representations of the British working class of the 1950s. In addition, Critcher notes that these books are not based on clear definitions of what constitutes working class or indeed, class in general. They often focus on particular indexes of class: for Young and Wilmott, it is the family; for Hoggart is the neighbourhood and a notion of working class culture; for Dennis *et al.*, it is working the mines, trade union membership, leisure and family, all under the umbrella of community. The books have the additional problem that they tend to portray working class people as passively determined by the social conditions in which they live. This notion of social reproduction is generally not presented as negative; rather it is constitutive of an organic community, providing a stable environment for its inhabitants.

Elsewhere, Bourdieu (2000) criticises researchers interested in the lives of working class people for effectively turning their research participants into people like themselves, as they 'credit working-class people with a "popular aesthetic" or a "popular culture"' (Bourdieu, 2000: 75) all of which involves 'a tacit universalization of the scholastic [academic] viewpoint', but does not really get to the heart of how the people being researched actually live or think. For Bourdieu, this is naïve operation at best, and a cynical one, if we adopt a more negative interpretation. For, as he explains, 'the economic privilege which makes the aesthetic viewpoint possible is granted by tacit implication to all men and women, but fictitiously, and only *on paper*' (Bourdieu, 2000: 75). And more forcefully, he concludes that '[o]ne cannot, in fact, without contradiction, describe (or denounce) the inhuman conditions of existence that are imposed on some, and at the same time credit those who suffer them with the real fulfilment of human potentialities such as the capacity to adopt the gratuitous disinterested posture that we tacitly inscribe – because it is socially inscribed there – in notions such as culture and aesthetic' (Bourdieu, 2000: 75). There is an element of researchers having their cake and eating it too here, basically saying that people are oppressed, but then portraying them as privileged in many ways. I will return to this point from a slightly different angle when I discuss the work of William Labov in Chapter 3.

In more recent books about working class life in Britain, authors have avoided to a great extent the pitfalls identified by Critcher and Bourdieu. Thus, they have been able to capture class-based experiences with references to neighbourhoods as physical places and community as more abstract, imagined places, while avoiding the excessive romanticisation of these experiences. And they have managed to limit the universalisation of the middle class academic's aesthetic (to paraphrase Bourdieu) in their work. Examples include Lynsey Hanley's (2007) history of housing estates in the UK and Michael Collins (2004) and Tim Butler and Chris Hamnett (2011) on how areas of London have become more multicultural and how this change, along with gentrification, has transformed what were once white working class neighbourhoods in south and east London, respectively.[12]

Running through such commentary is a view of class in affective terms as lived experience, or what Raymond Williams referred to as 'structures of feeling', described as the 'characteristic elements of impulse, restraint, and tone; specifically affective elements of consciousness and relationships; not feeling against thought, but thought as felt and feeling as thought: practical consciousness of a present kind, in living and interrelating continuity' (Willliams, 1977: 132). Crucially, structures of feeling are by no means effortless or smooth, or manifestations of an inner tranquillity. Indeed, given the basic conflict-laden nature of class relations in societies, class experience is all too often wrought with feelings of regret at having foregone what are perceived in the present as opportunities in the past and a general malaise among adults about their positions in societies and above all their positions in their families. Such feelings are captured well in Sennett and Cobb's (1972) *The Hidden Injuries of Class*, a book based on extensive interviews with working class adults at the end of the 1960s. The feelings of inadequacy that many of the interviewees felt about their positions in American society is captured well in the following quote in which a house painter describes his initial nervousness about being interviewed by a researcher:

> Um, let me try to explain to you why I was so nervous at the beginning of the interview, [...] It's not you, you're all right – but you see ... um ... whenever I'm with educated people, you know, or people who aren't my own kind ... um ... I feel like I'm making a fool of myself if I just act natural, you know? See, it's not so much how people treat you, it's feeling like you don't know what to do. Like – see, I remember, for instance, going to a Knights of Columbus social, and there were all these people in suits and I had on a jacket, you know, a windbreaker, and somehow people were introducing themselves to each other all over the place, but nobody was introducing themselves to *me*. So, that's how it is.
>
> *(Sennett and Cobb, 1972: 115–16)*

It is easy to see how Sennett and Cobb's portrayal of class as lived and felt in late 1960s' America is part of a more general cultural approach to the topic which, as we have already observed, comes down through the work of Williams, Thompson and of course, Bourdieu. Bourdieu was especially adept at showing how in addition to property, occupation and income, there is neighbourhood and community (Bourdieu *et al.*, 1999). And above all, there are phenomena such as taste and legitimacy, framed in terms of cultural and social capitals, habitus and the notion of fields. I will not repeat what I have written earlier, but provide one example of how Bourdieu's thinking is useful and will be drawn on later in this book.

Education is often cited as an index of class in research and in many studies aiming to qualify class, using the likes of the CASMIN and NS-SEC schemes just discussed, there are often links established between educational level attained, occupation and income, all leading to a particular class position on a scale. In Bourdieu's work, there are questionnaires (see *Distinction* in particular), but beyond statistics a field of social activity like education is seen in a more social, more lived and more dynamic way, as '*institutionalized* cultural capital' (Bourdieu, 1986: 47). Weber (1968) wrote about an increasing credentialisation of industrialised societies and Bourdieu (1984, 1986, 1996) has taken this notion forward, writing about the importance of 'academic capital' as a commodity that can be traded for access to higher level study or for a job in employment markets and which as a habitus (an acquired set of embodied dispositions) confers onto its holders status and prestige independent of its usefulness in employment markets. However, one of the more interesting aspects of the relationship between cultural capital, in all its forms, and class position, is how in many contexts the former can be separated from economic capital. In effect, there are many cases in which those who have postgraduate degrees may not earn nearly as much money as others who have low academic qualifications, but work in skilled jobs that are in high demand. For example, an experienced train driver on the London underground system often makes more money than an experienced secondary school teacher. Meanwhile, a successful house decorator can command a yearly income that is far higher than that of an academic with a PhD and a trained welder may earn more than a middle-range manager with an MBA.

In addition, it is worth considering the ways in which a lack of academic capital reflects a different kind of class habitus, one which confers onto individuals lower status and prestige in society as a whole while also conferring greater status and prestige in the working class cultures into which they are socialised. Sennett and Cobb (1972) discuss a grammar school in a large American city attended by the children of manual labourers from a range of European backgrounds (e.g. Irish, Italian, English). The authors set the scene, describing in detail the spatial relations which the school children encounter both in their homes and at school, conveying to the reader how social constraints are part and parcel of spiritual and intellectual constraints. There is great deal of self-fulfilling prophesy at work in the school: 'the teachers act on their expectations of the children in such a way as to *make* the expectations become reality' (Sennet and Cobb, 1972: 81). In effect, the children are positioned as problematic, both for the school and for society, before they can even begin to disprove any preconceived notions which teachers and society at large might harbour about them. As Sennet and Cobb explain:

> [T]eachers restrict the freedom of the children because ... figures of authority have a peculiar fear of the children. It is the mass who seem to the teachers to threaten classroom order, by naughty or unruly behaviour; only a few are seen as having 'good habits' or the right attitude. As one teacher explained, 'These children come from simple laborers' homes where the parents don't understand the value of education.'
>
> *(Sennet and Cobb, 1972: 80–81)*

In such an environment, the boys fall into two polarised groups: of the majority 'ordinary' group and the minority 'stuck-up' group. The former are disinclined to cooperate with schooling as an institution, and they 'act as though were serving time, as though schoolwork and classes had become something to wait out, a blank space in their lives ... to survive and then leave' (Sennett and Cobb, 1972: 82–3). Meanwhile, the more academically oriented students are positioned by the ordinary students as 'docile', 'weak' and even 'homosexual' (the reader is left to imagine the kinds of homophobic epithet used by the ordinary students to describe the stuck-ups). Ultimately, working class solidarity develops among the ordinary students, one based on precocious sexuality (publicly always within the confines of heteronormativity) and activities like smoking cigarettes, underage drinking, drug taking and cutting class.

Elsewhere, in *Learning to Labour: How Working Class Kids Get Working Class Jobs* (1977), Paul Willis presents similar findings based on his ethnography of a secondary school in the English Midlands, carried out between 1972 and 1975. In this study, Willis explores why working class boys end up with working class jobs, in other words, why they do not succeed in school and how school, in effect, becomes a training ground for their actual place in society as workers in local factories. As is the case with Sennett and Cobb, Willis's study is in some ways dated, as its backdrop is something of a bygone era in the UK, of relatively stable working class communities that were decimated by neoliberal economic policies from the early 1980s onwards. However, the study demonstrates all too well how class habitus is acquired through lived experiences and above all is about individuals' understandings of what lived experiences mean, and in this sense, it is in the tradition of Williams's and Thompson's views of class discussed already (even if Willis does not explicitly acknowledge such a link).

Willis's 'lads' manifest a negative attitude towards formal schooling and all activities deemed to support education as an institution. And they are keen to advance their entry into the adult world around them, engaging in activities they associate with their older siblings and parents, such as smoking and drinking. They show an acceptance of a certain predestination and a cynicism vis-à-vis notions such as upward mobility and the idea of the meritocratic society, as they prepare themselves for the manual jobs that await them when they leave school. All of their attitudes and behaviour contrast with those of the 'ear'oles', their more school-oriented classmates, whom they do not respect due to their conformity and what is seen as the futility of their attempts to escape their destinies as manual workers. As Willis notes, the lads walk a fine line between 'self-damnation' and 'resistance':

> In a sense ... it is their own culture which most effectively prepares some working class lads for the manual giving of their labour power [and] we may say that there is an element of self-damnation in the taking on of subordinate roles in Western capitalism. However, this damnation is experienced, paradoxically, as true learning, affirmation, appropriation, and as a form of resistance.
>
> *(Willis, 1977: 3)*

In her later in-depth study of a high school in suburban Detroit (United States), carried out in the early 1980s, Penelope Eckert did not encounter 'lads' and 'ear'-oles'. But she did come into contact with two prototypical school-based identities in the form of 'jocks' and 'burnouts'. Eckert observed and documented the social and linguistic practices of the students attending Belton high school, a school serving an overwhelmingly white community with middle class and working class residents. In her 1989 book, *Jocks and Burnouts*, she outlines in detail how the two identities existed for all students in the school although few students actually affiliated to or embodied either one completely. Eckert explained as follows:

> In the early 1980s, the stereotypic Belton High School Burnout came from a working class home, enrolled primarily in general and vocational courses, smoked tobacco and pot, took chemicals, drank beer and hard liquor, skipped classes, and may have had occasional run-ins with the police; the Jock was middle class and college bound, played sports for the school, participated in school activities, got respectable grades, and drank beer on weekends. The Jock had a cooperative, the Burnout an adversarial relationship with the school.
>
> *(Eckert, 1989: 3)*

As was the case in Willis's study, the cooperative and adversarial relationships to the school carried with them their respective consequences, not just with reference to what happened on a moment-to-moment basis within the school, but as regards what happened when the students reached school leaving age, notionally at 18. Willis writes about 'how working class kids get working class jobs'; Eckert writes about how jocks develop a very different orientation to life than the burnouts. She explains:

> The Jock category, based on participation in school activities and closely articulated with the adult power structure of the school, develops a corporate orientation that yields hierarchical social networks and instils corporate values in personal relations. The Burnout category, focusing on the more immediate development of adult status as defined in the working class world, develops egalitarian social networks focused on transcending the school context.
>
> *(Eckert, 1989: 22)*

Within these two distinct orientations to their eventual adult lives, conformist and corporate for the middle class students and resistant and egalitarian for the working class students, Eckert also found different consumption patterns in terms of clothing, music and recreational substance use. We saw earlier how Veblen was instrumental in introducing the importance of consumption as an index of class positions in societies. But not all consumption need be conspicuous in the extreme and obvious sense and in our day-to-day, mundane activities we position ourselves in class terms via the banal and routine consumption patterns we adopt, something Bourdieu (1984) was very adept at explaining. As Eckert noticed in her fieldwork in early 1980s American suburbia, it is not the same to wear one type of t-shirt as it is to wear another (a sports themed t-shirt may index a jock subject position while a heavy metal rock band t-shirt may index a burnout subject position). And in current times, in countries like the UK, it is not the same to buy food at a supermarket that positions itself as 'cost-cutting' as it is to do so at one that specialises in higher range products.[13] However, consumerism has evolved in such a way that the current economic crisis notwithstanding, the prices of many commodities have been driven down and this has made it more possible than in the past for a person of modest means to consume above his/her normal class position. A good example of this phenomenon was air travel in Europe, which during the 1990s and 2000s went down in price as low-cost airlines made flying to a long list of European cities affordable for people with modest incomes.

The opposite tendency obviously occurs, and has become the focus of much attention in recent years in the theory of the 'cultural omnivore', which maps the growing tendency among middle class individuals in late modern societies to experience and show appreciation for a wider variety of cultural options – low brow, middle brow and high brow – than was perhaps the case decades ago (see Peterson, 1992, for the original idea; Warde, Wright and Gayo-Cal, 2007, for a challenge to this thesis; and Friedman, 2012, for a refinement of it). But class boundaries survive such adjustments and more typical of class positioning through consumption is the following description of how middle class Americans might acquire distinction through their eating habits:

> It has not always been the case in America that an appreciation of *haute cuisine* was a marker of intellectual and aesthetic achievement, but that is the case in many social milieu today; and consequently, being able to participate knowledgeably and volubly in the discourse of food, and knowing how to make sense of the menus and recipes one encounters, marks one as a serious person in the twenty-first century.
>
> *(Lakoff, 2006: 165)*

Another traditional marker of distinction has been travel and out of an interest in travel has grown an interest in the more general topic of mobility as central to understandings, not only of societies, but how individuals and collectives live in them. John Urry (2007; Elliot and Urry, 2010; Grieco and Urry, 2012) has developed the idea that mobility is a central feature of culture and ultimately identity in late modern societies. And he sees it as intimately wrapped up with issues that fall under the general heading of political economy in that it is about how access to and the ability to exploit economic resources is directly related to the degree of mobility, or what Urry calls the 'network capital' of individuals and collectives, in parallel with Bourdieu's notions of cultural and social capital. Urry's starting point is the way in which '[h]istorically much literature on social inequality ignored the complex ways in which "space" makes significant differences to understanding economic, political and cultural processes that produce and reinforce social inequality' (Urry, 2007: 185). For while in past decades it might have made sense to centre on the local, carrying out research on close-knit working class communities as we observed above, certainly since the rise of 'disorganised capitalism' (Lash and Urry, 1987), this is no longer the case. In the neoliberal age of deregulation and the transnational financialisation of economies around the world, there is now the necessity to move beyond the local, and indeed the national, to the transnational. The latter term refers to how progressively more and more social phenomena are re-centred, with the origin more likely in cyber space than in a particular city in a particular nation-state. And with transnationalism come changes in affiliations. And here Urry connects his thinking to the work of Reich (1991) on 'symbols analysts' and the work of Sklair (2000) on the 'transnational capitalist classes', in both cases making reference to individuals and collectives who 'are highly mobile, detached from national class contexts and [who] ... through their "mobile habitus" develop global solidarity and cohesion' (Urry, 2007: 186, see Carroll, 2010, for a more recent discussion). These new classes obtain status not only in their local contexts but also, and perhaps more importantly, in global contexts. And in this sense, they are the citizens of nation-states who literally and psychologically leave their local contexts behind, and as a consequence, contribute directly to the increasing gap between the haves and have-nots in contemporary societies.

The key to mobility is access to economic resources that enable one to buy a car, pay for airfares and even pay for technology (e.g. a computer with an internet connection making the buying of movement easier). There is also the physical side to movement in that one must be sufficiently fit to walk, to fly, to drive and so on, as well as organisation, that is, how one is situated with reference to effective means of transport. And finally there is timing, or whether one moves when it is most possible to do so. It is no good trying to catch a bus at 5 am if the bus service does not begin until 5:30. All of this leads to Urry's grand idea of 'network capital', which is meant to be an adjunct to Bourdieu's cultural capital, as well as his related concepts of field and habitus:

> [M]ultiple mobilities set up new kinds of distinction of taste, between the modes of movement, the classes of traveller, the places moved to, the embodied experiences of movement, the character of those moving and so on. More generally, mobilities develop into a distinct field with characteristic struggles, tastes and habituses. It is site of multiple intersecting

contestations. This field has spun off from economic, political and cultural processes and is now self-expanding and gives rise to an emergent form of capital, network capital, that is a prerequisite to living in the rich 'north' of contemporary capitalism.

(Urry, 2007: 196)

In this way, Urry places mobility at the centre of increasingly unequal societies, with the amount and nature of network capital being a prime indicator of class.

Finally, class must be understood as embodied, multimodal symbolic behaviour (e.g. how one moves one's body, the clothes one wears, the way one speaks, how one eats, the kinds of pastimes one engages in, etc.) and, in part, a matter of style. One way to approach the notion that class is embodied and realised multimodality is to go back to Bourdieu's key constructs, habitus and body hexis, framing the former as 'embodied, turned into a permanent disposition, a durable way of standing, speaking, walking and thereby of feeling and thinking' (Bourdieu, 1990: 69–70), and the latter as a 'sense of acceptability' or a developed feel for what constitutes appropriate and legitimate behaviour in different social contexts. In essence, it is about knowing how to comport oneself, a point which was made all too clear to me one day, when a fellow academic who came from a working class background explained her experience with ongoing class positionings at an Oxbridge college at which she worked. My colleague found that she was often tested in very subtle ways to see if she could fit in, or form part of the Oxbridge in-group, in terms of her embodied multimodality. For example, at formal events, such as a banquet, she would need to know how to dress for the occasion, how to hold cutlery when eating and a glass when drinking, how to stand 'just so' and how to engage in conversation with other guests. All of this so as not to upset the established and expected norms of behaviour. Bourdieu explained such matters somewhat elaborately as follows:

> If a group's whole life style can be read off from the style it adopts in fur-
> nishing or clothing, this is not only because these properties are the objecti-
> fication of the economic and cultural necessity which determined their
> selection, but also because the social relations objectified in familiar objects,
> in their luxury or poverty, their 'distinction' or 'vulgarity', their 'beauty' or
> 'ugliness', impress themselves through bodily experiences which may be as
> profoundly unconscious as the quiet caress of beige carpets or the thin
> clamminess of tattered, garish linoleum, the harsh smell of bleach and
> perfumes as imperceptible as a negative scent.
>
> *(Bourdieu, 1984: 77)*

Conclusion: class and identity

In the previous section, I have discussed what I believe are the key dimensions of class, based on my reading on the topic over the past several years. One issue that arises in discussions of class is the connection between class and identity and, further to this, a long list of identity inscriptions, such as race, ethnicity, gender, sexuality, nationality, religion and so on. In this, the final section of this chapter, I address this point briefly, although I will come back to it again in the final chapter of the book.

As has been noted by several authors (Duff, 2012; Norton, 2010, 2011; Norton and Toohey, 2011; Noels, Yashima and Zhang, 2012), identity – in plural as *identities* – is generally understood by applied linguists today along the lines of the following definition from my book *Second Language Identities* (Block, 2007a):

> [I]dentities are socially constructed, self-conscious, ongoing narratives that individuals perform, interpret and project in dress, bodily movements, actions and language. Identity work occurs in the company of others – either face-to-face or in an electronically mediated mode – with whom to varying degrees individuals share beliefs, motives, values, activities and practices. Identities are about negotiating new subject positions at the crossroads of the past, present and future. Individuals are shaped by their sociohistories but they also shape their sociohistories as life goes on. The entire process is conflictive as opposed to harmonious and individuals often feel ambivalent. There are unequal power relations to deal with, around the different capitals – economic, cultural and social – that both facilitate and constrain interactions with others in the different communities of practice with which individuals engage in their lifetimes. Finally, identities are related to different traditionally demographic categories such as ethnicity, race, nationality, migration, gender, social class and language.
>
> *(Block, 2007a: 27)*

This definition is meant to capture what one might mean by identity, following the fundamental principles of poststructuralism, as outlined in Chapter 1. It is based on the work of a long list of social theorists, sociologists and anthropologists (some more poststructuralist in their orientation than others), such as Bauman, Bourdieu, Butler, Giddens, Hall and Weedon and it is the understanding of identity that many applied linguists have adopted in their work (Block, 2006; Byrd-Clark, 2009; Edwards, 2009; Harris, 2006; Jule, 2006; Kamada, 2009; Kanno, 2003; Kramsch, 2009; Pichler, 2009; Preece, 2010). And as has been the case in the social sciences in general, applied linguists have tended to adopt a culture-based view of identity. This view is consistent with goings-on in the economically advanced nation-states of the world (and particularly in the Anglophone world), where there has been a growing interest in what is commonly known as 'identity politics', although another and perhaps more appropriate term used by Nancy Fraser (2003) is 'recognition'. This recognition-based approach to identity has revolved around particular inscriptions – such as nationality, gender, race, ethnicity, and increasingly, religion and sexuality – and more sociologically informed applied linguistics research has explored how these inscriptions index individual and group positioning in socioeconomically stratified societies. However, in this research, what has too often been left to the side is what Fraser calls 'distribution', that is, a concern with identities linked to the material bases of human existence in twenty-first-century societies, in particular class-based subject positions. Fraser articulates this philosophical dilemma as follows:

> The discourse of social justice, once centered on distribution, is now increasingly divided between claims for distribution, on the one hand, and claims for recognition, on the other. Increasingly, too, recognition claims tend to predominate. The demise of communism, the surge of free-market ideology, the rise of 'identity politics' in both its fundamentalist and progressive forms – all these developments have conspired to decenter, if not extinguish, claims for egalitarian distribution.
>
> *(Fraser, 2003: 7–8)*

Elsewhere, along similar lines, Andrew Sayer formulates the problem as follows:

> Recognition at the level of discourse and attitudes is of course important, but it is not enough, and at worst may be tokenistic. It is easy for the dominant to grant discursive recognition and civility to the dominated or socially excluded; giving up some of their money and other advantages to them another matter.
>
> *(Sayer, 2005: 64)*

Fraser's solution to this problem (and Sayer would concur) is not to abandon recognition claims, which are ultimately about Weberian status positions in society, but to explore how these recognition claims interrelate with inequalities arising from the material bases of our existence, a more Marxist inspired position. For Fraser, recognition and redistribution can take place in very different ways. On the one hand, they can be 'affirmative', providing 'remedies aimed at inequitable outcomes of social arrangements without disturbing the underlying framework that generates them' (Fraser, 2008: 28). With recognition, this is what happens when diversity and difference are supported and even promoted in societies with a multicultural ethos. With redistribution, this is what happens when the liberal welfare state collects taxes and then provides resources to the most needy, although nothing is done to deal with the underlying conditions which lead to the needy existing in the first place. On the other hand, is affirmation enough if we wish to explore the roots of inequality? For Fraser, it is not, and so recognition and redistribution need to take place in a way that she calls 'transformative', providing 'remedies aimed at correcting inequitable outcomes precisely by restructuring the underlying generative framework' (Fraser, 2008: 28). Transformative recognition means problematising and undermining group differentiations, such as gay vs. straight, male vs. female, black vs. white and so on. Meanwhile, transformative redistribution means the arrival of socialism, as a deep restructuring of the political economy of a nation-state.

If we are to combine recognition and redistribution, it becomes a matter of how to engage in a form of 'intersectionality' (Crenshaw, 1991; Hill Collins, 1993), that is how to take into account the ways that different types of discrimination and inequality overlap and/or are inextricably linked. For example, it is impossible to develop a full and deep understanding of the discrimination and marginalisation that a 30-year-old female immigrant from Ecuador might suffer in Barcelona if one does not take into account a series of overlapping and interlinked social dimensions. These dimensions include (1) the ways that this woman is positioned in class terms in Catalan society (as a lower class person doing low level service jobs like cleaning); (2) her institutional and social status as an *immigrant*, that is someone who is progressively more unwelcome as the economic crisis deepens; (3) the fact that she is a person of colour, a visible minority with an Andean appearance, whose physical features are not valued in mainstream Catalan society; (4) her status as someone who is *culturally* different, someone with a worldview and behaviours that are not considered 'Catalan' or even 'Spanish'; and (5) her immersion in gender regimes in her home life (with her Ecuadorian husband) and in mainstream Catalan society, which are differentiable but which in both cases work against her attempts at self-fulfilment.

It is worth bearing in mind that these different dimensions of discrimination and marginality do not impact on this woman with the same force; neither are they all equally oppressive. And as they are all situated in the realm of the social, and in Marxist terms are superstructural, there is need to combine a focus on them with an understanding of the economic base, as elaborated by Marx. Thus if we return to Wright's (2005: 20–21) summary of key elements in the Marxist understandings of class, we see the need to explore two very basic ones: (1) 'class interests', based on aspects of the material foundations of class, such as 'standard of living, working conditions, level of toil, leisure, material security' and so on; and (2) 'class consciousness', as 'the subjective awareness people have of their class interests and conditions for advancing them' (see the discussion of Marx's 'class in itself' and 'class for itself' earlier in this chapter).

In addition, intersectionality would help to move researchers away from a tendency in the Anglophone world (especially pronounced in the UK) to assign class designations to so-called 'white people', while reserving for 'non-whites' ethnic, racial and nationality-based identity inscriptions. Or, as Rogaly and Taylor put matters:

> [D]iscussions of working class lives in Britain are too often elided with discussions of whiteness, so that working class black and minority ethnic people in Britain are defined by their ethnic heritage alone. Indeed white Britishness is often seen as being exclusively working class.
>
> (*Rogaly and Taylor, 2009: 4*)

In the process, social class is excluded from discussions of the lives of 'non-whites' and in lay and academic circles in Britain there is a 'white working class' and a 'white middle class', but there does not seem to be a 'Pakistani working class' or 'Indian (Gujarati) middle class'. This, despite the fact that these class positions no doubt exist objectively in British society, *in themselves*. As Rogaly and Taylor (2009: 14) argue, '[c]ontrary to what is implied in much British academic writing, working class does not necessarily mean "white" working class' and we could make the same point with regard to 'middle class'. However, if we work in an intersectional manner, we can perhaps avoid this tendency towards class erasure. For me, intersectionality means attention to and the problematisation of different identity inscriptions, as well as an engagement with the material base of human existence and the social relations emerging from this material base. In short, it means an engagement with social class articulated with a broader view of identity.

To conclude, I would say that in any attempt to understand how individuals and collectives live their lives in increasingly more complex twenty-first-century societies, there is a need for intersectional thinking. Above all, there is a need to introduce social class as a key construct in a context where it has not heretofore figured as a factor, as is the case of public discussions of immigrants in Catalan society. With cases like this one in mind, in Chapters 3, 4 and 5, I examine how class has and has not been a key construct in three key areas of applied linguistics research, sociolinguistics, bilingualism research and second language acquisition and learning.

Notes

1 I do this fully aware that many contemporary economists have no time at all for Marx's theory of value. I briefly cover it here because it is foundational to Marx's understanding of alienation, a concept that is perhaps more widely accepted, if not in economics circles, then among those who actually experience it.

2 Indeed, it includes a veritable paean to London, which I reproduce so that the reader might better grasp the passion with which Engels wrote his book:

> A town, such as London, where a man may wander for hours together without reaching the beginning of the end ... This colossal centralization, this heaping together of two and half millions of human beings ... has raised London to the commercial capital of the world, created the giant docks and assembled the thousand vessels that continually cover the Thames ... all this is so vast, so impressive, that a man cannot collect himself, but is lost in the marvel of England's greatness ...
>
> *(Engels, 2009: 68)*

3 *Capital 2* was written between 1863 and 1878 and first published in 1885, while *Capital 3* was written between 1864 and 1865 and first published in 1894.

4 A definition of communities of practice looks as follows:

> Communities of practice are formed by people who engage in a process of collective learning in a shared domain of human endeavor: a tribe learning to survive, a band of artists seeking new forms of expression, a group of engineers working on similar problems, a clique of pupils defining their identity in the school, a network of surgeons exploring novel techniques, a gathering of first-time managers helping each other cope. In a nutshell: Communities of practice are groups of people who share a concern or a passion for something they do and learn how to do it better as they interact regularly.
>
> *(Wenger, 2006: 1; available at www.ewenger.com/theory/; accessed 1 March 2012)*

5 Durkheim was born in 1858 and died in 1917. Weber was born in 1864 and died in 1920.
6 In *Economy and Society*, Weber actually devoted just 21 pages out of a total of over 1400 pages to the specific discussion and explanation of his two key constructs, class and status: pages 302–7 in Volume 1 and pages 926–40 in Volume 2.
7 *The Protestant Ethic and the Spirit of Capitalism* (Weber, 2002), a more concise and focused book, is generally considered his single greatest contribution to social theory and sociology in terms of quality.
8 The full statement contrasting 'class in itself' and 'class for itself', reads as follows:

> The economic conditions have in the first place transformed the mass of the people of a country into wage-workers. The domination of capital has created for this mass of people a common situation with common interests. Thus this mass is already a class, as opposed to capital, but not yet for itself. In the struggle of which we have only noted some, this mass unites, it is constituted as a class for itself. The interests whom it defends are the interests of class.
>
> *(Marx, 2005: 188–89)*

9 But see Block (2012b, 2013a) for a discussion of structure and agency.
10 It is worthwhile to distance Bourdieu, and his use of 'social capital', from managers, politicians and educators who have used the same term in recent years, but with a very different meaning. While Bourdieu's 'social capital' is social, relational and ultimately grounded in material conditions of people's lives, 'social capital' in current marketised educational discourses is a new way of framing workers. It is what Bonnie Urciuoli (2008: 211) terms the 'worker-self-as-skills-bundle', which is about 'not only … the worker's labour power as a commodity but [also] the worker's very person … defined by the summation of commodifiable bits'.
11 In this sense, and indeed here and elsewhere, Bourdieu writes about social ontology in a way that is consistent with Roy Bhaskar's critical realism, discussed in Chapter 1.
12 It is perhaps worth mentioning that Bourdieu *et al.* (1999) manage to do the same with regard to working class people in late twentieth-century French society in their massive *The Weight of the World*.
13 This notion is captured well in the following quote from an article by Stuart Jeffries, which appeared in the *Guardian* newspaper 12 March 2004:

> In one of Alan Bennett's Talking Heads dramas, someone exposes themselves in a branch of Sainsbury's. 'Tesco's you could understand,' says an elderly woman tartly. It's a remark that neatly sums up both the British obsession with class and our almost tribal attachment to specific supermarket brands. Tesco, the implication goes, is for commoner people who are slightly more likely to drop their trousers in public than Sainsbury's shoppers. By extension, Waitrose is for those more likely to have second homes in Chiantishire than the first two; Asda for people who aspire to have a second home anywhere but probably never will; Lidl for people who have never heard of Chiantishire; Marks and Spencer for those who affect to have never heard of Lidl. That kind of thing.
>
> *(Jeffries, 2004: NPN; available at www.guardian.co.uk/lifeandstyle/2004/ mar/12/foodanddrink.shopping; accessed 10 January 2013)*

More recently, Jan Moir, writing in *The Daily Mail* on 6 October 2012, follows the same logic that says that supermarkets index class positions. However, she adds that the economic crisis may be having the levelling effect of forcing middle class shoppers into shopping below their station:

> Apart from the names you give to your children, nothing says more about you than your choice of supermarket. Asda, Waitrose, Sainsbury's, Tesco, Morrisons? For

years, allegiance to any of the big boys has marked us out along tribal factions as neatly and distinctly as woad body markings. Asda devotees are cost-conscious shoppers; Waitrose customers are top-of-the-range aisle-rovers who don't mind paying for premium goods; Sainsbury's is the haunt of young professionals who find comfort in authentically sourced mozzarella; the Tesco tribe ranges from mothers in pyjamas shopping for cheap fags to anyone with an eye for a keenly-priced bargain, while Morrison's customers have solid, northern values and – according to their adverts – a fondness for 'fresh-cut' meat and cream cakes. But what could shopping at Aldi say about you? Sales at the budget German chain store are soaring – up by more than 500 per cent in the past year. A rise attributed to an influx of once-affluent posh shoppers who are desperate to cut their weekly grocery bills.

*(Moir, 2012: NPN; available at www.dailymail.co.uk/femail/
article-2213694/Aldi-More-middle-class-shoppers-lured-stores-
bargains-So-did-picky-JAN-MOIR-make-it.html; accessed 10
January 2013)*

3

SOCIAL CLASS IN SOCIOLINGUISTICS

Introduction

Given its strong historical links to the social sciences, and sociology especially, sociolinguistics has always been uniquely positioned to incorporate social class as a key construct, far more than other areas of applied linguistics. And many early sociolinguists were drawn to social class as a construct central to understandings of the social life of language use, following dominant trends in sociology in the 1960s, when it was a key construct. Still, as I will argue at the end of this chapter, in recent years there has been something of a shift away from social class in terms of its importance as a construct and in some cases outright erasure. In the sections that follow, I propose to take the reader through some of the key sociolinguistics research that has had social class at its centre, critiquing this work as I proceed. I end with some suggestions about future research. First, however, I would like to clarify what I mean when I make reference to the term 'sociolinguistics'.

In an early sociolinguistics textbook entitled *Sociolinguistics: An Introduction*, Peter Trudgill describes what he calls 'sociolinguistics proper' as follows:

> This covers studies of language in its social context which (whether they be sociological, anthropological or geographical in emphasis) are mainly concerned with answering questions of interest to linguistics, such as how can we improve our theories about the nature of language, and how and why does language change.
>
> *(Trudgill, 1974a: 33)*

Subsequently, Trudgill goes on to discuss the interaction between language and social class, language and ethnic group, language and sex, language and context, language and nation and language and geography, exploring, as he does all of this, 'the ways in which society acts upon language and, possibly, in which language acts upon society ... [and] the number of ways in which language and society are inter-related' (Trudgill, 1974a: 32). Significantly, 'language' always comes first in chapter titles, which is consistent with the linguistics-centric approach to sociolinguistics that is integral to Trudgill's notion of 'sociolinguistics proper'.

However, not all authors writing at the same time about sociolinguistics sub-scribed to Trudgill's relatively narrow view of what constituted and what did not constitute sociolinguistics. In his programmatic *Foundations of Sociolinguists*, Del Hymes writes:

> 'Sociolinguistics' could be taken to refer to the use of linguistics data and analyses in other disciplines, concerned with social life, and conversely, to [the] use of social data and analyses in linguistics. The word could also be taken to refer to correlations between languages and societies, and between particular linguistic and social phenomena.
>
> *(Hymes, 1974: vii)*

Hymes was, of course, interested in changing sociolinguistics, which as Trudgill's definition shows, was very much linguistics led. He argued for three changes in particular. First, sociolinguistics obviously should be about the study of language, but it should also be about what Hymes called the 'social as well as the linguistic' (Hymes, 1974: 195). This means the study of language not only as a linguistic phenomenon (meaning the analysis of formal features: morphology, syntax, lexis, phonology), but as an integral part of social phenomena. And this also means research on language use embedded in social context. Second, and as a corollary to the previous suggestion, sociolinguistics research needed to be more 'socially rea-listic', that is, it needed to be based not primarily or exclusively on samples elicited from language users in laboratory type settings, but on samples collected, *in situ*, from within existing speech communities. This means planned and controlled data collection in real-life situations (see Labov's work discussed later in the chapter), but the suggestion also points in the direction of more ethnographies (and exten-sive ones, at that), which came to be common in sociolinguistics as the field became more linked with sociology and anthropology from the 1970s onwards.

Third and finally, Hymes argued that sociolinguistic research needed to be 'socially constituted', beginning with a thorough understanding of 'the social', not only as a backdrop to language use, but as firmly integrated with language use. Hymes saw this suggestion as his most radical one, stating that '[s]uch a point of view cannot leave normal linguistic theory unchanged ... because its own goals are not allowed for by normal theory and cannot be achieved by "working within the system"' (Hymes, 1974: 196). In this vein, Hymes sees a linguistics without this social constitution in a way that parallels Marx's discussion of how human beings become alienated from the objects of their labour, from the processes involved in making these products, from themselves as human beings and ultimately, from their fellow human beings (Marx, 1976, 1988; see also Chapter 2). In short, the kind of idealised and abstract linguistics practised by Chomsky and others at the time that Hymes was writing, abstracted its object (language) from its producers (human beings), thus 'divorcing it from its roots in social life' (Hymes, 1974: 85). In writing these words, Hymes was clearly opening the door to a more multi-disciplinary research (research which draws on multiple established disciplines) *and* interdisciplinary research (research involving researchers from different established disciplines).

Their different approaches to sociolinguistics notwithstanding, Trudgill's rather narrow linguistics-based view and Hymes's broader socially informed one, there was general agreement in the early days of sociolinguistics that the project was about a group of like-minded linguists who had come to reject the then-dominant Chomskyan paradigm in linguistics and its socially disembedded, idealised notion of language (although, in defence of Chomsky, it should be noted that he never claimed to be doing anything other than this). These early sociolinguists effected a return of sorts to the older tradition in linguistics, which was always social and historical, with a sensitivity to communicative context (e.g. Jakobson, 1990). And one of them, William Labov, became known as the founder of the variationist school, which to this day is influential in sociolinguistics. Indeed, for many, Labov is one of the key founding figures of sociolinguistics, if not the key figure. It is with his work that I begin my discussion of social class in sociolinguistics.

In the beginning: Labov

Labov began his professional career as an industrial chemist, working in this capacity for over a decade, before completing in short succession an MA and then a PhD in linguistics. Labov's MA research, carried out in 1961, focused on sound changes in Martha's Vineyard, an island off the northeast coast of the US (Labov, 1963). The site of a growing tourist industry at the time of Labov's study, the island had a permanent population of about 6,000 people. Labov found that above all among the permanent residents who were 31–45 years of age and worked in the fishing industry, there was an ongoing shift in pronunciation of certain vowels, a shift in pronunciation which meant that these residents sounded very different from the tourists who came to visit the island. For example, words like 'house', 'out' and 'trout', generally pronounced with /aʊ/ as the principal vowel, came to be pronounced with a more elongated centralised vowel, /əʊ/, which means they sounded more like 'huh-oose', 'uh-oot' and 'truh-oot' than 'howss', 'owt' and 'trowt', respectively. Labov's research was unique for many reasons, among which were the innovative interview techniques that he used to prompt his research participants to speak in a relaxed style and his attention to detail in both the collection of linguistic data and their categorisation. However, the most important feature of Labov's study for the purposes of this book is to be found in how he linked linguistic features and language practices to social identities, in this case his documentation of how members of the fishing community who had come to resent the presence of so many tourists talked differently to mark a clear insider/outsider boundary.

This sensitivity to the interaction between social identities and linguistics was fundamental to Labov's next piece of research, the study of diverse and shifting pronunciation patterns in New York, which was eventually published as *The Social Stratification of English in New York City* (Labov, 1966). Labov examined in detail how a cohort of residents of the Lower East Side of New York pronounced a range of items across different speech styles ranging from informal to vernacular. Consistent with Marxist thinking on the relational nature of class and class positioning (although not in the least acknowledged as such by the author), Labov wrote the following early in his book:

> For a working class New Yorker, the social significance of the speech forms that he uses, in so far as they contain the variables in question, is that they are not the forms used by middle class speakers, and not the forms used by upper middle class speakers. The existence of these contrasting units within the system presupposes the acquaintance of speakers with the habits of other speakers. Without necessarily making any conscious choice, he identifies himself in every utterance by distinguishing himself from other speakers who use contrasting forms.
>
> *(Labov, 1966: 8)*

Labov saw the social stratification of New York in terms of two dimensions. First, there was what he called 'social differentiation', which is about how individuals are situated vis-à-vis particular variables deemed to index social class. Second, there was the 'social evaluation', that is the kinds of value that individuals attach to social differences. As regards the variables that construct social differentiation, the first one is income. However, Labov was intent not to adopt a one-dimensional approach to class and therefore occupation, educational level and housing were factors to be considered. Drawing on the work of Joseph Kahl, the author of a classic text entitled *The American Class Structure* (1957), Labov used the breakdown of American society outlined in Table 3.1.

As we observed in Chapter 2, such categorisation schemes do not come without problems, not least because education, occupation and income do not constitute the totality of social factors that index class positionings in a given society and in addition, they do not map onto one another as neatly as this table suggests. Nevertheless, the scheme does contain some subtlety. For example, in the middle of the scale, it shows nascent upward mobility in American society, noting how high school educated lower middle class parents save money for the university education of their children. At the top of the scale, it shows how class position can be linked to *which* university was attended, as members of the upper class are 'graduates of the *right* school'. Finally, it makes two interesting (and often interrelated) points about those classified as 'lower class'. On the one hand, they can be labourers who feel Marx's alienation as they work routine jobs for low pay,

TABLE 3.1 Distribution of the [US] population and their educational, occupational and income characteristics according to Kahl's social class divisions

Class title	Educational characteristics	Occupational characteristics	Income characteristics	% national population
Upper class	College graduate of the *right* school	First-rate professional manager, official or proprietor of large business	Do not bother to count it	1
Upper middle class	College graduate	Careermen in professions, managerial, official or large business positions	Equally high but they count it	9
Lower middle class	High school graduate, frequently with specialised training thereafter	Semi-professionals, petty businessmen, white collar, foreman and craftsman	Enough to save for children's college education	40
Working class	Some high school	Operatives: blue collar workers at the mercy of the labour market	Enough for cars, TV, etc.	40
Lower class	Grade school or less	Labourers: last to be hired and first to be fired Frequent job shifts	Struggle for bare existence	10

Source: Labov, 2006: 138

with little job security. On the other hand, they can be itinerant labour power, experiencing 'frequent job shifts', that is, moving from low level job to low level job.

In his research, Labov attempted to gather together a cohort of research participants who were a representative as possible of Kahl's scheme. In the end, he had an equal percentage of lower class (10 per cent); an over-representation for working class and upper middle class (46.5 per cent and 12 percent, respectively); an under-representation for the lower middle class (22.5 per cent); no one from the upper class (members of this class did not live in the catchment area); and a hybrid category of lower middle class/working class at 9 per cent (Labov does not explain how he came to create this category). Thus there was a general bias towards the lower end of Kahl's scale, which could not be helped given the geographical location that was the focus of his research. Importantly, as Labov notes, he found consistencies linking class positions to certain pronunciation features of American English, such as 'th' and 'r' production.

Labov also noted statistically significant above-their-class pronunciations among some of his lower middle class participants, referring to the 'profound linguistic insecurity' (Labov, 1966: 475) of members of this category. Labov suggested that the behaviour of these individuals was 'perhaps an inevitable accompaniment of social mobility and the development of upward social aspiration in terms of socioeconomic hierarchy' (Labov, 1966: 475). Such aspirations led to inconsistent linguistic behaviour as these individuals sometimes produced pronunciations that were more prototypically upper middle class, while on other occasions they produced what might be seen as anomalous or 'hypercorrect' forms. Labov defines hypercorrection as follows:

> [It is] the familiar tendency of speakers to overshoot the mark in grammatical usage; in attempting to correct some non-standard forms, they apply the correction to other forms for which the rules they are using do not apply. Common examples of such hypercorrect forms are *Whom did you say was calling?* [and] *He is looking for you and I.* The tendency to spelling pronunciations such as [ɔft-n] for *often*, or [pɑlm] for *palm* is another expression of the same process.
>
> *(Labov, 1966: 475)*

Most of *The Social Stratification of English in New York City* is about quantifying speech so as to establish links between statistically verifiable trends and class positions as determined by questionnaires. However, it would be an error to say that all of this classic work is devoted to statistics and what in essence is a rather unidirectional view of the world (social class exists and it determines speech patterns). As I stated previously, Labov was interested in 'social evaluation', that is the kinds of value that individuals attach to social differences. In the case of accent and the pronunciation of different variables, Labov found a good deal of self-awareness and seemingly as a result, self-criticism among many of his informants. Many made reference to how they did not speak 'good English' and when asked to judge others, they applied similar criteria. Still, there was some loyalty to participants' 'roots' and even a tendency to exaggerate their local New York accent when in the presence of outsiders. All of this is not particularly surprising and the kinds of observations made by Labov's informants have emerged in a wide variety of attitudinal research, not least in the 'matched guise' tradition (e.g. Lambert *et al.*, 1960).

At times Labov provides the reader with graphic depictions and commentary that lend life to the individuals who participated in his research and in this sense he follows a tradition begun by Engels (2009; see also Chapter 2). For example, in the following quote about the Lower East Side tenement dwellings in which many of his informants resided, Labov captures very well how class is a multimodal experience, in this case in terms of space, smell and overall affective orientation to one's environment.

> The tenement apartments usually consist of one to three small bedrooms in a straight line, barely furnished and neglected by the landlord. The smell of garbage and urine which pervades the halls can creep into the homes of the cleanest housekeepers. The contrast between living in a tenement house of this type, and in the best of the middle class apartment houses, illustrates the full range of stratification in the society of the Lower East Side.
>
> *(Labov, 1966: 166)*

In addition, Labov emphasises that he was as interested in 'deviant cases' a\
in cases that conformed to expected patterns. He discusses the case of Na\
an academic described by Labov in the 2006 edition of his book as 'a case …
[which] illustrates the fundamental Durkheimian notion of social fact: we are free
to talk in any way we want, but there will be social consequences if we depart too
strongly from the norms' (Labov, 2006: 157). Specifically, Nathan produced several
features of lower class speech regularly, despite his high educational (PhD), occupational and housing level (he lived in upper middle class housing). These included
DH stopping (the use of /d/ for word-initial /ð/) and the replacement of the
voiceless dental fricative /θ/ with a voiceless labiodental fricative /f/. These two
patterns meant the production of 'den' for 'then' and 'faif' for 'faith', respectively.
Labov shows himself to be agnostic when it comes to the physiological and/or
social origins of Nathan's 'deviant' middle class speech in that he does not know if
it is due to what some would call a 'speech impediment' or if it is due to the fact
that Nathan grew up on the Lower East Side and therefore was immersed in these
and other socially stigmatised speech patterns in his childhood and adolescence. He
sums up his surprise at these speech patterns when he says that the replacement of
the voiceless dental fricative with a voiceless labiodental fricative ('faif' for 'faith')
'appears to be a common trait of young children of 4 or 5, who are still learning to
pronounce (th)' (Labov, 1966: 251).

This discussion of *The Social Stratification of English in New York City* is not meant
to be exhaustive. Indeed, my aim has only been to provide the reader with
something of the flavour of Labov's landmark study, pinpointing a few links to
how we understand class and its relationship to language practices. The influence
of his work can be seen in research taking place elsewhere at more or less the
same time. For example, in the early 1970s Peter Trudgill documented and analysed the English spoken in Norwich, a small city in the east of England, focusing
on 16 pronunciation features, which included 'ing' vs 'in' endings on continuous
verb forms and third person 's' or its absence (Trudgill, 1974b). Like Labov,
Trudgill based his study on a social class categorisation system then in vogue in
British sociology, in this case a scale classifying individuals and households into
five class positions – middle middle class, lower middle class, upper working
class, middle working class and lower working class – based on occupation,
income, neighbourhood and type of housing. Drawing for the most part on 50
interviews with a random sample of Norwich residents, Trudgill found strong
correlations between class positions and the pronunciation of the 16 features
examined.

Trudgill was but one of many researchers around the world who were to follow
in Labov's footsteps, thus contributing to the generalised view that Labov was the
founder of variationist sociolinguistics. Nevertheless, there are numerous shortcomings in the Labovian paradigm, identified particularly by those who have not
followed the variationist tradition which he established. One shortcoming is his
relative lack of interest in how class systems work in societies at a macro level,
a more sociological view of world that would offer possible explanations not

only for the existence of the language practices he examined but also for their relative stability as mediators of the reproduction of class-based stratification in society. As John Rickford (1986) notes, in basing his theory of social class on the Kahl scheme (see earlier), Labov followed a:

> multi-index approach ... commonly associated with a functional or order paradigm ... which focuses on society as an integrated system, its different parts (classes) performing different functions and receiving differential awards according to the importance of their functions to the system and the level of education or skill which they require.
>
> *(Rickford, 1986: 216)*

This approach, most associated with Talcott Parsons (1951) and which derived from Durkheim's holistic view of societies, contrasts, as Rickford notes, with what are known as 'conflict' theories of class. Most of my discussion of class in the previous chapter would be classified as conflict theory, as running through the work of Marx, Weber and Bourdieu, and many scholars not cited in my discussion (e.g. Collins, 1975), there is a tendency:

> to focus on the schisms in society rather than the whole, stressing divergences in interests and values between classes rather than commonalities, and seeing change as the result of class struggle and the transformation of society as a whole rather than individual effort.
>
> *(Rickford, 1986: 216)*

In addition, as Glyn Williams notes, Labov is interested in 'the manner in which differences exist between objective groups rather than on the nature of power relations that exist between them' (Williams, 1992: 81). These differences are ultimately about language users slotted into different normative systems and the overall framing of the issue becomes highly individualistic: the individual and his/her class position are defined by affiliation to and participation in a set of linguistic norms. In the meantime, the bigger social and economic backdrops to all activity are left out of analysis. Of course, there are other ways to go about exploring how social class and language practices interrelate that differ from how Labov went about this task. And in the next section, we examine a different model, one put forth by Basil Bernstein, a contemporary of Labov working in the British context.

Bernstein: families, codes and debate (and Labov)

Bernstein somewhat defied disciplinary description, despite the fact that those who have written about him generally classify him as a sociologist (Atkinson, Davies and Delamont, 1995; Sadovnik, 1995), albeit one with a PhD in linguistics and a great deal more interest in language than most sociologists. And as a sociolinguist (or, in any case, someone who was read by sociolinguists), he certainly took on the interrelationship between social class and language in a very different way from Labov. In particular, and perhaps more in line with what Hymes (1974) had in mind when he wrote about a 'socially constituted sociolinguistics', Bernstein (1971, 1973, 1975, 1990, 1996, 2000) started with social structures in society and argued that particular language practices not only contribute to the constitution of these structures, but they also mediate the maintenance, reproduction and strengthening of them. The social structures that most interested Bernstein were those associated with social class in socioeconomically stratified societies, including the UK.

Part and parcel of Bernstein's thinking about class was a theory of socialisation, which argued that it is in the family, among peers and in schools that children come to master different ways of communication that serve different functions in their lives. And in the long run, schools exert far more influence on the child than the family, mainly because it is in schools that what he calls the 'three main message systems' come to structure most activity: curriculum, pedagogy and evaluation. For Bernstein (1975: 85) '[c]urriculum defines what counts as a valid knowledge, pedagogy defines what counts as a valid transmission of knowledge, and evaluation defines what counts as a valid realization of this knowledge'. And through these three message systems, there is the shaping of what might be understood as a culture, consisting of a worldview, patterns of behaviour and a value system, derived from curriculum, pedagogy and evaluation, respectively.

However, not all children encounter these message systems on equal footing and it is here that class as lived experience, as integral to the background which one brings to school, comes into play. Pre-school children spend a greater proportion of their time with their families and families are classified by Bernstein according to two extreme types: 'position-oriented' families and 'person-oriented' families. The former live in smaller dwellings than the latter, doing so according to stricter rules about who has authority and a general rigidity of roles across individuals and activities in the family structure. All of this occurs in conditions of intimacy, which comes with the physical proximity of smaller dwellings, and children grow up in greater proximity to their siblings and parents and therefore experience less personal privacy. In Bernstein's framework, these children are prototypically working class and their lives contrast markedly with those of children who grow up in person-oriented families. The latter live with a greater amount of personal space for each family member and although lines of authority are clearly drawn, there is a great deal more dialogue leading decisions that concern both the family as a whole and individuals as members. Due to more space and more liberal parenting, for children in person-oriented families there is more development of independent play and abstract thought and there is more explicit and contest-free communication. These children are prototypically middle class.

As a sociologist, Bernstein could have stopped at this point. He could have devoted his efforts to the sociology of the family, exploring in detail how the socialisation of children in different types of family articulates with class position in society. However, he did not stop at this point and further to his family dichotomy, he developed a theory about social class and language use. In this theory, he attempted to link class positions in society with particular ways of using language in the production of meaning. Embedded in the ways that language is used are class positions linked to individuals' relations to the means of production (*pace* Marx), their position in the social division of labour in society (*pace* Durkheim) and their differentiated access to and positions in markets (*pace* Weber). To capture such notions, Bernstein developed a contrast between: (1) 'elaborated code', which is associated with middle class families and their children and an affiliation to the institutionalised discourses of education and (2) 'restricted code', which is associated with working class families and their children and a lack of affiliation to institutionalised discourses of education. In Table 3.2, I outline the key features that serve to differentiate these two codes.

Dichotomies are always problematic, but to be fair to Bernstein, this one, along with the two types of family and indeed a long list of auxiliary constructs that he formulated in his work spanning over four decades, should be viewed as a set of ideal types, as polar extremes between which the linguistic repertoires of individuals can be situated. Still, on reading his early publications, many saw his theorising as overly simplistic categorising. And to make matters worse, his work was appropriated by the 'wrong people' in the form of conservatives in the US who saw it as a way of capturing what for them were the intellectual deficiencies of the lower classes, or more specifically African American school children (see Edwards, 2010, for a recent account). Thus apart from misreading Bernstein as an élitist who denigrated working class language and culture, they also turned a denunciation of class structure into a highly racialised condemnation of African Americans. In addition, many scholars who never actually read any of Bernstein's work, were content to accept a version whereby he was an ultra-conservative and even a racist (Sadovnik, 2001).[1] All of this ensued despite the fact that Bernstein never wrote

TABLE 3.2 Elaborated and restricted code

Elaborated code	Restricted code
Middle class	Working class
Individualistic	Collective
Institutionalised, school	Vernacular, community
Formal	Informal
About the abstract, eternal	About the concrete, immediate
Public oriented	Intimate oriented
Context independent	Context dependent
Syntax: complex, extensive use of conjunction and coordination	Syntax: short utterances, few conjunctions, little subordination
Pronoun use: I	Pronoun use: you, they
Vocabulary related to standard English	Vocabulary related to non-standard English

Source: Based on Bernstein, 1971, 1973, 1975, 1990, 1996/2000

about the US and indeed, had very little, if anything, to say about race. To make clear how much Bernstein managed to get on the wrong side of debates in the US about the relatively poor academic performance of African American children, I reproduce the following excerpt from an article by Labov, published in 1972:

> The most extreme view which proceeds from this orientation – and one that is now being widely accepted – is that lower-class black children have no language at all. Some educational psychologists first draw from the writings of the British social psychologist Basil Bernstein the idea that 'much of lower-class language consists of a kind of incidental "emotional accompaniment" to action here and now.' Bernstein's views are filtered through a strong bias against all forms of working-class behavior, so that he sees middle-class language as superior in every respect – as 'more abstract, and necessarily somewhat more flexible, detailed and subtle.' One can proceed through a range of such views until one comes to the practical program of Carl Bereiter, Siegfried Engelmann, and their associates. Bereiter's program for an academically oriented preschool is based upon the premise that black children must have a language which they can learn, and their empirical findings that these children come to school without such a language. ... Bereiter concludes that the children's speech forms are nothing more than a series of emotional cries, and he decides to treat them 'as if the children had no language at all.' He identifies their speech with his interpretation of Bernstein's restricted code: 'The language of culturally deprived children ... is not merely an underdeveloped version of standard English, but is a basically non-logical mode of expressive behavior.'
>
> *(Labov, 2004: 136–37)*

In this way, Bernstein came to be pigeon-holed – above all in the US, but also in the UK and elsewhere (see Rosen, 1974) – as a card-carrying deficit theorist who only saw merit in the language practices of the privileged and condemned the underprivileged to the status of uncommunicative brutes. Labov's demolition here is more aimed at Bereiter and Engelmann (1966), even if he is not averse to tainting Bernstein along the way. However, Bernstein did himself no favours in the way he presented his thoughts, particularly in his early publications. The items in Table 3.1 capture the relative crudeness of Bernstein's terminology well.

Meanwhile, working against the backdrop of the civil rights movement in the US, Labov was involved in his long-term commitment to a good cause, that is, the habilitation of AAVE (African American Vernacular English). But for Bernstein, the son of a working class Jewish family from East London and a man with left-wing political views and convictions, the association with deficit theories and conservative politics, and above all the very idea that he harboured 'a strong bias against all forms of working-class behavior' (Labov, 2004: 136) were all criticisms he found very hard to take. And, it should be added, he did not take any of the criticism that he received lying down, as up to his death, he wrote what were often poignant defences of his work, sometimes acknowledging his propensity to score own goals through his dense and often clumsy writing style. Unfortunately, constant reformulations and restatements of his theories and concepts, such as the following one in which he makes clear his rejection of both difference and deficit framings of discourse, were generally not taken on board by his critiques:

> The code theory asserts that there is a social class regulated by unequal distribution of privileging principles of communication […] and that social class, indirectly, effects the classification and framing of the elaborated code transmitted by the school so as to facilitate and perpetuate its unequal acquisition. Thus the code theory accepts neither a deficit nor a difference position but draws attention to the relations between macro power relations and micro practices of transmission, acquisition and evaluation and the positioning and oppositioning to which these practices give rise.
>
> *(Bernstein, 1990: 118–19; cited in Sadovnik, 2001: 613)*

Bourdieu: a comment on Labov and Bernstein

One scholar who noted the contrast between Labov and Bernstein's respective approaches to social class and language is Bourdieu. Bourdieu in effect issued a challenge to sociolinguistics in the Anglophone world with two publications, 'The economics of linguistic exchanges' (Bourdieu, 1977b) and *Language and Symbolic Power* (Bourdieu, 1991), in which he applied his thinking about social class to language practices in society. His challenge to sociolinguistics can in part be encapsulated in his attack on both Labov and Bernstein. In *Language and Symbolic Power*, he identifies two ill-chosen paths for those interested in exploring the interrelationship between society and language use. On the one hand, he warns against an ignorance of how uses of language deemed to be legitimate, are not legitimate due to any absolute properties they may have but because of a range of factors in the social contexts in which they arise. Thus 'dominant usage', the language of the powerful, holds this status not because it is intrinsically better than other varieties but because it is used by those who hold positions of power and are able to impose reception of it and the particular values attached to it. For Bourdieu, not recognising this basic reality is Bernstein's sin, as he 'fetishises' elaborated code as the legitimate variety of English in Britain and he fails to relate codes to 'the social conditions of this production and reproduction, or even … to its academic conditions' (Bourdieu, 1991: 53). I will return to this view of Bernstein and whether or not Bourdieu was right about him later in this chapter.

As regards Labov, Bourdieu positions him as a scholar who avoids Bernstein's error of reifying the speech of the powerful as he makes the case that AAVE is not a deficient code from a linguistic, cultural or even logical perspective; rather, it is positioned as deficient by those in power in an inherently racist society. In what is perhaps his best known publication on this topic, 'The logic of nonstandard English', Labov (1972) presents and analyses two responses to a question about the existence of god, contrasting what is said by Larry, a 15-year-old boy from a poor background, and Charles, described as 'an upper-middle class college educated Negro man' (Labov, 1972: 197). I reproduce these two responses here:

[LARRY]

JL: What happens to you after you die? Do you know?

LARRY: Yeah, I know.

JL: What?

LARRY: After they put you in the ground, your body turns into–ah–bones, an' shit.

JL: What happens to your spirit?

LARRY: Your spirit–soon as you die, your spirit leaves you.

JL: And where does the spirit go?

LARRY: Well, it all depends ...

JL: On what?

LARRY: You know, like some people say if you're good an' shit, your spirit goin' t'heaven ... 'n' if you bad, your spirit goin' to hell. Well, bullshit! Your spirit goin' to hell anyway, good or bad.

JL: Why?

LARRY: Why? I'll tell you why. 'Cause, you see, doesn' nobody really know that it's a God, y'know, 'cause I mean I have seen black gods, pink gods, white gods, all color gods, and don't nobody know it's really a God. An' when they be sayin' if you good, you goin' t'heaven, tha's bullshit, 'cause you ain't goin' to no heaven, 'cause it ain't no heaven for you to go to.

(Labov, 1972: 193–94)

[CHARLES]

CR: Do you know of anything that someone can do, to have someone who has passed on visit him in a dream?

CHAS. M.: Well, I even heard my parents say that there is such a thing as something in dreams some things like that, and sometimes dreams do come true. I have personally never had a dream come true. I've never dreamt that somebody was dying and they actually died, (Mhm) or that I was going to have ten dollars the next day and somehow I got ten dollars in my pocket. (Mhm). I don't particularly believe in that, I don't think it's true. I do feel, though, that there is such a thing as – ah – witchcraft. I do feel that in certain cultures there is such a thing as witchcraft, or some sort of science of witchcraft; I don't think that it's just a matter of believing hard enough that there is such a thing as witchcraft. I do believe that there is such a thing that a person can put himself in a state of mind (Mhm), or that – er – something could be given them to intoxicate them in a certain – to a certain frame of mind – that – that could actually be considered witchcraft.

(Labov, 1972: 197–98)

After a long and detailed analysis of the relative logic of these two excerpts, Labov describes Larry's speech as 'quick, ingenious and decisive' (Labov, 1972: 196) and he writes that Charles 'succeeds in letting us know that he is educated, but in the end we do not know what he is trying to say, and neither does he' (Labov, 1972: 200). In his short discussion of Labov, Bourdieu suggests that, like Bernstein, he fetishises a language variety. The difference is that he chooses to do so with a non-standard and denigrated variety, while making suspect generalisations, more from the heart than from the mind, about middle class varieties of standard American English. Interestingly enough, it was Bernstein himself who made this point in one of his last publications:

> It is of interest that in the endlessly recycled account of Larry's discussion … it is rarely noted that Larry is given five probes to assist in the structuring of his argument. … In contrast, the question to the black middle class speaker is … [n]ot the clearest question to answer. The respondent is given no probes to assist in the structuring of his reply. … In light of the question, [his is] perhaps not a bad effort. However, this is not Labov's view, nor of those who recycle the quotations and interpretations unmediated by analysis. The 'liberal' ideology of white sociolinguistics paradoxically here transforms difference into deficit.
>
> *(Bernstein, 2000: 151)*

For Bourdieu, Labov falls into the trap of 'the naivety par excellence of … scholarly relativism' as he 'overlooks the fact that … the linguistic "norm" is imposed on all members of the same "linguistic community", most especially in the educational market and all formal situations in which verbosity is often *de rigueur*' (Bourdieu, 1991: 53). Or, put another way, '[a]rguments about the relative value of different languages cannot be settled in linguistic terms: linguists are right in saying that all languages are linguistically equal; they are wrong in thinking they are socially equal' (Bourdieu, 1977b: 652). In short, for Bourdieu, Labov tries too hard to habilitate AAVE and in so doing he falls into a form of romanticism, which becomes asocial and ahistorical, ignoring the bigger picture of how language and symbolic power function in contemporary societies.

Against the backdrop of the critiques of Labov by Rickford (1986) and Williams (1992) cited already, such an assessment seems fair enough if we frame his discussion in terms of Fraser's recognition and redistribution distinction (see Chapter 2). In short, Labov seems to have ignored the redistribution issue here: class divisions are mediated by language practices and therefore are part and parcel of differences in the communicative resources and styles employed by lower class and middle class individuals. And this has led him to frame his discussion mainly in terms of a recognition and respect of linguistic difference. In Fraser's terms, he takes 'affirmative' action, providing 'remedies aimed at inequitable outcomes of social arrangements without disturbing the underlying framework that generates them' (Fraser, 2008: 28). He does not therefore take 'transformative' action, providing 'remedies aimed at correcting inequitable outcomes precisely by restructuring the underlying generative framework' (Fraser, 2008: 28). Of course, we need to take into account that Labov was researching and writing about AAVE in the mid- to

late 1960s, in the midst of the American civil rights movement and from this perspective he was engaging in what would have been considered radical politics,
advocating on behalf of the language practices of an oppressed minority. Nevertheless, from Fraser's perspective, a question remains: if Labov could convince
American educational authorities to recognise AAVE as equal to standard English
in linguistic terms, and get them to respect it as well, would such measures remove
the conditions that have shaped Larry's life and made him someone who 'causes
trouble in and out of school ... [,] was put back from the eleventh grade to the
ninth, and has been threatened with further action by the school authorities'
(Labov, 1972: 193)? My response is 'probably not', unless Labov and the authorities
whom he is able to convince go back to the material conditions of Larry's existence, perhaps to the tenement apartments he described so well in *The Social Stratification of English in New York City* (seen earlier). In this sense, Labov perhaps
needed to be more like Bernstein, who, Bourdieu's comments notwithstanding,
did start at the base of the class system in Britain in his concern with language
practices in families and schools.

Meanwhile, not everyone agreed with Bourdieu's assessment of Bernstein's
work. In a book written before Bernstein had published the bulk of his work, A.
D. Edwards sums up his approach to class and language as follows:

> In Bernstein's analysis, the class system acts on the 'deep structure' of com-
> munication. It is through talk that the child discovers the nature and
> requirements of his world. He learns to look at and talk about things and
> events as others do, and so act with them to 'produce and perform social
> order' (Cook-Gumperz 1973, p. 7). The 'focussing and filtering' of his
> experience within the family is seen as a 'microcosm of the macroscopic
> orderings of society', and a fundamental part of how the class structure affects
> the distribution of 'privileged meanings' (Bernstein 1973, p. 198).
>
> *(Edwards, 1976: 107)*

This view contrasts markedly with Bourdieu's assessment of Bernstein as a scholar
who 'fetishiz[es] the legitimate language' and 'describes the properties of the elaborated code without relating this social product to the social conditions of this
production and reproduction, or even ... to its academic conditions' (Bourdieu,
1991: 53; see earlier in the chapter). So if Labov and his followers were overhasty
in their dismissal of Bernstein as a deficit theorist, where does Bourdieu stand given
his portrayal of Bernstein as asocial? Hymes takes Bernstein's side in this affair,
suggesting that because:

> Bernstein has independently pursued a path parallel to that of Bourdieu [,] ...
> perhaps that is why Bourdieu has misrepresented Bernstein's work ... [by]
> stating ... that Bernstein does not relate the elaborated code to social
> conditions of production and reproduction.
>
> *(Hymes, 1996: 188)*

For his part, Bernstein was perplexed by Bourdieu's attack, citing several examples where he clearly does relate codes to 'the social conditions of their production and reproduction' (Bourdieu, 1991: 53), as well as noting that Bourdieu had been instrumental in the French translation of *Class, Codes and Control, Volume 1* (Bernstein, 1971), and seemed to be in broad agreement with Bernstein's approach to social class and language.

Discussing Labov and Bernstein in tandem, we are thus faced with several alternatives. For a start, there might be an attempt to arrive at some kind of decision as to who was right or at least *more* right. However, I am not inclined to go in this direction. Instead, I prefer to stay focused on the discussion of social class in sociolinguistics, seeing what I can take from the two scholars' work. First, I see Labov as having started with a view of social class based at least to some extent in the material conditions of people's lives but then as having evolved into a concern with recognition, which consequently led him to the virtual abandonment of social class as a central construct in his work in favour of race. Meanwhile, for all his faulty writing, and – in retrospect – unfortunate terminology, Bernstein is far more in line with the discussion of class developed in Chapter 2, as he seems more concerned with redistribution than recognition. Indeed, the problem that so many researchers past and present have with Bernstein is that he seems to have little interest in the respect for difference in terms of race, ethnicity and gender, which has become so central to so much work.

In this sense, perhaps Bourdieu's work may be seen as a remedy of sorts. Like Bernstein, he showed himself to have a keen eye for macro-level social structure and also like Bernstein, he was manifestly lacking in any kind of romantic spirit that might lead him to over-argue the case for the downtrodden in societies, as Labov did. Above, I cited his 1977 paper and his 1991 book as the key media through which he has entered the world of many sociolinguists. Above all, in the former he proved himself to be especially prescient as regards the ways in which he conceptualised language use in context and how he discussed dominant state ideology and how language practices mediate power relations and class structure in capitalist societies, with late twentieth-century France being the focus of his attention. He highlighted the importance of context, which he understood not only in terms of the physical and social setting, but also in terms of one's interlocutor. Bourdieu noted how '[u]nderstanding is not a matter of recognising an invariable meaning, but of grasping the singularity of a form which only exists in a particular context' (Bourdieu, 1977b: 647), adding that 'competence is always the capacity to command a listener' (Bourdieu, 1977b: 648) and '[l]anguage is not only an instrument of communication or even knowledge, but also an instrument of power' (Bourdieu, 1977b: 648).

With reference to the bigger issue of how class systems are dominated from the top, how ideology undergirds and mediates policy and practice in capitalist states in favour of the dominant class and to the detriment of the dominated classes and how language used in a range of contexts serves both to index and to constitute class systems, he wrote:

[T]he dominant usage is the usage of the dominant class, the one which presupposes appropriation of the means of acquisition which that class monopolizes. The virtuosity and ease which figure in the social image of linguistic excellence require that the practical mastery of language which is only acquired in a home environment having a relation to language very close to that demanded and inculcated by the school be reinforced but also transformed by the secondary pedagogy which provides the instruments (grammar, etc.) of a *reflexive mastery* of language.

(Bourdieu, 1977b: 659)

And to sum up how the macro and the micro are interconnected, how society at large is in every single instance of interaction, Bourdieu wrote:

Thus the whole social structure is present in the interaction (and therefore in the discourse): the material conditions of existence determine discourse through the linguistic production relations which they make possible and which they structure.

(Bourdieu, 1977b: 653)

Post-Labov and Bernstein

Since Labov, many sociolinguists have kept alive an interest in social class, although they have moved in different directions. In this section, I discuss two lines of research, both of which have taken very different tacks. First, I examine Leslie Milroy and James Milroy's work on social networks and social class in neighbour-hoods in Northern Ireland, which links back to the variationist tradition of Labov and Trudgill. Second, I consider Shirley Brice Heath's work on the emergence of literacies in social activity occurring at the crossroads of race and class in the southern United States, which many today see as foundational to 'new literacies' studies (Street, 1985).

Milroy and Milroy on social networks and social class

Like Trudgill, Leslie Milroy and James Milroy had an interest in urban dialects and how they interrelate with class positions in Britain. In a series of publications (e.g. Milroy, 1981, 1991; Milroy, 1987; Milroy and Milroy, 1978, 1985), they examined class-based differences across particular features of English in Belfast, Northern Ireland. However, they explicitly distanced themselves from what Rickford (1986: 216; see earlier) termed the 'multi-index ... functional or order paradigm'. They made their position clear as follows:

[T]he model of social class to which we have appealed here is not the stra-tificational consensus-based model that has been generally favoured by

Western sociolinguists. Whereas Labov's view of speech community has emphasized shared norms throughout the community and is thus related to a consensus model of social class, we have preferred to emphasize the conflicts and inequalities in society that are symbolized by opposing linguistic norms. This analysis emphasizes the basis of personal social networks in consensus, whereas class differences involve not consensus but conflict.

(Milroy and Milroy, 1992: 23)

In addition, they aimed to explain language related differences across class lines and therefore they adopted a very different tack from that adopted by Labov and Trudgill, who tended to remain at the level of description. In one study, Lesley Milroy collected data from 46 men and women from three neighbourhoods in Belfast, Northern Ireland. Each participant was graded according to criteria linked to membership in particular networks, that is the 'personal communities' of various sizes and intensities, created by individuals in their day-to-day interactions with others. These criteria included the amount of extended family there was in the same neighbourhood; the proportion of men and women in the neighbourhood who worked in the same place; the amount of workplace segregation there was; the type of same-sex activities that participants engaged in; and participation in activities tied to specific locations (e.g. bingo, football, drinking). The basic organising feature in this study was the neighbourhood and class position was established, a priori, by the fact the residents lived in particular areas dominated by public housing, as part of the government construction boom in the decade immediately after World War 2 (Hanley, 2007). The authors were also interested in showing how other identity inscriptions, such as gender and religion, intersected with and inflected class positioning in such a way as to contribute to the constitution of subgroups. Thus all participants in the study were classified as working class; however, there were major differences across the three communities. A breakdown of the three areas in the study, along with how they rated with regard to membership criteria in networks, is outlined in Table 3.3.

In a later publication (Milroy and Milroy, 1992), the authors provide something of a definition of social class, as used in their analyses of the speech patterns of these neighbourhoods:

TABLE 3.3 Three areas in the Belfast study

Area	Religion	Unemployment	Social networks	Gendered work/ activities
Ballymacarrett	Protestant	Low	Strong	High
Clonard	Catholic	High	Weak	Low
Hammer	Protestant	High	Weak	Low

Source: Milroy and Milroy, 1992

Social class is not conceived of here as a graded series of pigeonholes within which individuals may be placed. Following the analysis of the Danish Marxist anthropologist Thomas Hojrup (1983), a view of social class more consistent with network analysis conceives of it as a large-scale and ultimately economically driven *process* that splits populations into subgroups. The groups sharing certain social and economic characteristics and lifestyles that emerge from this split may loosely be described as classes, but as we shall see Hojrup offered a more explicitly motivated description in terms of *life-mode*. The attraction of this analysis from our point of view is that different types of network structure emerge from the conditions associated with the life-modes of these subgroups, and local and individual social behavior is seen as mediated through these smaller scale structures rather than directly related to class.

(Milroy and Milroy, 1992: 18)

In this quote, the authors no doubt wish to escape from some of the more rigid and fixed models of social class that had appeared in Labov's work, as well as that of Trudgill. Importantly, they attempt to move from a notion of class generating linguistic behaviour to a more fluid notion of class as a social marker constituted through the day-to-day practices, including linguistic practices, of individuals who purportedly occupy a particular class position in society. Nevertheless, as Williams (1992) notes, there are problems in this line of research. Williams is scathing as he remarks that network analysis 'has received attention far in excess of its theoretical merits ... for its attempt to introduce methodological novelty [network analysis] into sociolinguistic research' (Williams, 1992: 191). Paralleling his critique of Labov's work (see earlier in this chapter), he finds fault with what he sees as its tendency to see communication solely in terms of surface interaction; the way the research is grounded in a functionalist view of society that does not give adequate attention to (class) conflict; and the preoccupation with normativity or how individuals conform to the norms of a community encountered in interactions with members of the community.

Heath on the development of literacies in communities

Elsewhere, a far more detailed account of how social class is constituted through day-to-day practices, including linguistic practice, can be found in Shirley Brice Heath's classic ethnography of textile mill workers in the Piedmont area of South Carolina in southeast United States. Heath observed, interviewed and collected speech samples from the residents of Roadville, a white community, and Trackton, an African American community, for nearly a decade, from 1969 to 1978. Roadville residents had worked in the mills for at least two generations at the time of the study, while Trackton residents, benefitting from relatively recent anti-discrimination and desegregation legislation, were new arrivals to this form of employment, which had come to replace sharecropping and other farming jobs. The focus of Heath's research was on how the cultural environment enveloping children impacts on their language development and ultimately their performance in school where language – and particular ways of using language, it should be added – mediates most activity. As Heath puts it, she was interested in how 'the place of language in the cultural life of each social group is interdependent with the habits and values of behaving shared among members of that group' (Heath, 1983: 11). Social class is not explicitly invoked very often in Heath's book, although we do understand that the residents of Roadville and Trackton are differentiable by not only race but also by social class: the residents of Roadville are identified as working class but as noted already, their employment history in the mills goes back further than the residents of Trackton, who are identified as working class, but more specifically as workers who have fairly recently moved from farming to the mill.

Focusing on the childrearing practices of the two communities, Heath observed very different general patterns. In Trackton, parents took little direct responsibility for their children's education and development, as these took place in the extended family and the community as a whole. When parents and other adults interacted with children they generally did so talking in third person – talking *about* them rather than *to* them – and this meant that children were unaccustomed to interacting directly with adults. Crucially, there was very little provision of space and time constraints on children and the general idea was that children would 'come up' rather than be raised by parents or other adults, an ethos consistent with the message delivered in the church on Sunday, that life should be taken and accepted as it comes. Children were expected to learn by observation rather than participation and overall there was very little activity observed by Heath that would be seen as guided learning (e.g. a parent and child reading a story together or assembling a model together). All of these factors in the pre-school experiences of Trackton children meant that when they entered school, they were ill prepared for what awaited them: in essence, their values and behaviour were very different from what was expected in school.

Meanwhile, in Roadville, childrearing practices and childhood experiences were very different. Parents took direct responsibility for their children's education and development. They adapted how they spoke to their children, while inculcating in them individualism and the will to overcome their weakness, two messages that came through in church sermons every Sunday. In general, parents provided the frameworks and orientation to life experiences, which were valued in school environments far more than their Tracktown counterparts. The fact that children were used to predictable space and time barriers, often interacted directly with adults and were regularly encouraged to participate in activities and learn from their experiences, meant that by the time they entered school, their values and behaviour were aligned with what was expected in school.

In effect, parental activity and children's behaviour in Roadville were more similar to what Heath found in a smaller third cohort, the 'townspeople', who represented the more established middle class, or local élite, consisting of managers and other professionals living in the vicinity. Townspeople children were said to 'bring with them to school linguistic and cultural capital accumulated through hundreds of thousands of occasions for practicing the skills and espousing the values the schools transmit' (Heath, 1983: 368) and what we see in Roadville are attempts to emulate such behaviour as a way towards upward mobility. As noted already, Roadville adults had worked in the mills for longer than their Trackton counterparts and they were more oriented towards an exit from this type of employment and a more middle class lifestyle. However, we should not forget that race was another factor in all of this as years, decades and over a century of post-civil war racial apartheid meant that the black residents of Trackton were that much more isolated from the white middle class values of the townspeople. Thus Roadville's residents were working class, but they were also white and therefore more easily able to share social space with the middle class counterparts, the townspeople and, above all, they could far more easily imagine themselves as future townspeople. At the time of Heath's study, this was surely not the case with the Trackton residents, who were much more occupied with maintaining their newly won working class status and who certainly had little or no prospect of sharing social space with the local white middle class.

Heath's ethnography was something of a landmark in sociolinguistics, combining as it did anthropology with concerns about language and education. And, as I noted earlier, it was a precursor to what was eventually to be called 'new literacies studies' (Street, 1985). It was also important in situating class issues at the forefront of discussions of the relative achievement of different social and cultural groups in education, even if it did not always do so explicitly enough. Indeed, one could argue that Heath's work was always far more about race than it was about social class. In keeping social class at a distance, however, Heath was doing no worse than most of her contemporaries and indeed the vast majority of sociolinguistics who have done ethnographic fieldwork over the past four decades. However, in recent years an exception of sorts to the trend towards class erasure can be found in the work of Ben Rampton, a researcher who has done ethnographic work with class as a central construct.

Ben Rampton and a more class-centred sociolinguistics[2]

Over the past decade Ben Rampton (2003, 2006, 2010) has consistently put social class at the centre of his work. And, he stands out as the only scholar to have produced a sustained discussion of what class is for the purposes of his research, doing so in three lengthy chapters (6–9) of his 2006 book *Language in Late Modernity*. This, in contrast to other researchers who have taken one of two paths: either they introduce social class into their discussions with absolutely no indication of what it might mean, or they follow fairly limited frameworks derived from questionnaire-based sociological work, with the listing of the general indicators income, occupation and educational level sufficing as an explanation.

Rampton adopts as the site of his research the educational system and schools in particular, which scholars ranging from Bernstein to Bourdieu have identified as one of the key sites (or fields) of the reproduction of and struggles over social class. He situates himself at the crossroads of several traditions in sociolinguistics. First, he has been in recent years one of the forces behind the establishment of linguistic ethnography as a methodological subfield of sociolinguistics (Rampton, 2007). Second, he acknowledges his conceptual and methodological debt to the variationist sociolinguistics of Labov (1966) and Trudgill (1974b) and their quantitative work on the interrelationship between formal features of English and class structures in the US and the UK, respectively. He also situates himself in another tradition of sociolinguistics, one more about social structures interacting with micro-level activity. In this regard, there are his references to Bernstein's early work (e.g. Bernstein, 1971) and Heath's ethnographic research (1983). He sums up his debt to Bernstein as follows:

> Bernstein's analysis of language and class starts with macro-social structure and the division of labour, moves into the institutional organization of family and education, homes in on interactional practices deemed critical in socialization, and from there looks for links to the communicative disposition of individuals and their impact on school achievement. In doing so, Bernstein spans most of the levels where researchers have located class processes – the economy, the community, occupations, families, activity, discourse, language, consciousness and school careers.
>
> *(Rampton, 2010: 5)*

Nevertheless, although Rampton sees certain merits in Bernstein's work, he is also critical of it. Indeed, he takes Bernstein to task for not taking on how social class is necessarily interrelated with other identity inscriptions, such as gender, race and ethnicity. He also notes that in his work there is a lack of engagement with ideology and class struggle, which would have allowed him to develop a more clearly articulated theory of power and resistance, Finally, he sees Bernstein as a poor ethnographer (or more specifically, not as an ethnographer at all), as his analytical work lacks the systematicity and attention to detail that one finds in the work of researchers like Labov and Heath. To be sure, Rampton sees similarities between Bernstein's work and Heath's, especially the latter's interest in how different language practices, both in homes and in communities at large, interact and often come into conflict in more institutionalised settings such as schools. However, Heath was an anthropologist by training while Bernstein, for all intents and purposes, belonged to no clearly defined research tradition, as I have explained already. As Rampton puts it, while Heath 'describes people in their individual and contextual particularity' (Rampton, 2010: 8), bringing to the fore the 'literacy event' as a key construct, Bernstein's work seems somewhat stuck in a more macro level model which can become one-dimensional, despite its internal complexity. Rampton speculates about how things might have been different had Bernstein come onto the scene a decade or two after he actually did:

Maybe if the ethnography of communication had been fully invented when Bernstein did his work on language and class ... , or if he had been less attracted to models of knowledge production propounded in formal linguistics, we would have had something like *Ways with Words* in England in the 1970s and 1980s.

(Rampton, 2010: 9)

In the development of his theory of social class, Rampton draws on the work of a range of scholars, which includes Raymond Williams (1977), Edward Thompson (1980), Valentin Voloshinov (1973) and Michel Foucault (1962), elaborating a two-part view of class, which looks as follows:

1   material conditions, ordinary experience, and everyday discourses, activities and practices – the 'primary realities' of practical activity which are experienced differently by different people in different times, places and networks; and
2   secondary or 'meta-level' representations: ideologies, images, and discourses about social groups, about the relations of power between them, and about their different experiences of material conditions and practical activity.

(Rampton, 2006: 222–23)

This two-part distinction is consistent with Thompson's (1980) and Bourdieu's (1990) discussions of the objective and the subjective realms of class experience as outlined in Chapter 2. And it is consistent with Bhaskar's (Bhaskar, 1998: 36–37) view that '[s]ociety ... provides necessary conditions for intentional human action, and intentional human action is a necessary condition for it' (see Chapter 1).

In his research, Rampton monitors the everyday experiences and practices of a cohort of London secondary school students via recordings of their classroom interactions which are both on-task (when students are participating in teacher-led activity) and off-task (when they are talking among themselves, often about topics which have nothing to do with teacher-led activity). In particular, he examines their use of what he calls 'posh' and 'Cockney' Englishes, although a better term for the latter would be 'slang', the term used by young people in London to describe their day-to-day speech, as Roxy Harris (2006) and Siân Preece (2010) have noted. In their work, 'posh' refers not so much to received pronunciation (RP), which is about an élite accent (and register), but to a more generalised educated southern variety of English, while 'slang' refers to the emergent post-estuary English vernacular of young people in London (more on this later). Rampton monitors the switching back and forth between the different English codes, arguing that they are significant because each code shift marks a change in voice from insider (Cockney) to outsider (posh). More importantly, the students are deemed to inhabit working class subjectivities as they use both varieties, showing themselves to be multivocal and creative in their usages: they use Cockney to talk as working class youth and they use their mock posh to voice either an anonymous middle class, distant and distinct from the students and their day-to-day lives, or anyone whom they wish to position simply as distant from their interests and day-to-day practices. Thus for example, on one occasion, two girls imitated one of their teachers by putting on mock posh accents. However, as Rampton notes, the teacher in question 'actually spoke with … a noticeably [non-southern] regional accent' (Rampton, 2006: 287) and employed none of the supposedly posh features that the two girls attributed to him.

Rampton describes in detail how activity mediated by teachers, students and curriculum serves to reproduce class positionings. In addition, these class positionings are presented to the reader as effects created by the uses of communicative resources (linguistic and other semiotic forms) during participation in ongoing classroom interactions and informal conversations with peers. However, for Rampton these class positionings are not merely made up, haphazard or accidental; rather, given his approach to social structure outlined earlier, he argues that the actual class positionings being reproduced exist independently of the activity reproducing them. He opts for what he calls an 'ontological realism', echoing Bhaskar's (1998) thinking on critical realism discussed in Chapter 1, whereby there is assumed to be a reality outside of the researcher's ability to describe, analyse or interpret it.

Another point of interest arising from Rampton's research is how class is not explicitly evoked very often by teachers or students in their classroom-based interactions. Effectively, this means that while there may be class *in itself*, there is not necessarily class *for itself* (Marx, 2005; see also Chapter 2). And where it is invoked, this is done with negative connotations, as when a teacher warns a group of students about using the English that they normally speak during a university entrance interview:

> [L]isten (2) to get a level Five it starts […] to be a little more difficult because […] the words Standard English start to crop up […] and […] so […] sort of people who er answer every question […] with lots of aints and innits […] are in fact handicappin' 'emselves […] so unfortunately […] because you're all from […] London […] you're handicapped to a certain extent.
> *(Rampton, 2006: 277–78; all interruptions and false starts*
> *have been edited out of this excerpt)*

Here the teacher delivers a message about speech-based social class distinctions in Britain, the rather gloomy 'you're handicapped to a certain extent'. Meanwhile, seemingly in an attempt to make his message more effective, he interjects from time to time his own form of mock Cockney. He thus engages in final consonant dropping (handicappin') and word initial /ð/ dropping ('emselves), although the latter might have been more authentically uttered with DH stopping, that is the use of /d/ for word initial /ð/: /d/emselves for *themselves*.

Alternatively, references to social class may be included in a school-sanctioned respect agenda, according to which social class is another way of being, along with ethnic and gendered subjectivities, which must be acknowledged and valued in the school context. And this latter point leads to another finding by Rampton, namely the by-now much discussed way in which it is extremely difficult to discuss one identity inscription without invoking others. Thus, as Beverley Skeggs (2004) notes, class in modern Britain is inflected by race and ethnicity (e.g. white English) as well as gender (working class women), a point which hooks (2000) makes as well about the United States.

It is perhaps due to this inflection that the very class-based nature of London English, as it is spoken by young people today, may be called into question, a prospect that Rampton shows himself to be all too aware of when he notes how 'it may be harder than it used to be to treat particular non-standard variants as being typically working class' (Rampton, 2006: 255). As more and more Londoners see themselves in terms of nationality, race and ethnicity, supported by schools championing diversity in such terms, there is an issue that arises as to how we associate ways of speaking, including not only accents but any number of other semiotic forms accompanying speech, with class positions. In this sense, some of the recent work on accents in London (Cheshire *et al.*, 2008, 2011) and other parts of the UK (Moore, 2010, 2012; Snell, 2011, 2013) is instructive. I made reference earlier to 'slang' as an emergent post-estuary English vernacular of young people in London. This emergent variety has been given the name 'multicultural London English' (MLE) by Cheshire *et al.* (2011: 154) 'to refer to the overall range of distinctive language features used in multiethnic areas of London ... as a repertoire of features'. This 'new' London English includes traditional Cockney features and other influences from the Caribbean and South Asia, as well as from the United States. All of this means that the shorthand use of 'Cockney' by Rampton – or even the aforementioned 'slang', used by young people themselves – may be too narrow. Some of the key features of multicultural London English, including additional features from American Englishes (e.g. AAVE – African American Vernacular English) are listed in Table 3.4.

Cheshire *et al.* (2008, 2011) are not clear when it comes to how this emergent new English indexes class position, given that young people across London seem to pick up and use the same forms as they go about their day-to-day business. Indeed, the use of MLE is more identified with urban culture and urban cool and thus comes to be understood as a communicative resource that individuals and collectives can deploy in ongoing communicative events. Its use is then no longer linked strongly to social class: neither as emergent *from* relatively stable social structures and class positions in society, nor as the creator of social class as an effect arising in communication. In a sense, it enters the realm of recognition (Fraser, 2003), as its Cockney roots are disembedded and extracted from the realm of the distribution of economic resources and relations to the means of production. This framing of MLE as a communicative resource, among other communicative resources forming repertoires, is consistent with a general trend in sociolinguistics, whereby communication is seen as being about style and stance taking. It is to repertoire, style and stance that I now turn.

TABLE 3.4 Some features of London English

Feature	Examples
Glottal stop /ʔ / for voiceless dental plosive /t/	'I can wri[ʔ]e like simple le[ʔ]ers bu[ʔ] not technical ones like my sister she carried on yeah and she's just done her GCSE Gujara[ʔ]i ...' (Harris, 2006: 95) ... Oi Señori [ʔ] a
Voiced dental fricative /ð/ replaced by voiced labiodental fricative /v/	'bruver' for 'brother'; 'togever' for 'together'; 'wiv' for 'with'
Voiceless dental fricative /θ/ replaced by voiceless labiodental fricative /f/	'fing' for 'thing'; 'fink' for 'think'; 'frough' for 'through'
h dropping	'e's from 'ackney innit? It's 'orrible
l vocalization /w/	milk [mɪwk], fill [fɪw], alright [ɒlwajt]
DH stopping: the use of /d/ for word-initial /ð/	'dat' for 'that' 'dese' for 'these'
[tʰ], which is an aspirated /t/, for word-initial /θ/	'ting' for 'thing' 'tief' for 'thief'
the all-purpose tag question 'innit'	'You live in London innit' 'He's a teacher innit'
non-standard negation, e.g. ain't and double negation	'I ain[ʔ] seen im' 'I don[ʔ] wan[ʔ] no one to know'
'was' for all grammatical persons	'We was talkin' 'They was there'
Quotative THIS IS + SUBJECT	This is them 'what area are you from . what part?' this is me 'I'm from Southwark' This is her 'that was my sister' (Cheshire et al., 2008: 17)
Quotative BE LIKE	'He's like .. and I'm like ...'
Uptalking i.e., the use of rising intonation at the end of statements	'So we fough[ʔ] we'd go out[ʔ] ? An we wen[ʔ] to a par[ʔ] y? And we saw Jim there? ...'

Source: Cheshire et al., 2008, 2011; Harris, 2006; Rampton, 2006

Repertoire, style and stance in sociolinguistics

In recent years, many sociolinguists have contributed to what constitutes a reconfiguration of our understandings of how meaning is made via the use, in context, of language and other semiotic resources (e.g. Blommaert, 2005, 2010; Canagarajah, 2013; Pennycook, 2012). This reconfiguration has brought to the fore *repertoire* as a key term used to describe the resources that individuals bring to the communicative events in which they participate. And basing discussions of communication on the concept of repertoire implies an embrace of three further notions that are accepted by more and more sociolinguists today. First, it means a shift in how languages are framed: from seeing them as integral, free-standing entities to seeing them as both emergent and ever evolving. Second, it means a move from the study of communication exclusively in terms of language and language use to the view that individuals and collectives come to interactions with a multitude of semiotic resources at their disposal, including language, which they can draw on in their ongoing constructions of self, embedded in their participation in a range of activities. Third, and finally, the shift to repertoire means that new terms such as style and stance (a discussion follows) are now employed to describe what individuals do when they communicate using a range of resources, replacing earlier terms such as 'code', which only referred to linguistic features.

In a recent article both explaining and exemplifying the move from a traditional approach to variation to a repertoire-based approach, Julia Snell writes the following:

> The use of repertoire has several advantages over the traditional difference approach to language variation. The first point to note is that repertoire refers to the set of resources that a speaker actually commands rather than to abstract linguistic models. In this way, it can account for speakers who draw upon and mix resources associated with a range of linguistic varieties. Secondly, the use of repertoire invokes Hymes' […] notion of 'communicative competence' in that it links linguistic resources with knowledge of how to use these resources.
>
> *(Snell, 2013: 115)*

Elsewhere, Eckert provides an interesting discussion of how we have arrived at this particular phase in sociolinguistics, arguing that there have been three waves in '[t]he treatment of social meaning in sociolinguistic variation'. She writes:

> The first wave of variation studies established broad correlations between linguistic variables and the macrosociological categories of socioeconomic class, sex, class, ethnicity, and age. The second wave employed ethnographic methods to explore the local categories and configurations that inhabit, or constitute, these broader categories. In both waves, variation was seen as marking social categories. This article sets out a theoretical foundation for the third wave, arguing that (*a*) variation constitutes a robust social semiotic system, potentially expressing the full range of social concerns in a given community; (*b*) the meanings of variables are underspecified, gaining more specific meanings in the context of styles, and (*c*) variation does not simply reflect, but also constructs, social meaning and hence is a force in social change.
>
> *(Eckert, 2012: 87)*

In earlier sections in this chapter, I have discussed the first two waves, perhaps best exemplified by Labov and Heath, respectively, although I have obviously done so with neither the authority nor the depth provided by Eckert. Here my concern is with the third wave and, in particular, what I see as two important developments: (1) the use of 'style' (and derived terms – 'styling' and 'stylisation') and 'stance' to capture what people do or achieve in language use, and (2) the incorporation of multimodality in sociolinguistics analysis.

In Chapter 2, it was observed that Weber introduced 'style' and 'stylisation' into his analysis of industrialised societies in the late nineteenth and early twentieth centuries, using the terms to refer to the norms of social interaction. In recent years, and as part of a very different research agenda, 'style' (and its derived forms) and 'stance' have entered the sociolinguistic lexicon with great force coming, as they have, with new ways of conceptualising meaning making in context. Nikolas Coupland (2007: 1) opens his in-depth monograph entitled *Style: Language, Variation and Identity* by defining style succinctly as 'a way of doing something', before going on to explain, among other things, that style: (1) emerges from among alternatives (one chooses one style over other possibilities); (2) has a social meaning, which, in turn, has a history; and (3) is domain specific, i.e. it can be situated in what Bourdieu would call a field (see Chapter 2).[3] There is a general consensus among researchers focusing on style (e.g. Coupland, 2007; Eckert, 2008) that there has been an evolution in understandings of the construct. Thus, in Labovian variationist sociolinguistics, style was understood in the following terms:

> *There are no single style speakers.* ... By 'style shifting', we mean to include any consistent change in linguistic forms used by a speaker, qualitative or quantitative, that can be associated with a change in topics, participants, channel, or the broader context. ...
>
> *Styles can be arranged along a single dimension, measured by the amount of attention paid to speech.* ... Attention paid to speech appears to be mediated by the process of audio-monitoring, which can be blocked by a range of factors. ...
>
> *The vernacular, in which the minimum attention is paid to speech, provides the most systematic data for linguistic analysis.* ... The 'vernacular' is defined as that mode of speech which is acquired in pre-adolescent years.
>
> *(Labov, 1984: 29)*

This is a view of style that Scott Kiesling describes as 'intraspeaker variation', that is, how '[i]ndividuals use variants at different rates depending on the situation, broadly speaking' (Kiesling, 2009: 173). It contrasts with a more recent version of style that 'focuses not on the use of a single variable by an individual speaker in different situations, but on the use of more than one linguistic variable by one speaker' and therefore how 'a single variant is seen as part of a more complete *personal style* or *persona*' (Kiesling, 2009: 173). Importantly, it sees 'speakers not as passive and stable carriers of dialect, but as stylistic agents, tailoring linguistic styles in ongoing and lifelong projects of self-construction and differentiation' (Eckert, 2012: 97–98).

Taking an historical perspective with regard to the term, Rampton suggests that there are three general routes via which 'style' has been used in sociolinguistics. These are:

> S1: as 'style-shifting' in the tradition of variationist sociolinguistics: patterns of phonological variation identified with different situations by analysts using quantitative correlation ... S2: as 'enregistered style'/'register': distinctive forms of language, speech and non-linguistic semiosis associated by users with differentiating typifications of person, situation, relationship, behaviour etc, used as a normal part of social interaction ... S3: as 'stylisation': more reflexive communicative action in which speakers produce specially marked and often exaggerated representations of languages, dialects, accents, registers or styles that lie outside their habitual repertoire (at least as this is expected within the situation on hand).
>
> *(Rampton, 2011: 3)*

S1 is the most basic and perhaps least common approach to style in sociolinguists today, if one is to judge by what is published in journals such as *Language in Society*, *Discourse and Society*, *Journal of Sociolinguistics* and *Journal of Linguistic Anthropology* and it is S2 and S3 around which most research is carried out. As we move deeper into the twenty-first century and deeper into what has in recent years been understood to be 'late modernity', there is by now a well-established interest in how identity is made in interactions and how the latter are the sites of multilingual and multimodal meaning and identity making.

Elsewhere, researchers have proposed an additional term, 'stance', to capture how meaning and identity are made in context (Engebretson, 2007; Jaffe, 2009a). For Kiesling (2009: 172), stance is 'a person's expression of their relationship to their talk (their epistemic stance – e.g., how certain they are about their assertions), and a person's expression of their relationship to their interlocutors (their inter-personal stance – e.g., friendly or dominating)'. In her introduction to the edited volume, *Stance: Sociolinguistic Perspectives*, Jaffe (2009b: 4) defines 'speaker stances' as 'performances through which speakers may align or disalign themselves with and/or ironise stereotypical associations with particular linguistic forms'. However, if I take this definition of stance, examine Jaffe's more detailed discussion of the stance in general in the same publication (Jaffe, 2009b: 14–17) and then go back to the discussion of style from earlier in this chapter, I find that it is not always easy work out the how style and stance are different.

It does not help matters that there is a fuzziness in the way that some authors use the two terms. This being the case, it is perhaps best to see style as a reference to communicative processes and stance as adopted and achieved positions of varying permanence or ephemerality arising from communicative processes. In any case, it is not my intention here to develop an in-depth discussion of these two constructs; rather, I am more interested in how analyses framed in terms of style or stance inform us about how social class 'gets done' in interactions.

As indicated already, the turn to repertoire means not only the incorporation of style and stance as key terms, but also a full embrace of multimodality, that is, the view that that language practices must be examined, not in isolation, but as part of the employment of assemblages of semiotic resources. As Carey Jewitt (2009: 14) puts it, multimodality is about 'approaches that understand communication and representation to be more than about language, and in which language is seen as one form of communication ... among other modes such as image, gesture, gaze, posture, and so on'. In this way, communication is seen as far more than the various linguistic means which can be drawn on to mediate self-expression (accent, pronunciation, lexical choice, syntax, morphology); in addition, it is about a range of multi-sensory accompaniments to the linguistic, such as hairstyle, clothing, ornaments, facial expressions, posture, gait and so on. Multimodality is an area of research that has grown exponentially in recent years, much of it concerned with the analysis of relatively inert 'texts', such as children's drawings, textbook illustrations, photographs, paintings, sculptures, toys and webpages (e.g. Kress and Van Leeuen, 2013). However, there is also a growing interest in the multimodal analysis of activity and interaction. Thus, in Kress *et al.* (2005) and Jewitt (2011), we find fine-grained analyses of how subject English is taught in London secondary school classrooms, with a focus on 'how modes and semiotic resources feature and are orchestrated in the production of school knowledge' (Jewitt, 2011: 185).

As I note elsewhere (Block, 2013b), there is a line of thought running through Goffman (1981), Hymes (1974), Bourdieu (1991), Hanks (1996) and others, which informs current understandings of how embodiment and multimodality are constitutive of communication. The end result is analysis, such as that provided by Eckert:

> [T]he burnouts in each school lead overwhelmingly in the use of non-standard negation and in the advancement of the three sound changes that are moving outward from the urban end of the conurbation. And although some correlation exists between the use of negative concord and mother's education as well as social category, the sound changes correlate with social-category membership rather than either parent's class membership (or both), clearly showing that patterns of variation are not set in childhood but serve as resources in the construction of identity later in life. This finding indicates that broader class correlations are not simply the fallout of education, occupation, and income, but rather reflect local dynamics rooted in practices and ideologies that shape, and are in turn shaped by, class.
>
> *(Eckert, 2012: 92)*

Here Eckert rehearses some of her findings from earlier publications about her well-known study of 'jocks' and 'burnouts' in a secondary school in the United States (e.g. Eckert, 1989; see, further, Chapter 2). Crucially, she returns us to notion of language practices indexing social class. However, she adds to this the notion that social class is made not only in the ways that the students talk, but in how they *communicate*, drawing on a range of semiotic resources. All of this is fine, but reading Eckert's work, and indeed that of many other researchers who have followed the repertoire turn in recent years, one comes to an understanding of how 'middle class', 'working class' and 'social class' in general are constructed through style and stance, but one finds nowhere a clear presentation of what is actually meant by 'class'. Some examples follow in the next section.

Repertoire, style, stance and social class: two examples

Given the discussion thus far in the chapter, it is worthwhile to examine recent publications that clearly follow this trend towards putting repertoire at the centre of linguistic and semiotic analysis and which, at the same time, include social class as a working construct. A good example of this type of research in recent years has been the work of Julia Snell (e.g. 2010, 2013). Snell focuses on non-standard dialect use among adolescents in Teesside, in the northeast of England, a setting she describes as follows:

> The setting for the analysis is Teesside, north-east England, where I con-
> ducted a comparative ethnography of the language practices of 9- to 10-year-
> old children in two socially differentiated primary schools (Snell 2009):
> Ironstone Primary was situated in a lower working-class area of Teesside; and
> Murrayfield Primary served a predominantly lower middle-class area.
>
> *(Snell, 2013: 112)*

In an endnote, Snell expands on this statement, writing: 'Elsewhere (Snell 2009; see also Snell 2010) I make a detailed comparison of the two school areas using census data, indices of deprivation and OFSTED reports' (Snell, 2013: 124). This may be the case in the 2009 publication, Snell's PhD thesis, but it is not in the more readily available journal article by Snell (2010), in which there is no real clarification of what the author means by social class. Still, there is in this article an interesting question posed, which involves an understanding of behaviour associated with working class identity:

> Does habitual use of a particular kind of interactional stance by the partici-
> pants at Ironstone Primary cumulatively construct a particular kind of
> working-class identity (e.g. characterised by humour, playfulness, the poli-
> cing of social boundaries), or at least an aspect of that identity, which can be
> contrasted with the middle-class identity associated with Murrayfield Primary?
>
> *(Snell, 2010: 649)*

Here we see a link made between working class subjectivities and behaviour that Willis (1977; see also Chapter 2) found in his 1970s' study of working class adolescent males in the West Midlands area of England: 'humour, playfulness, the policing of social boundaries'. However, this type of description of behaviour does not constitute a definition of working class and nowhere in the article is any such clarification to be found.

In her research, Snell (2010, 2013) elaborates sophisticated and nuanced ways of seeing communication that have the potential to enhance our understanding of social class. However, the net effect of their analyses comes to be something more akin to class erasure, at least with regard to the usefulness of the construct as part of a broader redistribution agenda (Fraser, 2003). Indeed, the advocacy on behalf of working class forms of speech, very much aligned with Labov's earlier advocacy on behalf of AAVE, shifts the reader away from a redistribution agenda, which goes to the economic base and the heart of the socioeconomic inequalities generated by capitalism, to a recognition agenda dealing with superstructural linguistic prejudice. The proposed action arising as a result – that the dominant class should respect working class forms of speech – is, in Fraser's terms, only affirmative, as opposed to transformative. This, because it provides 'remedies aimed at inequitable outcomes of social arrangements without disturbing the underlying framework that generates them' (Fraser, 2008: 28). As noted already with reference to Labov's work, a question arises as to what would happen if we could convince the dominant class to respect working class dialects and not vilify and denigrate them. The question is: What would this achieve as regards the material-based deprivation and poverty which serves as the base-level shaper, not only of ways of speaking and communicating in general, but also of every other index of social class in socio-economically stratified societies? In addition, we must also take on Andrew Sayer's comment to the effect that '[t]he poor are not clamouring for poverty to be legitimised and valued'; rather, '[t]hey want to escape or abolish class position rather than affirm it' (Sayer, 2005: 53). Sometimes respect is not enough.

Far away from the British context, Jan Blommaert and Pinky Makoe (2011) set out to explore social class in the classroom in South Africa, or at least as much is suggested by the title of their article: 'Class in class: Ideological processes of class in desegregated classrooms in South Africa'. At the beginning of the article, the authors make a very interesting statement about adopting a class-based analysis in the context of South Africa:

> There is hardly any literature on post-Apartheid South Africa in which a class analysis is attempted. This is remarkable for several reasons. One reason is the continued presence and prominence of the communist party (SACP) and its affiliated trade unions in the South African political landscape; another one is the abundance of Marxist class analysis in the period prior to 1994 in international scholarship on South Africa as well as within the ANC 3 (see e.g. Curtis 1986). Current discourses on class are still connected to these older traditions, but they tend to be activist and veer towards overly simple and mechanistic views on class and class dynamics. A more fine-grained analysis is needed, one which avoids rapid associations between social groups and social classes but which delves into the fabric of class *processes* and their *effects*.
>
> *(Blommaert and Makoe, 2011: 2–3)*

Here the authors express surprise that there is not more class-based analysis in educational research in South Africa, especially given that such analysis exists in politics, via an active Communist party, and in a long tradition of class-based research during the apartheid era. They then suggest that what is needed is not 'overly simple and mechanistic views on class and class dynamics ... [with] rapid associations between social groups and social classes' – of which we are given no examples – but a 'fine-grained' approach, which examines classroom '*processes* and their *effects*'. The latter proposal refers to how social class is made in day-to-day interaction and engagement in social practices (cf. Thompson, 1980; see also Rampton, 2006).

In the main body of the paper, Blommaert and Makoe adopt, as we have just seen, a Bourdieusian approach to social class, even if they explicitly avoid defining the term: 'We shall abstain from definitional battles here and use the term class as shorthand (following Bourdieu) for material and symbolic social stratification' (Blommaert and Makoe, 2011: 3). From here they examine class in context as embodied and disciplined ways of being, which includes language used in particular ways, values and preferences, display of appropriate knowledge, dress and so on. Examining classrooms in a school that has moved from being exclusively white, as regards the student body, to being racially diverse (albeit with a majority black student body), the authors note a series of positionings and repositionings in observed lessons and they frame their understandings of what is observed according to a series of oppositions. One such opposition is an obviously racial one but in the context of South Africa, we can easily see the transformation of race into race/ social class as a recognisable and recognised stratifying element in early twenty-first-century South African society. Intrinsic to the transformation is the implicit notion that one can move beyond race in South Africa today via upward socioeconomic mobility. Apart from increased income and a likely change of neighbourhood, the latter involves adopting English as a dominant language, becoming an ordered and disciplined person, obtaining an education and acquiring a mobile and translocal disposition, all characteristics previously associated with the world of élite white South Africans. The acquisition of these marks of distinction allows for spatial and metaphorical transformation in the form of a move from the township to the suburb. As Blommaert and Makoe note, education in action is a rich environment for those interested in seeing how stratified race- and class-based systems are continually reproduced, despite also continually being altered by events in the world.

All of this is fine to a point, but as is the case with Snell's work, the authors do not clearly articulate a theory of class and this makes it difficult for the reader to know exactly what the documented interactions taking place in South African classrooms are constitutive of. And the relative vagueness of adopting a default Bourdieusian approach to social class is not sufficient to remedy this situation. For example, the authors note how classroom activities designed to inculcate white middle class embodiment and disciplined ways of being and using language 'recall Foucault's ... [1973] argument that institutions such as Melrose Primary are sites of control and surveillance that induct children into a specific "world view" of learning practices' (Bloommaert and Makoe, 2011: 9). However, in making this statement, the authors do not make reference to class-making activity (which these events surely show), but to race-making activity (which these events also surely show). Thus, they conclude that '[t]hrough recurring body-discipline, coupled with ideological discourses, we see how a group of black children are trained to "adjust" to the demands of ex-white education' (Bloommaert and Makoe, 2011: 9), leaving social class out of the analysis. My point is that surely social class is an issue here, or so we are led to believe in other parts of the article, and that a golden opportunity for working intersectionally is somewhat lost.

Blommaert and Makoe conclude their article with the following statement:

> The particular mode of occurrence of social class is in South Africa, as else-where, a matter about which only limited forms of generalisation will do. It is best to look at the concrete ways in which people orient towards stratify-ing diacritics (such as the ordered bodily hexis, the use of English, reading books, and so forth) in articulating images and patterns of social mobility before making general statements about class. This is one way of rescuing a hugely important analytical concept from totalising (and thus irrelevant) interpretations – the tendency, already observed by E.P. Thompson in 1963, 'to suppose that class is a thing'.
>
> *(Blommaert and Makoe, 2011: 13–14)*

This is an interesting point to make: it is best to work from data upwards, exam-ining links between activity emergent in ongoing classroom practices and 'stratify-ing diacritics' that index class. However, my point would be that proceeding in this manner does not preclude defining social class, and, at the same time, avoiding treating it 'as a thing'. Perhaps what is going on here is what Adam Jaworski (personal communication, 24 April 2013) describes as an avoidance of the essen-tialisation or reification of social phenomena at all cost. This avoidance leads many sociolinguists today away from entering into detailed discussions of key constructs such as social class and any suggestion that as a social structure, social class can exist independently of its invocation either by participants in interactions or researchers trying to make sense of data. I wonder if we need to be so careful.

I might add here that I am not singling out Bloommaert and Makoe or Snell as bad examples of how not to deal with class in sociolinguistics. On the contrary, I have chosen to focus on the work of these authors because they are among a minority of researchers who at least have tried to include social class as a worth-while construct in their work. In doing so, they avoid the trap of getting lost in detailed data analysis, connecting the latter to social issues in the real world. In addition, unlike Rampton, they seem to have returned to the advocacy agenda, which was so much a part of the early work of Labov and Bernstein discussed earlier in the chapter.[4] However, this agenda is limited somewhat by the lack of a clear articulation of what social class is, coupled with a tendency to turn it into an identity inscription instead of an indicator of the inherent contradictions and defects of capitalism.

Conclusion

In this chapter, I have taken the reader through a chronology of my selective reading of a small sample of major publications in sociolinguistics, always looking out for social class as a key construct informing analysis. As we observed, social class made it onto the agenda very early in the history of sociolinguistics, only to fade away somewhat as the field grew. In some cases, researchers (e.g. Labov) seemed to shift their emphasis, from the economic material bases of existence to the cultural bases of existence. In other cases (e.g. Bernstein, particularly in the United States), the research tradition has ceased to be of interest for many. All the while, and running parallel with developments in sociology, Bourdieu's ideas have become dominant in sociolinguistics and they have become the chief prism through which class-based analysis is framed. However, in contrast to what has happened in sociology, where there is still some theorisation of social class as a construct, researchers in sociolinguistics have tended to adopt a default Bourdieusian approach to the construct without including in their work much in the way of detail, critique, problematisation or application.[5] In my view, class-based work in sociolinguistics would benefit greatly from the inclusion of such background work.

None of what I write here is meant to detract from the great advances made in sociolinguistics over the past six decades as regards methodology and the application of research findings to real world contexts. Linguistic analysis in sociolinguistics has become increasingly technical and detailed and the terminology used to label what is going on in interactions and in written texts has become ever more sophisticated. The work on style and stance exemplifies these two trends well as researchers combine Labov-like attention to detail with a broad range of frameworks gleaned from social theory, sociology, anthropology, geography and other areas of the social sciences to embellish the analysis of language in society. Still, there is a danger that researchers may become so infatuated with linguistic analysis that they lose sight of bigger social issues, such as social class. In this vein, Rampton writes the following:

> Sociolinguistics (and linguistic anthropology) may be defined by their expert analyses of 'practices, discourses and textual play', but over-enthusiasm about these … could easily end up trivialising social class, neglecting its toll on individuals, lending support, indeed, to market ideologies which treat class position as a matter of individual will, effort and enterprise.
>
> *(Rampton, 2006: 235)*

Indeed, on the whole in this research, a political economy angle is conspicuous by its absence, an angle that would base sociolinguistics more firmly in a Marxist critique of capitalist society, which, in turn, would complement the already very strong culturalist orientation. This stronger political economy angle would make it possible for sociolinguists to inform those who wish not only to effect change in the sphere of recognition, but also those who seek the transformation of capitalist society.

Notes

1 Sadovnik (2001) writes the following about how Bernstein was positioned, and ignored, in the United States:

> Despite Bernstein's continued refutation of the cultural deprivation label, these distortions had profoundly negative consequences for his work. For example, Hymes reported: 'a young anthropologist recently told me that as a student she found Bernstein's account of restricted code to describe her own family but was told by a faculty member not to read him' (Hymes, 1995: 5). When Bernstein came to a United States university in 1987, an anthropologist asked why 'that fascist Bernstein [had been] invited'. When pressed, the anthropologist admitted that she had never read Bernstein's own work, but that she had read secondary sources accusing him of racism.
>
> *(Sadovnik, 2001: 613–14)*

2 This is a revamped and expanded version of my discussion of Rampton's work in Block *et al.* (2012).
3 Eckert prefers to situate style in Lave and Wenger's (1991) *communities of practice*. As she explains:

> Every speaker participates in a variety of communities of practice, or collections of people who engage together in a particular enterprise – a garage band, a family, a gang, a car pool, an office. The community looks out jointly on the social land-scape, interpreting the landscape, and constructing their place and stance within that landscape. And individuals' place in the community is closely related to their participation in that process of construction. An important part of this meaning-making is the social characterization and evaluation of people and groups out in that land-scape, and of their stylistic practices. It is in this process of meaning-making that speakers assign meaning to stylistic resources and assess them as potential resources for their own stylistic moves.
>
> *(Eckert, 2004: 44)*

4 Cathie Wallace (personal communication, 12 April 2013) suggests that perhaps what is needed is a more explicit '*applied*' sociolinguistics, which would address and involve itself more directly in projects of social change.
5 Despite the clearly materialist and class-based orientation to language in society that comes through in much of Bourdieu's work on language in society, many sociolinguists have tended to adopt his work primarily in a culturist vein. In this sense, they have decanted towards Fraser's (2003, 2008) recognition side of the inequality equation, leaving distribution issues relatively underdeveloped. Two recent edited collections devoted to Bourdieu and language bear this claim out. In Michael Grenfell's (2011) *Bourdieu, Language and Linguistics*, there is nowhere to be found a sustained discussion of Bourdieu on social class and how social class might be inserted into the discussions and arguments developed. The same applies to James Albright and Allan Luke's (2008) earlier collection, *Pierre Bourdieu and Literacy Education*. Here, according to the index, contributors make reference to or discuss social class on 58 pages. However, a detailed

examination of these pages reveals that social class is a term that tends to be used in passing and not one that is central to analysis. As I have argued previously, this is not a bad thing – it is just a partial thing – as it does not go to the heart of capitalism as the underlying base of so many social problems in societies in the past and the present, including inequality.

4

SOCIAL CLASS IN BI/MULTILINGUALISM RESEARCH

Introduction

> Within the upper ranges of socioeconomic status, bilingualism tends to be associated with some additional educational advantages; within the lower ranges, it often appears to result in an additional handicap. This picture ... should not be interpreted as any kind of explanation of educational achievement. It should, however, serve as a reminder of two important points: (1) In many educational outcomes affecting bilinguals, social class rather than bilingualism *per se* may be the factor of primary importance. (2) Findings concerning bilingualism and the effects of bilingual education are not necessarily transferrable across social class boundaries.
>
> *(Politzer, 1981: 3–4)*

> In contrast to the economic status of Mexican *braceros*, that of the elite of Cuban society who had fled to Florida following the Cuban Communist Revolution did much for the entrenchment and duration of Spanish bilingualism. The first wave of Cuban refugees included the cream of Havana's professional and business classes. They did more than pay their way, thus contributing to the ease and rapidity with which their language was accepted in Miami as a medium of instruction in bilingual schools.
>
> *(Mackey, 2003: 619)*

These two quotes, produced more than 20 years apart and with different intentions, both call for bi/multilingualism researchers to take social class into account in discussions of the life experiences of bilinguals. Politzer is interested in academic achievement and he warns against attributing relative success and failure in school exclusively to bilingualism. Although he does not draw on Marx, he notes that the material conditions of the children's lives, as the base of all social and cultural activity (the superstructural elements in individuals' lives), surely account for what goes on in schools far more than an attributed status of 'bilingual'. In the second quote, Mackey takes a different tack, critiquing the tendency of many bilingualism researchers to work according to the notion 'a bilingual is a bilingual is a bilingual ... '. Not all Spanish speakers in the United States are the same in terms of their social class positions in American society and there are differences that are often associated with nationality (Cuban vs. Mexican), which might be framed more appropriately in terms of social class. This means that while the majority of the Mexican-descendent population in the US came (and continue to come) from poor backgrounds, the Cubans who left their country after Castro came to power in 1959, and form the base of what is now a Cuban-descendent population of about two million, were, for the most part, professionals and members of the business community prior to emigrating.

In this chapter, my aim is to question bilingualism research along similar lines, focusing on educational settings. I have chosen to limit my discussion to educational settings for three principal reasons. First, most research into bi/multilingualism that I come across is carried out in educational settings. Second, education is, for many researchers, the key institution in which social class is made during the first 20 years of individuals' lives. This said, we should not lose sight of how social class emerges from the economic base of societies and individuals and collectives' relationships to the means of production, and how children bring with them to school, in embodied form, the various factors indexing class position outlined in Chapter 2. These factors then hope to shape class as constructed in school-based processes. Third, and finally, discussions of naturalistic bi/multilingualism are not excluded from this book as they appear in Chapter 5, albeit under the heading of second language acquisition and learning. As was the case in Chapter 3, I will construct my discussion around a partial survey of publications that I think are representative of this area of applied linguistics.

Before beginning, however, it is worthwhile to explain what I mean when I refer to bi/multilinguals and bi/multilingualism in this chapter, starting with the two-way bi/multi prefix. I have opted to use bi/multi in my references to research, except where researchers cited have used another term (e.g. bilingualism, multilingualism, trilingualism, etc.) because I think it better reflects and represents the range of research being carried out today on language contact situations involving two or more languages. The work I cite here points to a certain terminological and conceptual evolution in the field, from an exclusive interest in dual language contact (e.g. Spanish–English bilinguals, Korean–English bilinguals, Catalan–Spanish bilinguals, etc.) to an interest in trilingualism (Basque–Spanish–English trilinguals; Portuguese–Spanish–English trilinguals, etc.) to an interest in multilingual repertoires, where the latter term is used to refer to the assembly and employment of multiple semiotic resources in communication and eschews the notion of languages as integral, unified and stable. In this vein, Adrian Blackledge and Angela Creese, drawing on Heller (2007a), call for:

> [A]n approach to researching multilingualism which moves from a highly ideologized view of co-existing linguistic systems, to a more critical approach which situates language practices in social and political contexts. ... [W]e adopt just such an approach. That is, in paying careful attention to the

language practices of young people in urban settings, we see new multi-
lingualisms emerging, as the young people create meanings with their diverse
linguistic repertoires. We see the young people (and their parents and teachers)
using their eclectic array of linguistic resources to create, parody, play, contest,
endorse, evaluate, challenge, tease, disrupt, bargain and otherwise negotiate
their social worlds.

(Blackledge and Creese, 2010: 25)

As for the nature of the relationship of bi/multilinguals to the languages and
communicative resources in general in their lives, views have varied. Much work
has been concerned with competence as a key defining notion and there has been
a range of views expressed in this regard, from Leonard Bloomfield's (1933) notion of
a full command of two separate languages to Carol Myers-Scotton's definition, some
70 years later, that it is 'the ability to use two or more languages sufficiently to
carry out limited casual conversations' (Myers-Scotton, 2005: 44). Myers-Scotton
goes on to note that while her definition does not 'set specific limits on proficiency
or how much the speaker in question is speaking or demonstrating comprehension
of another speaker' (Myers-Scotton, 2005: 44), it 'does rule out people who can
use a second language [only] in specialized ways … [, such as] being able to read a
menu and place an order in a restaurant' (Myers-Scotton, 2005: 44–45). In
between, we encounter Ute Haugen's (1953) modest standard that it means the
ability to produce 'complete and meaningful' utterances in more than one language; Jane Miller's notion that a bilingual is 'someone who operates during their
everyday life in more than one language and does so with some degree of self-
confidence' (Miller, 1983: x); and John Edwards' (1994) somewhat audacious suggestion that '[e]veryone is bilingual', justifying this statement by explaining that
'there is no one in the world (no adult, anyway) who does not know at least a few
words in languages other than the maternal variety' (Edwards, 1994: 55). What all
of these definitions of bi/multilingualism (and many others that I cannot include
here for reasons of space) have in common is that they contain judgments about
individuals' ability, knowledge, mastery – in short, what Leung, Harris and
Rampton (1997: 555) call 'language expertise', that is, 'how proficient people are
in a language'. Being a bi/multilingual is therefore about meeting a linguistic
standard set by the observer – seemingly fairly low for Edwards, quite high for
Bloomfield, and somewhere in between these two extremes for Myers-Scotton.

However, another issue that has traditionally interested those who study bi/
multilingualism, particularly those who work in the area of bilingual education
(e.g. Baker, 2011; Blackledge and Creese, 2010; Dewaele, Housen and L. Wei,
2003; Edwards, 2010a, 2012; Garcia, 2008; Martin-Jones, Blackledge and Creese,
2012; May, 2012; Valdes *et al.*, 2006), is the interaction between languages of host
communities and heritage languages. As regards the latter, the interest is in what
Leung *et al.* (1997: 555) call 'language inheritance', defined as 'the ways in which
individuals can be born into a language tradition that is prominent within a family
and community setting whether or not they claim expertise in or affiliation to that

language'. Particularly in multicultural environments, for example large urban areas with large immigrant and immigrant-descendent populations, researchers have focused on the home languages that students bring with them when they begin formal schooling. The language expertise and language inheritance of Leung *et al.* are just two perspectives on what might be called 'ethnolinguistic identity' or 'language identity'. While the former refers to an individual's 'sense of belonging to a language community ("speakers of X") and a sense of belonging to an "ethnic" community' (Blommaert, 2005: 214), the latter is about 'the assumed and/or attributed relationship between one's sense of self and a means of communication which might be known as a language (e.g. English) a dialect (Geordie) or a sociolect (e.g. football-speak)' (Block, 2007a: 40).

There is also a third aspect to consider, what Leung *et al.* call 'language affiliation'. Language affiliation is defined as 'the attachment or identification [people] feel for a language whether or not they nominally belong to the social group customarily associated with it' (Leung *et al.*, 1997: 555). And more broadly, a bi/multilingual identity cannot be understood exclusively in terms of external barometers and personal biography (i.e. language expertise and language inheritance); there needs to be this additional agent-driven perspective that can account for how individuals make their way through and make sense of their bi/multilingual lives.

This interest in identity and the general sociocultural orientation of the Leung *et al.* approach notwithstanding, a good proportion of publications devoted to the topic of bi/multilingualism tend to have a strong cognitive-linguistic orientation, one that parallels a similar trend in second language acquisition and learning research (see Chapter 5). Thus in recent edited collections (Cook and Bassetti, 2011; De Angelis and DeWaele, 2011; Pavlenko, 2009, 2011) and journals such as *International Journal of Bilingualism* and *International Journal of Bilingual Education and Bilingualism*, contributions tend to examine linguistic issues such as code switching and lexical choice, and there is a clear-cut and well-established interest in how individuals identified as bilingual take in, process and produce the two or more languages in their repertoires. In this chapter, I will not focus on this line of research, above all because it leaves little space for the consideration of social class and, indeed, anything social. Rather, I will focus on research that follows much more the agenda set out by Leung *et al.*, which seeks links between notions of expertise, inheritance, affiliation and other social aspects of bi/multilingual practices. Here there is far more fertile ground for the inclusion of social class as a viable and useful construct.

Seeking social class in bi/multilingual education research

Is bilingualism a problem?

- There is still a widespread view that bilingualism is disadvantageous to learning.
- Early research into bilingualism tended to reinforce this negative view, suggesting that monolingual students performed better than bilingual students in a range of cognitive and learning tasks.

- A 'container' view of the brain, where it was thought that learning another language impacted negatively on or 'pushed out' the existing language, reinforced the perception of bilingualism as a problem. It has since been found that this is not the way the brain works; rather, languages are linked in the brain by a central processing unit, meaning that people can easily learn two (or more) languages.
- Subsequent bilingual research has also discredited the early bilingual research, consistently demonstrating that bilingual people have clear cognitive advantages over monolinguals. (See also the inquiry *Is bilingualism an advantage?*)

(*LEAP webpage: http://leap.tki.org.nz/Is-bilingualism-a-problem;
accessed 30 March 2013*)

This text is taken from the New Zealand-based webpage of LEAP (Language Enhancing the Achievement of Pasifika), which defines itself as 'a professional learning resource developed for New Zealand teachers ... who have bilingual Pasifika students in mainstream classrooms ... in which English is the language used for instruction' (LEAP; accessed 30 March 2013). Its aim is to contest notions held by many in New Zealand and beyond that bi/multilingualism is a disadvantage in education and that it is, on the whole, a negative force in societies, costing money and making social cohesion difficult. On the whole, the concerns and aims of LEAP are shared by many academics who have written about bi/multilingualism in educational contexts over the past several decades (e.g. Baker, 2011; Bialystok, 2001; Cummins, 2000; de Houwer, 2009; Edwards, 2010a, 2012). In such cases, there is often an emphasis on the 'cognitive advantages' bi/multilingualism affords to individuals. These cognitive advantages include greater metalinguistic awareness, enhanced overall analytical abilities when dealing with novel input and better memory skills. There is also an ongoing critique of policies such as sink-or-swim linguistic immersion programmes, which lead to subtractive bilingualism, and are deemed to be unfair to ethnolinguistic minority and immigrant children who in the past have not had contact with the host language. However, in the midst of concerns of this type and a tendency for some researchers to act as advocates for bi/multilingualism, class differences and conflict in contemporary societies are not mentioned or in any case do not figure prominently.

Nevertheless, it would be unwarranted to suggest or even imply that bi/multilingualism researchers, in a range of contexts around the world, have not been interested in inequality and injustice in societies. For example, Jim Cummins has written eloquently and passionately about these very issues and their relationship to bilingual children in Canada, the US and other contexts over the past four decades (e.g. Cummins, 1996, 2000). In *Social Justice Through Multilingual Education* (Skutt-nabb-Kangas *et al.*, 2009), an edited volume focusing on social justice in bilingual education worldwide, he makes reference to studies examining the impact of power relations on bilingual education:

These studies point to the clear centrality of societal power relations in explaining patterns of minority group achievement. Groups that experience long-term educational underachievement tend to have experienced material and symbolic violence at the hands of the dominant societal group over generations. A direct implication is that in order to reverse this pattern of underachievement, educators, both individually and collectively, must challenge the operation of coercive power relations in the classroom interactions they orchestrate with minority or subordinated group students. Challenging coercive power relations within the societal institution of schooling clearly also represents a direct challenge to the more general operation of coercive power relations in the wider society.

(Cummins, 2009: 27)

In this way, Cummins produces a call for educators to challenge and resist power in bi/multilingual societies, where the norm is for governments and educational systems to deny the elementary linguistic rights of children from minority ethnolinguistic backgrounds, thus inflicting on them what Bourdieu long ago termed 'symbolic violence'.[1] In Cummins's statement, there is a clear understanding of societies as stratified, if not class based, as he makes reference to a 'dominant societal group' and its 'operation of coercive power'. In addition, he refers to two ways in which power is exercised and in terms in which individuals and groups may be stratified: materially and symbolically. Ultimately, the type of stratification that concerns Cummins is that dealing with racial, ethnic and cultural difference. Indeed, in the remainder of his discussion, Cummins discusses inequality solely in terms of race, ethnicity and ethnolinguistic identity. In addition, he takes on power at the classroom level and, by implication, at the institutional level (education policy more generally), but not at the economic base level. The view is that changes at what is, in effect, the superstructure level will make their way into the base level and society will change for the better. However, another way to view matters is that unless there are major systemic changes at the base level (changes in the way that the economy is organised), changes at the institutional and educational practice level will alleviate immediate injustice but in the long run will not go to the heart of the problem, which is class divisions as the inevitable effect of capitalism, a system that depends on inequality in education. Following Fraser (2003, 2008), there may be changes in terms of respect and recognition, but not in terms of redistribution on a general scale.

In the same collection, Tove Skutnabb-Kangas (2009), another author well known for her work on language-related social issues (e.g. Skutnabb-Kangas, 2000; Skutnabb-Kangas and Cummins, 1988), begins a discussion of multilingual education for global justice with an introduction based in political economy. She cites Marx and Engels's succinct description of the logic of capitalism as a globalising force in the *Communist Manifesto*, specifically '[t]he need of a constantly expanding market for its products chases the bourgeoisie over the entire surface of the globe' (Marx and Engels, 1948: 12) and how this leads to conformity around work in terms of economic and cultural practices. The analogy with the spread of English in more recent times as the beachhead of globalisation, and capitalism, is then put forth. However, Skutnabb-Kangas does not sustain the political economy strand in her argumentation as she goes on to discuss linguistic and cultural diversity in the world today. Therefore, like Cummins, she adopts a more respect and recognition agenda than one that focuses on profound economic changes related to redistribution. And, in this way, the opportunity to make a stronger argument in favour of economic equality as a base for social equality is lost. For example, Skutnabb-Kangas could have fruitfully developed the notion of the 'neoliberal citizen', which links neoliberal economic policies with the development of cosmopolitan citizenship in education (Park, 2009; more on this later). In addition, there is no consideration or engagement with the argument that an embrace of neoliberalism is in no way inconsistent with a call for local languages and cultures to be protected. This because it will likely be local élites who take the lead in such matters and they are likely to have adopted wholesale the kinds of neoliberal values that Skutnabb-Kangas (rightly) decries (Block *et al.*, 2012; Holborow, 1999). Thus, while I agree with the thrust of many of Skutnabb-Kangas's arguments here and elsewhere, in particular the way in which she has identified how the spread of English does lead to a diminishing of other languages across a range of domains, what is needed is more follow-through as regards a political economy-based approach to such issues.

Elsewhere, in a series of books in which bilingualism takes centre stage (Edwards, 2009, 2010a, 2010b, 2011, 2012), the author hardly mentions class, although in one book, *Language and Diversity in the Classroom* (2010a), he devotes some space to a discussion of disadvantage and poverty. In doing so, he does enter the realm of social class, acknowledging that relative poverty is a factor in poor educational results, independently of whether or not other dimensions such as ethnicity and race are factored in. And he does seem to be making the point that social class is inseparable from other aspects of identity such as race and ethnicity and that the real challenge is to tease out the nature of such interrelations without leaving social class out of the equation, as is so often the case in discussions of language and identity. However, on the whole, I detect a resistance to social class as a construct to think with in bi/multilingualism research, as Edwards prefers to focus exclusively on ethnicity, race, gender and nationality. Indeed, in the following, he clearly argues that economic factors are far less important than social factors when it comes to inequality in the United States:

> Attempts have been made to control for environment by matching socio-economic-status levels across groups that are to be compared (black and white schoolchildren, for instance), but these cannot be very useful in contexts in which such matching does not really imply environmental equality. In societies where racial prejudice exists, for example, it is obvious that gross similarities in socioeconomic status may only mask the effects of that prejudice; thus, it would be naïve to accept that matching the educational and income levels of blacks and whites in America implied the establishment of environmental equality between them.
>
> *(Edwards, 2010a: 72–73)*

From a Marxist (and indeed Weberian and Bourdieusian) perspective, this is a remarkable statement. In making it, Edwards seems to rule out the prospect that a profound economic change in the United States, one which would lead to parity in 'educational and income levels of blacks and whites', would have any effect whatsoever on 'environmental equality', since racism is so deeply ingrained in American culture. This stance ignores how fundamental changes in the economic base of society *necessarily* have profound effects on superstructural phenomena such as racism. So while it is no doubt the case that white-on-black racism are unique in the US context in terms of how it manifests itself and is reproduced, and that racism runs very deep as a shaper of behaviour and events, its survival is surely in part due to the lack of economic progress among the majority of African Americans since the abolishment of slavery a century and a half ago. And while the African American middle class has grown significantly both in terms of absolute number and percentage, the vast majority of African Americans are still classified as working class and poor (US Census Bureau, 2012). Indeed, as the economic crisis has deepened, it is working class and poor African Americans above all who have paid the price, suffering proportionately higher rates of home repossession and job loss than other sectors of the American population (Harvey, 2010a; Reed and Chowkwanyun, 2012). In this sense, we see very clearly the links between the effects of decades of neoliberal policies (and indeed, centuries of capitalism) and historically embedded, institutionalised racism in the United States.

In more general textbooks and textbook-like collections on bi/multilingualism, there is very little mention of class. However, there are exceptions regarding the degree to which this is the case. For example, in the index of the fifth edition of Colin Baker's (2011) *Foundations of Bilingual Education and Bilingualism*, there are 42 entries for 'socioeconomic/sociocultural class'. And while most of these entries point to passing comments (e.g. as part of a list of factors impacting on an issue related to bilingualism), there are occasions on which Baker goes into more detail about class-related issues. So, there are comments with regard to the relationship between relative poverty/wealth and how much funding schools receive in the US (p. 255); the relationship between poverty and lack of achievement among Latino students in the USA (pp. 255–56); how French immersion education in Anglophone Canada is often a way for local élites to reinforce their relative positions of power in Canadian society (p. 271; more on this later); and how class power may be reinforced by managers who do not learn a local language spoken by the staff whom they supervise (p. 423). However, none of these discussions go beyond a few sentences in length, which is perhaps due, at least in part, to the fact that Baker's book is a general survey in which the author is trying to expose the reader to as broad a range of ideas and research findings as possible.

When Baker moves to discuss socioeconomic factors more explicitly, and hence when he moves closer to using social class as a key construct, he is rather vague about what he might mean by it. He writes that 'socioeconomic status' constitutes 'a definite cause of language minority underachievement', making reference to 'relative economic deprivation, material circumstances and living conditions'

(Baker, 2011: 202). He then suggests the these factors are intertwined with 'psychological and social features such as discrimination, racial prejudice, depression and a sense of immobilizing inferiority' (Baker, 2011: 202). Making this link is wise, but there is then no discussion of how all of these factors interrelate. Still, at one point, Baker makes a very good point about social class and the importance of home life when he writes:

> [U]mbrella terms like socioeconomic status need to be deconstructed into more definable predictors of underachievement, (e.g. parents' attitudes to education, literacy environment, material and emotional home conditions). Home factors will then interact with school factors providing an enormous number of different routes that may lead to school success or failure.
>
> *(Baker, 2011: 202)*

Here links to Bernstein's (1975) work on 'position-oriented' and 'person-oriented' families (see Chapter 3) might fruitfully have been drawn on. But Baker never really engages for long enough in this type of discussion to elaborate a possible explanation of what it is that holds back many ethnolinguistic minority students when it comes to educational achievement. So, while he writes that '[w]here the funding of schools is based on a local tax, then "per-student" expenditure in more affluent areas will be considerably greater than in less affluent areas' (p. 255), this somewhat obvious state of affairs is not linked to education policy emanating from a government that serves the interests of capitalism (and the dominant class) and not the interests of the population in general (and certainly not those of the lower classes). In this case, it would be interesting to explore the extent to which governments take on a redistributive function, topping up education budgets in poorer areas with federal funds. On the whole, then, what is missing throughout Baker's discussions of social class is any in-depth discussion of bigger economic issues, to say nothing of class-based lifestyles, behaviours and overall cultures, all of which are determinant factors in the education and life chances of children from working class and poor backgrounds.

Despite these shortcomings, Baker does better than most when it comes to acknowledging that such a thing as social class might intersect with bilingualism. For example, in an earlier book which he co-edited, *Encyclopedia of Bilingualism and Bilingual Education* (Baker and Prys Jones, 1998), and in Bhatia and Ritchie's substantial *Handbook of Bilingualism* (2003), there is not one developed discussion of social class. The same tendency towards class erasure applies to general texts and collections on bi/multilingualism that have come out over the years (e.g. Auer and Li Wei, 2007; Li Wei, 2009a, 2009b, 2009c, 2009d; Martin-Jones, Blackledge and Creese, 2012), as well as other books that are more specific in their focus. For example, Monica Heller's (2007b) edited volume, *Bilingualism: A Social Approach*, contains chapters written with reference to economic issues (e.g. Heller, 2007a; Pujolar, 2007; Stroud, 2007); however, social class, *per se*, is never taken on directly in the sense that it is never defined or problematised. In Martin-Jones *et al.* (2012), there are two chapters dealing with the economics of bi/multilingualism (e.g. Duchêne and Heller, 2012; Piller, 2012), but in neither of them does a sustained discussion of social class emerge. Meanwhile, *Language and Poverty* (Harbert *et al.*, 2009) is another edited collection which looks from the title as though it might contain some discussion of class as central to socioeconomic stratification. The editors open the collection of 12 chapters by stating that their intention is to 'address […] the question of how poverty affects language survival' (Harbert *et al.*, 2009: 1). The papers assembled are meant to examine issues such as how the shift from a minority language to a majority language is often about the relative economic weight of the two languages in question and how funding for bilingual education and other forms of minority language support are directly linked to available economic resources. However, these papers are ultimately about language maintenance and shift, and inequality and stratification in terms of language, ethnicity and culture. They do not, by contrast, or in addition, contain well-developed discussions of political economy and/or class-based inequality in contemporary multicultural and multilingual societies. Indeed, there is no discussion of social class in the entire book and no political economy sources are cited. All of this seems odd given that by the time the chapters were being written, neoliberal economic policies clearly had had an impact on all of the contexts explored in the book (e.g. several African nation-states, India, the United States), affecting education in general and activities such as language policy, specifically.[2]

Elsewhere, Martha Bigelow's (2010) *Mogadishu on the Mississippi* is a well-documented and compelling portrayal of the children of Somali migrants in a large city in the Midwest United States. Throughout the book, the informants in Bigelow's study are framed in terms of multiple identity inscriptions – race, ethnicity, gender, nationality, religion and language – but never in terms of social class, although it should be noted that Bigelow makes clear from the beginning that this will be her orientation. Her informants are phenotypically black and they have imposed on them the label 'African American' by educational authorities (with a census mentality), by the police (with a racial profiling mentality) and by an American society in general, in which one must always self-define in racial terms. While this label may be obviously accurate in bald physical appearance terms – the informants are of African origin and they are Americans – it is also linked with certain self positioning vis-à-vis ethnicity and culture in American society. And it is precisely at this point that it becomes problematic.

The Somali immigrant adolescents found themselves inserted into a highly racialised education system where 'acting white' (Ogbu, 1988) and 'becoming black' (Ibrahim, 1999) were often presented to them as the only two paths they might adopt. Most of the individuals interviewed by Bigelow and her colleagues strongly identified themselves as 'Somali', where this label was understood as a cultural and national marker. With regard to the latter, there is by now a considerable Somali diaspora in the world today, above all as the direct result of ongoing and incessant conflict over the last several decades. And this diaspora has Somalia and being Somali as key reference points. But in fact, it is not only the

Somali cultural identity or the somewhat vague Somali national identity that dominate the self-presentations of Bigelow's informants; rather it is a strong Muslim identity, which affords a feeling of difference vis-à-vis American society in general and, most importantly, serves as a tool of othering by other Americans.

In this context, where might social class, and specifically 'class in itself' and 'class for itself', come into the analysis? Interestingly, there is no discussion of Bigelow's informants in terms of their position in the American class system. Indeed, I can find nowhere in the book an explicit indication of how they are inserted into (or insert themselves into) American society in terms of economic stratification, although there is some suggestion that parents have a degree of class consciousness as regards what they want for their children. In this sense, there are glimpses of these individuals positioned as migrants and the parents are reported to be worried about their children 'acting black', as they react to cultural forms like hip hop, which they relate to low socioeconomic status in American society. So, to become 'black' equates to opting for a lower class position, while to become 'white' is to aspire to a middle class position. In addition, there are fears among parents of a total immersion in American culture, deemed as antagonistic to the values and maintenance of a Muslim identity. Ultimately, race and religion are complexly interrelated and come to be significant intracommunity as well as intercommunity markers for Bigelow's informants. At the same time, however, there is en ethic of upper mobility at work, as parents want their children to succeed in school and eventually in the American job market. Taking all of these factors into account, we see that there is space for a class angle here, albeit one that passes through the filters of race, religion and nationalism, all documented very effectively by Bigelow. However, this class-based analysis is never developed in an explicit manner.

By contrast, in a discussion of language minority students and their experiences in mainstream classrooms in the United States, Angela Carrasquillo and Vivian Rodriguez do manage to introduce two indicators of social class, relative poverty and unemployment, into their discussion:

> [A] significant percentage of Hispanic students are poor. In the 1998 census report the poverty rate of Hispanics at 29.4 percent compared to 13.3 percent for the whole United States population. The low status occupations and high unemployment rates among Hispanics translate into low income and high levels of poverty.
>
> *(Carrasquillo and Rodriguez, 2002: 42)*

Here the authors seem on the verge of suggesting that poverty (and, I would add, the relatively lower class position of a high percentage of Hispanics in American society) might be an important factor in their low educational achievement. Taking this tack means that educational underachievement among Hispanic children is not exclusively a matter of the historical and systemic discrimination against Hispanics due to their status of ethnolinguistic minority in the US. Social class and material factors need to be factored in, in particular how poverty undergirds a range of factors such as poor housing, cramped living conditions, absent parents, and a range of behaviours and actions (see Chapter 2) associated with poor people in the US. However, Carrasquillo and Rodriguez do not delve into these issues as the discussion in general frames inequality and discrimination almost exclusively in terms of language and ethnicity.

Covering contexts similar to those discussed in Carrasquillo and Rodriguez, but far more ambitious in scope, Ofelia Garcia's (2008) *Bilingual Education in the 21st Century: A Global Perspective* is a compelling account of bilingualism and bilingual education against the backdrop of globalisation in the new millennium. However, despite its concern with we might call 'big' issues (it does say 'global perspective' in the title after all), it includes just one foray into political economy and class issues. In a section devoted to 'socioeconomic status' as a factor shaping the cognitive and social development of bilinguals, Garcia writes the following:

> Often poor children attend schools in the communities in which they live, and the schools may reflect some of the poverty of the community – educational resources are of poor quality, classrooms are overcrowded, class size is large, and the school building is in need of repair. ... Poor families also cannot relocate to ensure that their children are receiving an adequate education. Poor bilingual families have to settle for the educational program that their local school offers, whether it is a monolingual or a bilingual program. ... Poor families also cannot afford the resources to support their children's education outside of school. They can rarely pay for tutoring and after-school or weekend supplementary classes or summer camps. ... When poor children are bilingual, their bilingualism is often *subtractive* because it is almost never supported and developed in schools. Often they are immigrants. And because their home language is not in any way supported in school or majority society, poor children can rarely enjoy the full range of cognitive and social benefits afforded to middle-class bilingual children.
>
> *(Garcia, 2008: 102)*

In this excerpt, which I have edited considerably, Garcia acknowledges the differences across individuals and families classified as bilinguals: there are three references to 'poor children' and 'poor families' here who presumably contrast with bilinguals and bilingual families who are not poor. Garcia seems to be referring exclusively to poor bilinguals and poor bilingual families here. Nevertheless, what she says about their educational opportunities applies equally to all poor children and all poor families, no matter what their ethnic or ethnolinguistic classification (Lareau, 2011; Weis, 2008). Thus, poor white monolinguals also live their lives under the constraints described by Garcia. Poor white monolingual families attend under-resourced schools in poor parts of towns and cities. They cannot move to an area with a better school because they do not have the economic resources or social and cultural capital necessary to do so. Indeed, they cannot even afford to pay for extracurricular activities. However, Garcia does not pursue this line of reasoning, one that would address the issue raised by Poltizer (1981) in the quote that opened this chapter, that is, of how social class intersects with bi/multilingualism. Instead, Garcia seems to want to stay focused on bi/multilingualism, avoiding this kind of foray into general education issues that transcend bilingualism, given that they relate to systemic class-based inequality in society.

Elsewhere, in the UK context, what are known as 'complementary schools' offer fertile ground for developing research that works intersectionally to examine how social class and bi/multilingualism interrelate, even if, as we shall see, there has been little if any class-based analysis of their constitution and goings-on within them. Complementary schools are:

> [V]oluntary schools, also referred to as community, supplementary or Saturday schools ... [which are] set up by specific linguistic, cultural or religious communities for a range of functions, particularly the maintenance of community languages and cultures for fear that these might be lost over the generations.
>
> *(Lytra and Martin, 2010a: xi)*

As Li Wei notes, the first cohort of such schools were set up in the 1960s as:

> [A] direct response by Afro-Caribbean parents who were very dissatisfied with what their children received from mainstream education at the time ... [and how] the mainstream school curriculum often failed to reflect the interests, experiences and culture of the Afro-Caribbean community.
>
> *(Li Wei, 2006: 76)*

Such schools were more culturally than linguistically oriented and in discussions of them, both in the public sphere and in academia, there was relatively little reference to social class as a key factor in the underperformance of children from African Caribbean backgrounds. This is interesting given the working class status of the majority of Afro-Caribbean families at the time. Social class also does not figure in discussions of the second wave of complementary schools that were set up from the late 1970s onwards by Muslim parents who:

> [W]anted separate, religious schools for their children because they believed that their children's religious traditions were more likely to flourish if taught by committed adherents in an environment free from what they regard as the antagonistic influences of either the Christian-dominated or secular ethos of mainstream schools.
>
> *(Li Wei, 2006: 77)*

Again the emphasis was on perceived cultural differences between an immigrant community and host community, but religion was the central focus, and as a consequence the Arabic language was a central part of the content of these schools.

The third wave of complementary schools also started in the late 1970s:

> At around the same time as the Muslim communities in the UK were urging
> for separate education for their children, a number of other immigrant
> communities began to set up their own complementary schools with an aim
> to maintain their linguistic and cultural heritage. For example, the Chinese,
> the Turkish, and the Greek communities set up a significant number of
> schools in England and Scotland for their British-born generations. These
> schools were really weekend classes and they were truly complementary in
> the sense that their organisers never asked for a separate education for their
> children. Instead, classes were run at weekends or outside normal school
> hours, i.e. after 3 p.m., to provide additional teaching of the community lan-
> guages and cultures. There are now more of this type of community language
> school and classes than separate schools for Muslims and Afro-Caribbeans
> combined.
>
> *(Li Wei, 2006: 77)*

At present, this is the type of complementary school that is currently attracting the
most attention from researchers as an ever expanding list of publications indicates
(Blackledge and Creese, 2010; Conteh, Martin and Robertson, 2007; Issa and
Williams, 2009; Lytra and Martin, 2010b). Underlying much of this work, there is
the notion that knowledge about one's heritage language and culture constitutes
cultural capital within one's ethnolinguistic community, and even in society at
large when multiculturalism is framed in a positive way. However, this phenomenon is not always examined in a clear manner (but see Blackledge and Creese,
2008, 2010) and in any case it is only a small part of a more ambitious research
agenda that would explore the intersectionality of social class, bi/multilingualism
and migration.

As in the case of the bi/multilingualism research previously cited, complementary schools research has tended to marginalise social class, and indeed the
material basis of the lives of stakeholders, in favour of an overwhelming multicultural frame. This orientation is useful in that it taps into ongoing debates and
society around social ills such as racism and discrimination. However, it does not
get to the heart of inequality, based in the capitalist system inside which minority
ethnic and ethnolinguistic communities live. And furthermore, it does not take on
another issue that is something of an elephant in the room. I refer to how individuals and collectives identified as bi/multilingual in contemporary multicultural
societies are also framed in society at large as having the status of immigrant, even
when the original migration is a generation or two in the past. There is, in other
words, the question of how to relate an immigrant status and being bi/multilingual
to social class. Of course, a first step in this direction is to bring social class into
discussions of immigration, something which has not happened as much as it might
have, as we shall now see.

Migration, social class and bi/multilingualism research

Given that in sociology there has always been a strand of thought and research philosophically grounded in the work of Marx and Weber which framed social relations in societies in terms of social class, it is perhaps surprising that there has been very little research that has married this strand with the considerable amount of research on immigration that has appeared since the 1950s. However, one publication from 40 years ago, Stephen Castles and Goudla Kosack's (1973) *Immigrant Workers and Class Structure in Western Europe*, stands out as unique because while it framed immigrant identity very strongly in terms of race, and in this way fitted comfortably into mainstream work on migration (and it should be added, the studies discussed above), it also showed how race and social class intersected in the lives of migrants. Castles and Kosack's research focused on four industrialised western European societies – Germany, France, Switzerland and the UK – all of which by the late 1960s had received a significant amount of immigration from a wide range of countries, both European and non-European. As the authors point out, migration to western Europe in the 1950s, 60s and 70s was leading to a certain destabilisation of societies that had evolved from nineteenth-century industrial revolutions to the post-World War 2 economic reconstruction with class systems populated by autochthonous peoples relatively intact. With the economic boom that began in western Europe in the 1950s, there soon came labour shortages and governments began to seek workers from abroad, in some cases, from ex-colonial nations (in the case of the UK, this meant migrants from South Asia and the Caribbean) and, in other cases, from southern Europe (in the case of Germany, this meant migrants from countries including Turkey, Greece and Spain). These migrants entered as *de facto* members of the working class in that they tended to take jobs associated with this class position in the host nations in which they settled – i.e. skilled and semi-skilled manual jobs. In this labour position, they openly competed for some jobs with the traditional local autochthonous working class and, in some cases, they did not. The more skilled the migrant and the job sought, the more likely he/she was to enter into open competition for work, factory assembly line work being a good example. By contrast, a good proportion of migrants took unskilled, low-level and poorly paid manual jobs (e.g. cleaning and serving) and therefore entered into no such conflict with the established local working class.

The extent to which migrants were racialised in such contexts further complicated matters. Castles and Kosack document how intra-European migrations (e.g. Greeks to Germany, Portuguese to France, Italians to Switzerland) developed differently from ex-colonial migrations (e.g. Algerians to France, Pakistanis and Jamaicans to the UK) and other migrations such as that which saw hundreds of thousands of Turks migrate to Germany in 1950s and 1960s. In this last case, racism was a key conditioning factor in the settlement and subsequent situating of individuals and collectives in the existing class systems of western European countries. This is not to say that southern Europeans did not face discrimination and racism of a sort; however, their stories did not contain the feelings of rejection and the violence that sometimes accompanied it, to the degree found in the accounts provided by migrants who were darker skinned.

Discrimination based on skin colour or perceived insurmountable cultural differences manifested itself in a variety of ways with respect to employment and class conditions. First, it meant that many employers simply refused to hire anyone who was not white and British or French or German, etc. Second, it meant that when immigrants were hired, they were expected – and, in some cases, were forced by employers – to do the jobs that autochthonous workers refused to do. Third, discrimination meant that when migrant workers performed well, they were denied promotion simply because they were not white or a national. Fourth, and finally, even when migrants had stable employment, they were often discriminated against when it came time to find housing for their families.

Discrimination also meant that migrants were more often than not excluded from trade unions, which faced the difficult balancing act between catering to their traditional and core constituency – the indigenous white working class – and showing class solidarity by inviting and incorporating migrants into the culture of organised labour. In many cases, not having a tradition of organised labour in the home country meant that immigrants had little or no experience of trade unionism and therefore were not interested in taking part. Legally, migrants were vulnerable to threats by employers who could fire them and, in doing so, jeopardise their permanence in their host countries. In some cases, where housing was provided by employers (as was the legal requirement in some sectors in Germany, France and Switzerland), the threat of a loss of employment would have meant the threat of a loss of accommodation, all of which made migrants feel vulnerable. And this vulnerability turned them into what was, in effect, a 'reserve army' of labourers (Marx, 1976: 781–94) more willing to take lower wages and put up with poor work conditions than autochthonous workers.

A very high proportion of all migrants came from rural areas in their home countries and brought with them relatively low levels of formal education and few or no vocational qualifications, that is, what we might call low cultural capital (Bourdieu, 1984). In most cases, the aim of migrants was not to stay in their new home countries, but to work enough years to save enough money so as to be able to go back home to buy property or to start a business. Migration was thus about bettering migrants' social and economic position back home and not the seeking of another home. This being the case, there was always the issue of how children fit in as for them there was far greater opportunity, through the educational system, for integrating to varying degrees with the established local population.[3]

Ultimately, migrant workers differed greatly from their indigenous counterparts in that they were tied to no particular community or location in their new home. And even in cases in which they might find an established enclave, heavily populated with people from their home country, they nevertheless showed a greater willingness to move to somewhere where they were not only a visible minority but perhaps the only individual from their home country, or in any case, just one of very few people from their home country. By contrast, indigenous workers often had roots going back several generations in their home communities and the thought of moving for employment was not attractive.

In this way, Castles and Kosack situated migrants to western Europe in the 1950s and 1960s in existing class systems in stratified societies. My aim in providing this somewhat detailed account of some of the main findings of their study is to bring to life and make vivid to the reader how existing material conditions and class intersected with race and otherness in shaping the lives of these migrants. And I would argue that the life conditions of these migrants, as synthesised here are: (1) hauntingly similar to those encountered by migrants today in many contexts (see Wills *et al.*, 2010, for a detailed snapshot of migrant workers' lives in contemporary London) and (2) strong shapers of how migrants live their lives in their new home countries. If we accept the latter point, the question then arises as to why more bi/multilingualism researchers interested in migrants only seem interested in them in terms of language and culture or in terms of race, ethnicity, nationality and gender, but not in terms of social class.

Bearing in mind the life conditions described by Castles and Kosack, migrants as bilinguals need first of all to be understood in terms of the class dimensions outlined in Chapter 2. This means taking into account what income, property and employment statuses predominate in migrant groups which are the focus of research. From this base, power relations both in the public sphere (workplace, engagement with institutions) and the private sphere (home/family life) may be considered. It becomes essential to examine the kinds of housing in which migrants live (house or flat/apartment, shared or not) and the kinds of neighbourhood in which they live: is a particular neighbourhood wealthy or poor? Also, is it segregated by income level, race, ethnicity or nationality?

Cultural, human and social assets, roughly corresponding to Bourdieu's cultural and social capitals, also need to be examined, which means that educational level, digital literacy, work-based skills and embodied ways of being may be considered in the light of the kinds of social groupings to which migrants have access (from church groups to trade unions). Ways of being include Weberian (and Bourdieusian) status markers such as consumption patterns (e.g. buying food at a 'cost-cutting' supermarket vs. buying food at one that sells 'healthy' and organic products) and symbolic behaviour (e.g. how one moves one's body, the clothes one wears, the way one speaks, how one eats, the kinds of pastimes engaged in, etc.). Prestige, status and legitimacy, both intracommunity and extra-community, are also important, as are what kinds of social grouping these assets are associated with.

Significantly, I am not the first person to make such a call for research situated at the intersection of social class, migration and bi/multilingualism. Collins, for example, makes the following statement in a paper published in 2006:

> For the sake of brevity let us accept that the United States is a highly class differentiated society, with large social and economic differences between the owning and managing elites and the working-class majority, and a widening

gap between the incomes and education of middle class and working-class households (Henwood, 2003; Zweig, 1999). Let us also accept that immigrant populations are sharply differentiated with, for example, wealthy entrepreneurs, middle class professionals, and low-wage service workers found among most groups. Put briefly, class is a significant structural feature in the contemporary US, and it is a significant 'category of difference' in immigrant communities. There is, in addition, quantitative evidence that social class influences second language learning. In a recent dissertation on national patterns of language shift among U.S. Hispanics, Lutz (2002) shows that both upper class and working-class Hispanics are more likely to retain Spanish than their middle class counterparts. She also reports that 'fluent bilingualism' is strongly associated with middle and upper class resources.

(Collins, 2006: 3)

The Lutz (2002) study to which Collins makes reference shows how there is a statistical correlation between Latino groups' language maintenance and shift and their social class position in American society. However, it is a complex relationship and by no means one way. On the one hand, members of the middle and upper classes are often more comfortable in their class situation in society and engage with phenomena such as bi/multilingualism with the kind of self-confidence manifested by Carlos, the main informant in my study of Spanish speaking Latinos in London (Block, 2006; see Chapter 5). In the context of the United States, this kind of self-confidence might lead middle and upper class Spanish speakers to maintain Spanish as a home language and indeed they may see Spanish as a prestige marker as well. On the other hand, as Lutz (2008) notes elsewhere, middle class Latinos may see Spanish as a language holding them back. For example, the work-based interactions in which it is useful to speak Spanish may be with interlocutors from a low socioeconomic stratum, such as cleaners. This type of bilingual practice is not of interest to middle class Latinos in terms of career advancement, and it may even work against them as monolingual colleagues who harbour negative attitudes about the use of Spanish may look down on them or take them to task for using Spanish. In addition, there are cases in which middle class Latinos come to believe that their use of Spanish is affecting their accent in English, which provides yet another reason not to promote Spanish–English bilingualism in the home or for their children.

Meanwhile, working class and poor Latinos find themselves in a bind as they tend to live in segregated neighbourhoods with other working class and poor Latinos. The latter speak a non-standard English that is stigmatised in American society in general and their Spanish is highly localised and generally has little value outside the Latino community. Thus while they may be in favour of Spanish in the home and bilingual education at school, the latter perhaps as a way of validating what is the dominant language in their communicative repertoire, they generally suffer the negative consequences of their Spanish-dominant lives, such as limited job prospects and less prestige in society at large. In any case, the social class–bi/multilingualism nexus seen through the prism of migration is complex to an extreme. The key is to recognise this complexity in attempts to understand how class position shapes how bi/multilingualism is lived by Latinos in the United States. This point is made well elsewhere by researchers such as Urciuola (1996) and, of course, Politzer (1981), whose statement about this complexity opens this chapter.

Who benefits most from bilingual education?

Another question arising from Garcia's mention of poverty is who benefits most from bilingual education. On the one hand, there are the poor or poorer students to whom Garcia refers; but, on the other hand, there are middle and upper class families who are English speaking at home but who wish their children to develop a more international profile, to become cosmopolitan global citizens and learning another language – Japanese, Spanish, French – may be conceptualised as the kind of cultural capital that would be part of this citizenship. This would be the kind of family described as follows:

> Two-way bilingual immersion programs, where English- and Spanish-dominant students are combined into one classroom to receive instruction in both languages, have recently received increasing numbers of students from affluent families with high levels of formal education. These children are often put on a waiting list, while educators simultaneously struggle to fill a class with native Spanish-speaking Latino children. ... The stark differences in Spanish bilingual program enrollment create a dichotomy in terms of whose bilingualism is valued. Students from poor, immigrant and Spanish-speaking homes are often viewed as needing bilingual education as a reme-dial program. At the same time, Spanish–dominant students are necessary for two-way bilingual immersion programs to succeed. Since two-way programs are also viewed as enrichment education by many middle- to upper-class English monolingual parents ... , program designs and goals will depend upon whom they are intended to serve.
>
> *(Kelyn and Adelman Reyes, 2011: 215)*

Elsewhere, Deborah Palmer (2009) discusses her research on a dual immersion Spanish–English bilingual programme at a primary school in northern California in similar terms. The school in her study was 'dual' in two distinct ways. First, it was 'dual' because subjects were taught in two languages, Spanish and English. Second, it was 'dual' because it served two different purposes for two very different sets of students. On the one hand, it provided Spanish first language maintenance for the poor and working class children of Latino and Latino-immigrant backgrounds. On the other hand, it provided the middle class children, most of whom were white, with an 'enrichment "foreign" language immersion experience' (Palmer, 2009: 177). In principle, this mix of students was not a problem, and indeed the school as whole was exemplary in terms of racial integration, with 38 per cent of the students classified as Hispanic or Latino, 30 per cent as African American and 28 per cent as White. However, only focusing on the race or even ethnolinguistic identities of the children (Latino/Spanish–English bilingual speaker, contrasted with white monolingual English speaker) obscures a very real problem with this type of school, one that Palmer pinpoints all too well in her study.

As we observed in the work of Bernstein, Heath, Bourdieu and other researchers cited in Chapter 3, poor and working class children bring a very different set of dispositions and cultural capital to schools than do their middle class counterparts. The latter grow up in homes that inculcate the kind of values and behaviour that will later be appropriate in school settings. And middle class students develop far more than their working and lower class peers the 'feel for the game' necessary for success in education. Meanwhile, schools, as institutions serving power, act in effect as willing receptacles of the kind of educational capital that middle class children bring with them to school. As Palmer notes, the middle class children in her school commanded different treatment and more attention from their teachers, among other things because they knew how to obtain both. These children took over the course of lessons unless the teacher took an active role in remedying this situation. In the following excerpt, the focal teacher in Palmer's study, Ms. Melanie, explains her dilemma:

> I think that in that unstructured environment then the white kids dominate … Because if … the teacher isn't consistent about not interrupting for example, it's the white kids who interrupt or most of the time. Or the boys who will interrupt and dominate. And so I think structure also facilitates equity … Whereas if you're just like, 'Oh speak your mind,' well the same people are always going to speak their mind and the kids who are not so feeling empowered in the environment never will. But the structure I think creates more equity.
>
> *(Palmer, 2009: 195)*

It is interesting to note how the teacher frames her discussion in terms of strict racial categories – 'white kids', whom she mentions, vs. Latinos, who exist by default as those who suffer if the former are allowed to dominate. The use of race as a central label is no doubt due to the teacher's individual experience as well as the general tendency in the United States for race to be used as a proxy for social class (a tendency that is noteworthy in the studies cited previously in this chapter). Nevertheless, there is reason to question using race as the central identity inscription in the analysis of two-way immersion programmes as these programmes come in many forms, with diverse student bodies, which cut across racial and class lines:

> Many two-way immersion bilingual programs are relatively divided in their populations. With half their students coming from a Latino immigrant, and largely working-class, background and the other half middle-class English

speaking and mainly White students, these programs work to bridge the race, class, and language differences between their two populations. Of course, this line is never perfectly clear; working-class and poor English speakers of many races and ethnicities, as well as middle-class Chicano bilingual and Spanish-speaking immigrant children, enter these programs as well. And there are plenty of schools in which the English dominant students are also Hispanic, or where students are all bilingual and language dominance is difficult to determine. ... However, it is difficult to ignore in some schools the disparity in class and race between English- and Spanish-speaking students.

(Palmer, 2009: 179)

In the end, Spanish–English bilingual families can be middle and upper class, and not just working class and poor, and this is the case far more than is acknowledged by most researchers. Families can have roots in Mexico or Central America or they may have recently migrated to the US from Spanish speaking countries further afield, such as Venezuela, Argentina or Chile. And the latter type of migration to the United States tends to be middle class. In such cases, we are talking about families who are more aligned with the dominant class in the US, and who are composed of parents and children occupying positions of relative power in their home countries, people who are used to having things their way. This being the case, immersion programmes, as Fred Genesee (2003) notes, do not necessarily serve to lift students from 'low socioeconomic status' backgrounds out of their lower economic and status positions vis-à-vis their middle-class classmates. Indeed, the gaps between students from these different class backgrounds remain relatively equal in both immersion and L1 monolingual schools. So once again education – and more specifically, innovative approaches to bilingual education – seem only a partial palliative for what are deeply rooted political, social, historical and above all, economic realities.

Further to this point, in Heller's (2006) study of a French immersion school in Toronto, *Linguistic Minorities and Modernity*, the middle class students once again do what Bernstein and Bourdieu argue that middle class students generally manage to do, that is, they benefit from education systems in capitalist economies while their working class counterparts do less well. Social class differences emerge at several points in Heller's study. First, there is the type of school she studies, a monolingual French school in Ontario, a predominantly English speaking province of Canada. Set up in 1968, Champlain, and others that followed it, were a response to a rise in *Québécois* nationalism and a heightened sense of *Québécois* identity, which came to the fore in Québec and other parts of Canada with French speaking minorities (such as Ontario), as the 1960s unfolded. When the school was established there were two general francophone groups with very different interests and stakes in the school, which, in turn, meant very different expectations about what kind of school it would be. On the one hand, working class Francophone parents, who in their day-to-day lives had less access to English, wanted a bilingual school, which would provide their children with access to English alongside French. This position was related to their desire for upward mobility, which in Ontario would mean being a competent user of English in a range of domains. On the other hand, middle class parents, who already had ample access to English in their day-to-day lives, preferred a monolingual French school, which would ensure a fuller knowledge of French to go along with English. Secure in their class position and secure in the knowledge that their children were already university bound, they were interested in the linguistic capital that the French language would represent in addition to their children's full knowledge of English, which they could take for granted. The difference in the two class positions is described by Heller as follows:

> Class positions with respect to Franco-Ontarian education tend to differ in important ways. Middle-class parents tend to focus on the preparation of their children for university studies and professional careers, in which domains they assume bilingualism (as parallel monolingualisms) will be valued, whether their children study in French or in English at university level. … Working class parents are more concerned about the exigencies of the job market, which, in the Toronto area, is dominated by English. Their tie to French has more to do with family identity than with the social, political and economic interests of the middle class.
>
> (Heller, 2006: 42)

Not surprisingly, it was the middle class approach that was adopted and Champlain was defined according to the dominant discourse of the 'bilingual student': competent in English away from institutionalised school activities and competent in standard French within institutionalised school activities. Those who spoke nonstandard French, that is, a good proportion of the working class students, were not *doing* the official bilingualism that the school recognised as legitimate.

Indeed, so strong was the rejection of vernacular French that it was even ridiculed on occasion by the middle class students who conformed to the official bilingualism of the school, which only recognised standard French as legitimate. For example, on one occasion, during an assembly organised to 'contribute to "school spirit" … [and] convince all students to participate in extra-curricular activities' (Heller, 2006: 126), some students performed sketches mocking nonstandard vernacular forms of French. The latter were linked to working class cultures via well-worn stereotypes such as the consumption of beer and heavy food, for men, and wearing 'rollers, [a] housecoat and fluffy pink slippers' (Heller, 2006: 126), for women. As Heller notes, however, this denigration of vernacular French, associating it with unattractive working class subject positions performed multimodally, meant that students were on shaky ground, as they upset a certain balance effected both officially and *de facto* within the school. This balance included the active (and official) promotion of standard French along with the passive (and quasi-official) tolerance of vernacular French as the symbol of the Canadian French identity on which the school was founded. In this way, there were two discourses in play here, a discourse of new French and a discourse of old French. The former is the standard of the school, the language variety that opens up to the future; the latter is a relic of the past, useful as a badge of (working class Francophone) authenticity, but not likely to travel very well outside of the contexts of its formulation and use.

It is also worth noting that class struggles within Champlain were not just about born and bred Canadian French–English bilinguals. There was a significant number of recent arrivals from Somalia, most of whom were from middle class backgrounds with well-educated parents. On entering the school, these students tended to be placed in general-level streams, as opposed to advanced-level steams, because school officials assumed that as non-native speakers of both French and English, they would need time to catch up linguistically with other students. However, as Heller (2006: 55) notes, '[s]taying in general-level courses means only that you fall farther and farther behind, or at least that you diverge more and more from what advanced-level students are learning'. It therefore was not, neither could it ever have been, a step on the way to full access to the educational resources that Champlain had to offer. This point was not lost on many of the affected students or their parents, who protested, although seemingly with little effect.

Towards the end of her book, Heller makes an interesting statement about how Champlain students showed little propensity to challenge authority or the system according to which the school was organised. They were even less inclined to overturn the growing marketisation of school content:[4]

> They have learned from the politics of identity that it is important to fight discrimination not on the grounds of collective rights, but on other grounds altogether. They prefer to alter the discourse, to move it to something plur-alist which might be a way-station to not caring at all any more about ethnicity, or race, or any other social category which might be used as a basis for social stratification. But they have no desire to alter the fundamental nature of the market they are engaged in; they are not trying to move into or build an alternative market ... , they are trying to get equal access to the dominant one.
>
> *(Heller, 2006: 218)*

The latter statement applies to much of what falls under Fraser's category of recognition, as actions taken on behalf of groups are all too often about individual rights, and they do nothing to overturn the capitalist system which is the base of all inequality in society. Clearly, the middle class dominance of Champlain was supported by such a liberal ethos of respect for others and individual self-development.

Heller's study is recognised as an important landmark in bi/multilingualism research, as it is a well-constructed, in-depth ethnography of a languages-in-contact setting with a well-developed socio-political backdrop. However, its potential as a study about social class and its interrelationship with bi/multilingualism is not as developed as it might have been. In fairness to Heller, her study is more about her emerging ideas with regard to critical ethnography and the evolution of French nationalism in Canada, as well as nationalism beyond this context, at the end of the twentieth century, two themes that come together in her later book, *Paths to Postnationalism* (2011). Still, more than other researchers in the field, Heller manages to situate social class as a key dimension of identity that intersects with bi/multilingualism, national identity, gender, race and ethnicity. And, above all, her findings resonate well with the work of Bernstein and Bourdieu (see Chapter 3), who argued that middle class students tend to take full advantage of what schools have to offer while working class children manage to do so to a considerably lesser degree. Indeed, this phenomenon is all pervasive in education, not least in bi/multilingualism, which involves one (or more) first language that is not English, with English as the main additional language.

English and global cosmopolitans

With the rise of English as the *de facto lingua franca* in the world today, a new bi/multilingualism has arisen, one in which English is the key language, added onto one or more languages acquired in early childhood, early socialisation and early education. Thus, while Mandarin in its multiple varieties can claim to be the most widely spoken language in the world, and French and Spanish can publish impressive statistics, as regards its numbers of users, English is, as so many authors have noted (Jenkins, 2009; Schneider, 2011; Seargeant, 2012), the global and international language *par excellence* and the most effective contact language in a range of contexts – in person and virtual – in which users of different languages meet and have a need to communicate. Making this point, however, is in no way to celebrate the rise of English and a good number of authors have investigated and discussed the dark side of the rise of English (Canagarajah, 1999; Pennycook, 1994, 1998; Phillipson, 1992, 2003, 2010). Pennycook, for example, usefully sums up a somewhat sobering view of the role of English in the world today as follows:

> English holds out promise of social and economic development to all those who learn it (rather than a language tied to very particular class positions and possibilities of development); and that English is a language of equal opportunity (rather than a language which creates barriers as much as it presents possibilities). By contrast with these myths around English, I would point to the collusionary, delusionary and exclusionary effects of English. This thing called English colludes with many of the pernicious processes of globalisation, deludes many learners through the false promises it holds out for social and material gain, and excludes many people by operating as an exclusionary class dialect, favouring particular people, countries, cultures and forms of knowledge.
>
> *(Pennycook, 2007: 100–101)*

Most of interest here is Pennycook's mention of the way that English is for many people associated with 'social and economic development' and 'equal opportunity' and how English often mediates practices that, ultimately, serve the interests of neoliberalism (English 'colludes' with neoliberalism); delude people when it comes to what English, or any other language, can actually *do* for them; and finally, lead to inequality, including the few and excluding the vast majority. In this vein, I aim here to examine the interrelationships between social class and L1(s) + English bi/multilingualism.

This kind of bi/multilingualism is different from the kinds of bi/multilingualism discussed thus far in this chapter, not least because it is a globalised phenomenon, involving an emergent global bi/multilingual élite consisting of 'generally well educated, upwardly mobile individuals who are proficient in two or more world languages ... [and who] in many cases ... have been in a position to forge a new global identity' (de Mejia, 2002: 51). In this context, the study of English is more often than not linked to notions of cosmopolitan citizenship, and the idea that children should learn to be 'global citizens' (Block, 2011; Guilherme, 2002). As educational goals go, becoming a global citizen is very much a middle class aspiration as it requires certain levels of symbolic capital – economic, cultural and social – as well as mobility (e.g. travel, study abroad programmes) and ready access to and knowledge of how to use advanced technologies. Such factors have led to a situation in which, outside of the historically Anglophone countries, there is a great deal of stratification based on the relative knowledge of and competence in English in societies (Blommaert, 2010). In short it is the upper and middle classes of countries around the world who have access to English, are successful learners of English and ultimately become effective users of English. Commenting on China as a relatively new frontier with regard to L1(s) + English bi/multilingualism, Fuhui Tong and Qing Shi (2012: 168) make the point that '[f]or developed metropolitan cities in mainland China, including Shanghai, Beijing, and Guangzhou, bilingual education becomes a form of elite education which is associated with family income, hence, privileged to higher social classes'. And in a very timely paper appearing recently, Stephanie Vandrick comments on the presence in American universities of what she termed 'students of the new global elite':

> Universities in the United States and elsewhere are increasingly enrolling an elite group of international students who not only are able to pay the high tuition and other expenses of U.S.-based universities, but also are personally familiar with several countries and cultures. These students are part of a new global economic and cultural elite. They have lived, studied, and vacationed in various places throughout the world; they may carry passports or permanent visas from more than one country; their parents may have homes and businesses in more than one country; they may speak several languages; they have often been educated at Western high schools – frequently boarding schools – and colleges. There have always been affluent, well-traveled international students studying in the United States and other Western, English dominant countries. However, the students on whom I focus here are distinguished and defined by, first, having lived and studied in at least three countries; second, being affluent and privileged; and third, exhibiting a sense of global membership. Some of the contributing factors to the growth of this group are the increasingly wealthy

upper class in some non-Western countries, increased ease of world travel, and increased freedom of female students to live and study far from home. For this group of students, the world is their home. They often feel somewhat untethered, belonging both everywhere and nowhere.

(Vandrick, 2011: 160)

In this way, these global bi/multilingual élites show how language and social class interrelate and how English has become a communicative resource that indexes, along with many other social phenomena, class position in domestic and global markets. Taking English as a communicative resource that indexes middle and upper class positions in societies around the world, many researchers have followed a trend whereby English is seen as 'commodified' (e.g. Rubdy and Tan, 2008). But what does this actually mean?

Commodification: a terminological clarification[5]

Over the past two decades, Heller (e.g. 2002, 2003, 2010) has written a great deal about the 'commodification of language' and findings from her research on French in the Canadian context are applicable to English and other languages (Rubdy and Tan, 2008). With a degree of poetic licence, Heller has worked metaphorically, using the term 'commodification of language' to refer to an observed shift from the valuing of a language for its basic communicative function and more emotive associations – national identity, cultural identity, the authentic spirit of a people and so on – to valuing it for what it means in the globalised, deregulated, hyper-competitive, post-industrial 'new work order' in which we now live. This process may be conceptualised as a shift from language as use value to language as exchange value.

The notions of use value and exchange value are taken from Marxist theory, although Heller has seldom engaged in an in-depth discussion of the Marxist roots of her commodification metaphor, a section in Duchêne and Heller (2012) being something of an exception. Here the authors do not go into very much detail, passing in a rather cursory manner through Marx's writing on the topic in two paragraphs, stating that '[c]ommodities are in fact *things* that have value' and then ending with:

> Marx pinpoints the fact that, in the end, the structure of work is determined by the market and by the interplay between useful and exchangeable products, both of which are linked to time, availability of labour and the consumption of goods.
>
> *(Duchêne and Heller, 2012: 371)*

It should be noted that Duchêne and Heller do acknowledge that their discussion constitutes a '(too) short digression on the Marxist view of commodities' (Duchêne and Heller, 2012: 371), so here I will provide a slightly more extended one with a view to reaching something of an understanding of exactly what we might mean by the commodification of language.

In Marx's work (e.g. 1904, 1976), a commodity is a product of human labour. It has value, initially and at the most basic level, for the uses that can be made of it. This use value is reflected in how, for example, linen can be used as sheets on a bed, shoes can be used to protect one's feet, a fork is used to eat with and so on. All such objects mediate the satisfaction of basic biological and ideational needs and wants. From commodity production for such basic qualitative value, there is a shift as markets (and market-based economies) arise as sites from which individuals can acquire that which they need or want but which they cannot or simply do not produce themselves. In markets, commodities have exchange value, which means that they can be exchanged for other commodities, as would be the case in a barter economy. Crucially, with market exchange, there is the beginning of a separation between the social relationship of the individual in the production of a commodity and the act of its exchange. The acquirer of a commodity only comes into contact with the finished product but not the socially necessary labour expended by the person who produced it. This is the beginning of a disconnect between the social relationship of production processes and end products. As we observed in Chapter 2, alienation follows as the production of commodities escapes the control of the labourers/producers. The social relations of production become hidden as the market only shows the finished product to the person acquiring it. Marx explained matters as follows:

> As a use-value, every commodity owes its usefulness to itself. Wheat, e. g., serves as an article of food. A machine saves labor to a certain extent. This function of a commodity by virtue of which it serves only as use-value, as an article of consumption, may be called its service, the service which it renders as use-value. But as an exchange value, a commodity is always regarded as a result; the question in this case is not as to the service which it renders, but as to the service which it has been rendered in its production. Thus, the exchange value of a machine is determined not by the quantity of labor-time which it saves, but by the quantity of labor-time which has been expended on its own production and which is, therefore, required to produce a new machine of the same kind.
>
> *(Marx, 1904: 34–35)*

As noted earlier, Heller and others (e.g. Rubdy and Tan, 2008) have argued that languages, and English especially, are increasingly being treated as commodities in the world: in job markets, in educational systems, in the tourist industry. In all of this, the commodification of English refers to a process or change in how the English language is oriented to and appropriated by its increasing number of users in the world. But bearing Marx's definition of commodity in mind, can we talk of the 'commodification of English', or any other language, with authority? If we accept Heller's metaphorical shift, commodification works as a way to capture a move from English as having *use* value to English as having *exchange* value, or better to English having both types of value. It exists as a means of communication in ever changing social and geographical locations and as an objective skill that affords status, recognition and legitimacy to those who possess it. And can be traded in employment markets as it is often required for certain jobs (Heller, 2003, 2010).

However, if we stick to a narrowly Marxist interpretation of what is and what is not a commodity, we see that the metaphor LANGUAGE IS A COMMODITY does not hold up to scrutiny. I say this because language cannot be seen, strictly speaking, as the product of human labour, a condition *sine qua non* for commodity status in Marxist theory. In addition, if, as Marx argues, 'every commodity owes its usefulness to itself' and, for example, '[w]heat ... serves as an article of food' (Marx, 1904: 34–35), what does language 'serve as an article of', if it is a commodity? And then when we move from use value to exchange value, we see, following Marx, that 'as an exchange value, a commodity is always regarded as a result' (Marx, 1904: 34–35) with a value commensurate with the cost of its production. What then is the cost of production of language as commodity? Or are we talking about an instance of language use and not language in its entirety (whatever that might mean), as a commodity? But even in the case of an instance of language use, or even a 'chunk' of language use, the question remains as to how we grasp the 'labour-time' involved in the production of language. A language is not a machine, a piece of linen, a bed sheet made from linen, or wheat, or anything else material, what Holborow (2007: 56) calls the 'real products' on which capitalist systems are dependent. And this is a problem.

Bonnie Urciuoli (2008) goes some ways towards resolving this problem, providing a very convincing account of the move from commodity, based in the material, to commodity based in the abstract. She manages this because she subsumes language under skills and then argues that there has been a commodification of the latter. Urciuoli charts the move in developed economies from 'hard skills' to 'soft skills', the former being 'the technical requirements of the job' and the latter 'the cluster of personality traits, social graces, facility with language, personal habits, friendliness, and optimism that mark each of us to varying degrees' (Menochelli, 2006: npn; cited in Urciuoli, 2008: 215). She discusses the way in which one item in the soft skills cluster, 'facility with language' (or perhaps better, knowing how to communicate), has come to be valued as something that can be broken down into component parts and measured. However, this objectifying of language notwithstanding, two caveats are in order. First, as Cameron notes, communication is still cultural and 'not a natural phenomenon with objective existence in the world' (Cameron, 2000: 145). Second, as Holborow notes, even if 'language is used and inculcated in people for the purposes of selling, this does not in itself make language a product' (Holborow, 2007: 68).

Still, framing different types of communication as skills sets, such as 'effective public speaking', allows for the itemisation of component parts, which can be assembled so that there is a product, the well-delivered speech. As the move to soft skills has become all pervasive, there is, therefore, room for adapting Marx's thinking about labour processes and products to the present. As Urciuoli argues, '[i]n skills discourses, social acts are cast in a transactional or entrepreneurial frame and actors' segmented selves are recast as assemblages of productive elements, as bundles of skills' (Urciuoli, 2008: 224). The bundles of skills, in turn, act as:

> [C]ommodities insofar as they are aspects of productive labor with market value: as aspects of self that enhance theory possessors' worth on the labor market and as products sold by their inculcators, which command hefty fees for some hours or days of skills workshops.
>
> *(Urciuoli, 2008: 224)*

English as academic capital: two exemplary cases

The relevance of all of this to the discussion of English as a mediator of class division in societies around the world is to be found in how languages, and in particular the English language, are the key mediators of skills sets. Indeed, English has taken a position as the essential means of delivery of skills sets around the world. And this in turn has led to a situation in which knowing how to use English is the most basic of soft skills and the most important one as regards how it provides access to a wide range of skills sets, which have become commodities in global markets.

It is precisely this point that a good number of scholars (Abelmann, Park and Kim, 2009; Park, 2009, 2010, 2011; Park and Abelmann, 2004; Piller and Cho, 2013) have highlighted in their work on English in South Korea. The authors examine and analyse the growing importance of English in recent years in South Korea, during which time there has been a 'key cultural change', which has meant 'the elevation of competitiveness and competition to a core value of both individuals and the state' (Piller and Cho, 2013: 28) and the development of the 'neoliberal citizen' (Park, 2009), linking neoliberal economic policies with the development of cosmopolitan citizenship in education. In South Korea, English is portrayed as a key skill to have in the Korean job market and it is seen as the key constituent of the idealised and much coveted status of the cosmopolitan global citizen. 'English fever' and 'English frenzy' are the terms used to describe the Korean obsession with learning English, which means, in part, that adults obsess about their children's English when they are not obsessing about their own. The real and tangible benefits that English can offer to many Korean citizens notwithstanding, Park and others challenge the common assumption that English language competence automatically leads to better employment in the job market and, ultimately, upward mobility in class terms, where the latter is understood, as explained in Chapter 2, to include a series of indicators, ranging from income, education and occupation, to housing, neighbourhood and multimodal behaviour. However, as Park makes clear, we should not believe that all Koreans accept without question many of the ideas emanating from officialdom about the inevitability and naturalness of (global) competition, the need for competitiveness that derives from an embrace of competition and, finally, the national obsession with

English that is part and parcel of competitiveness. He notes how most South Koreans know that studying English does not in and of itself guarantee that one will find secure and well remunerated employment. And many are aware of the class divide, which determines who has access to English (access via the money required to pay for high-quality courses both inside and outside South Korea) and who does not, and which results from different competences school and university leavers take with them into the job market. Indeed, it is here that English becomes relevant to his book.

In the midst of the English fever/frenzy, there is a need to develop

> a deeper understanding of how English language skills of workers come to be evaluated within the political-economical context of the capitalist market. It is only when we understand the mechanisms by which linguistic competence is measured and valued under these conditions that we can properly comment on the underlying problems and policy implications of the pervasive promise of English, without being under the illusions of elusive claims to social and economic development generated by English.
>
> *(Park, 2011: 445)*

This means being attentive to how well (or not well) different Englishes travel. As Blommaert notes in his analysis of a letter written by Victoria, a Tanzanian friend's daughter:

> [A]s soon as the document moves across the world system and gets transplanted from a repertoire in the periphery to a repertoire in the core of the world system, the resources used by Victoria would fail to index elite status and prestige … The indexicalities of success and prestige, consequently, only work within a local economy of signs, that of Tanzania, an economy in which even a little bit of English could pass as good, prestige-bearing English.
>
> *(Blommaert, 2003: 618–19)*

And despite the liberal ethos underlying many publications appearing under the banner of ELF (English as a *lingua franca*), whereby there *should be* respect for the many different ways that English is used around the world, the hard reality is that there is a great deal of stratification when it comes to which English is up, which English is down, which English is valued and which English is denigrated, and so on.

Elsewhere, in a discussion of the interrelationships between English and vernacular languages in India, Vaidei Ramanathan (2005) presents a very different set of issues, although her conclusions are similar to those of Park and Piller and Cho with reference to the ways in which English mediates class divisions in societies today. Ramanathan contrasts vernacular-medium (VM) education, where the term 'vernacular' refers to forms of Gujarati used in the Gujarat region of India, with English-medium (EM) education, where 'English' refers to 'Indian/South-Asian English' (Ramanathan, 2005: vii). Among other things, she examines how university-bound students are placed in education according to the English–vernacular distinction/ division and how an early choice in one direction or the other both reflects class positions in Indian society and strongly orients the eventual class positions of young adults once they have finished their education. Simply stated, EM education allows access to a whole range of academic disciplines and the knowledge associated with them, while a VM education does not. Given their stronger background in English during the early years of their lives,

> middle class EM students have easier access to EM colleges and, thus, to all disciplines. Lower income VM students who, because of their relative lack of fluency in English, … have access only to 'lower-level' disciplines which … do not get them the jobs they seek or the social standing they desire.
>
> *(Ramanathan, 2005: 34)*

As Ramanathan describes so well in her book, class divisions in India run deep. First, they emerge out of the caste system, which though weaker than it once was, still exists. In discussions of caste, there have tended to be two broad and often conflicting versions, one 'idealistic' and the other 'material'. In the former case, 'caste is cultural construct and … people are placed on a higher or lower scale based on religiously sanctioned notions of purity and impurity' (Ramanathan, 2005: 95). Meanwhile, in the materialist version, 'caste is simply a rationalization and obfuscation of more basic inequalities: those higher on the caste scale are generally wealthier than those who are lower … [and] [i]n hegemonic terms, the higher castes have more access to the means of production, including better schooling, better jobs and more social goods' (Ramanathan, 2005: 95). Both in colonial and postcolonial times, members of the higher castes have always existed in the idealistic realm, and with the economic development from the late colonial period onwards, they have existed in parallel with the merchant and professional class which arose during the colonial period and then vied with the higher castes for power in postcolonial India.

A second way in which class divisions run deep is to be found in class habitus, which is so well established as to go unrecognised by those in positions of power. Interestingly, in her discussion of this phenomenon, Ramanathan draws not on Bourdieu but on Berger and Luckman (1966) and their work on 'habitualization', which captures how the repetition of particular actions in the same or similar contexts 'can then be reproduced with an economy of effort … [and] may be performed again in the future in the same manner and with the same economical effort' (Berger and Luckman, 1966: 70; cited in Ramanathan, 2005: 36). From such thinking, she develops her own term, 'assumption nexus', which she defines as follows:

> '*[A]ssumption nexus*' is intended to capture the vast array of class-based social practices both inside and outside the home that privilege the middle-class and that by its very existence subordinate low-income groups. The term includes

everything in class-based conventions that inform how and why particular class groups live and make the choices they do in almost every realm of everyday existence, including those related to schooling, child-rearing, literacy practices at home, clothing and public appearances, food, how money gets spent, body sizes, weight, health, nutrition, hairdos and most importantly, ... opting for fluency in English.

(Ramanathan, 2005: 37)

How this works in practice is portrayed vividly when Ramanthan contrasts female students at a women's college (WC), most of whom are from working class and poorer backgrounds, with the middle and upper class students attending an EM coeducational business college. The former university and its students exist in a context of lack and austerity – there is not a lot of anything. The students attending classes in relatively poor facilities are subject to many time and spatial constraints. For example, the university operates a timetable that begins late morning so that the students have time to attend to the 'local, class-related, cultural demands on women' (Ramanathan, 2005: 68) and 'there are no campus grounds to speak of, just a tall three-storey building that one enters through a parking lot filled with scooters and bicycles' (Ramanathan, 2005: 68). From Ramanathan's description, we see how such students are on the path to what Bourdieu (1984) called a 'taste of necessity', which arises from *lived necessity*, and means 'a form of adaption to and consequently acceptance of the necessary, a resignation to the inevitable' (Bourdieu, 1984: 372). In other words, the modest conditions of their day-to-day lives help to shape a habitus of lower expectations among these students as to what life can offer and what one can expect.

In stark contrast to this state of affairs, the business school is a more spacious and inviting venue and its students are freer in terms of the organisation of time and space. As a result, their lives are far more aligned with the notion of the cosmopolitan global citizen when it comes to a wide range of behaviour and practices. We see here stylisation and stance that conveys class position in Indian society, as students inhabit a universe of choice, which contrasts markedly with the students in the WC described earlier. Ramanathan describes this context and the students in it as follows:

> Located in the 'better' part of town, the business college (BC) is not nearly as engulfed in traffic as the WC is. Set amidst trees, the institution itself is far removed from the street and, for the most part, secluded from street noise. This institution seems to have everything that the WC did not: quiet, space, a canteen for students to hang out in, a well-stocked library, drinking fountains. Groups of students mill at the entrance of the driveway, several stand in groups at tea stalls sipping tea, some sit on benches under trees. ... [T]he students seem to tote clear markings of an upper-middle-class culture: a high degree of westernization (evidenced partly in the extensive amount of English spoken among teachers and students), relatively easy interaction

between the sexes, the clothes (with all the young men in jeans and the young women in an even mix of jeans, and skirts, and Indian outfits), the generally un-oiled hair and the comparatively fancy shoes (no rubber flip-flops here).

(Ramanathan, 2005: 69)

WC students study English as an important subject alongside their other subjects. Pedagogically, classes are very much teacher led with lecturing and choral work but little in the way of group discussions or individual interventions. The content is at times very far removed from the students' day-to-day lives, which in itself is not a problem if the pedagogy employed serves to move students into the world of the author and, in the process, a work of literature. However, in this context, a book such as *The Importance of Being Earnest* is required reading and is handled in such a way that it comes to mediate the alienation of students, as Ramanathan explains vividly:

[T]he general alienation that these students experience is caused by several competing factors, all tied to the English-vernacular gulf: the content is culturally alien and far removed, the language in which the play is written is one they are not familiar with and the language in which the content is explained reduces a really funny scene to dullness and tedium, with traces of humor completely erased. The conflict between mediums – English in the text and the Vernacular in class – among other things does not help them gain fluency over either the language or the content/culture of what they are reading.

(Ramanathan, 2005: 75)

In addition, the teaching practices employed in this setting tend to be teacher fronted with little opportunity for pair or group work. There is a kind of connection between the vernacular base and the WC being local and therefore more bound to tradition. This contrasts with the BC, where being EM means easier and more fluid contact with the world beyond Gujarat. As Ramanathan explains, '[i]n the WC, the cultural models are more oriented to the vernacular; in the BC, the cultural models seem to be more oriented to westernized pedagogical practices' (Ramanathan, 2005: 78). In this way, class differences, based in the material existence of these young people living in Gujarat, are mediated by the English language: ideas about it, access to it, success in learning it, prospects for using it and so on. Despite all of the positive press around English in the world today, we should not lose sight of the Pennycook quote reproduced earlier, to the effect that English 'colludes with many of the pernicious processes of globalisation, deludes many learners through the false promises it holds out for social and material gain, and excludes many people by operating as an exclusionary class dialect, favouring particular people, countries, cultures and forms of knowledge' (Pennycook, 2007: 101).

Conclusion

In this chapter, I have discussed bi/multilingualism in a partial way, focusing primarily on educational contexts, with a heavy concentration on research in the United States. However, by the end of the chapter, I have moved to a more global perspective, examining a phenomenon that perhaps falls more under the general heading of 'world Englishes' than 'bi/multilingualism' – L1(s) + English bi/multilingualism. Taking on board all factors as an initial way into bi/multilingualism research is, of course, a tall order. As I suggested in Chapter 1, it involves putting sociology more clearly at the centre of such research, something that is anathema to researchers more wed to cognitive/linguistic approaches and a seemingly wilful ignorance of all things social. Going back to Fraser's work, I can only appeal to the necessity of considering the material conditions of bilingual lives as it is my view that these serve as a baseline for all that ensues, as much, if not more, than pervasive racism in twenty-first-century societies. If we want to obtain a more complete understating of bilingualism as a social phenomenon, we need to move in this direction.

To conclude, I would say that it is essential to examine social class in terms of how bi/multilinguals in a range of contexts are positioned in society and how individuals act according to generative and dynamic Bourdieusian habituses. In addition, when bi/multilinguals are framed in terms of their migrant status (either as the children of immigrants or immigrants themselves), there is room for an historical perspective, drawing on notions such as Williams's 'residual' culture. Residual culture means values, attitudes, behaviours and other aspects of culture that have been 'effectively formed in the past, but ... [which are] still alive in the cultural process, not only and often not at all as ... element[s] of the past, but as ... effective element[s] of the present' (Williams, 1977: 122). Rephrasing Williams somewhat, I would say that this means examining what migrants take with them in terms of culture when they migrate. But more specifically, it means examining class habituses that are transportable and transported in migratory processes. Finally, as regards the study of L1(s) + English bi/multilingualism, there is the need to consider not only how access to English is variable and this variability indexes class positions in societies, but also how the acquisition of English language competence, usually by individuals who already possess a great deal of economic, cultural and social capital, serves to strengthen the dominant positions of the powerful in societies.

Notes

1 Although it is worth noting that Bourdieu's conceptualisation of symbolic violence was initially about stratification and class in societies, as the following quote shows:

> The different classes and class fractions are engaged in a symbolic struggle properly speaking, one aimed at imposing the definition of the social world that is best suited to their interests. The field of ideological stances thus reproduces in transfigured

form the field of social positions. These classes can engage in this struggle whether directly, in the symbolic violence of everyday life, or else by proxy, via the struggle between the different specialists in symbolic production ... , a struggle over the monopoly of legitimate symbolic violence ... , that is, of the power to impose (or even to inculcate) the arbitrary instruments of knowledge and expressions ... of social reality – but instruments whose arbitrary nature is not realised as such.

(Bourdieu, 1991: 167–68)

Bourdieu also saw gendered-based stratification in terms of symbolic violence, as the following quote shows:

Symbolic violence is instigated through the adherence that the dominated cannot fail to grant to the dominant (and therefore to the domination) when, to shape her thought of him, and herself, she has only cognitive instruments that she shares with him and which, being more than the embodied form of the relation of domination, cause that relation to appear as natural.

(Bourdieu, 2001: 35)

However, it is difficult to find in Bourdieu's work any discussion of symbolic violence in terms of race, ethnicity or ethnolinguistic identity. And so it has been left to scholars, particularly in fields such as sociolinguistics and bilingualism, to develop this link.

2 It should be noted, however, that in sociology and the social sciences in general there has been a tendency for scholars to leave entire parts of the world out of discussions of neoliberalism, as they follow a bias that leads them to examine the wealthier parts of the world, which are seen as the most exemplary laboratories for neoliberalism. Mathieu Hilgers argues that this bias needs to be overturned and that the focus needs to shift to parts of the world like Africa, which:

[h]as been on the vanguard of austerity and reforms of the kind now affecting such European nations as Ireland, Portugal and Greece. In Africa, the 1980s were marked by policies of stabilisation and structural adjustment. ... These interventionist policies led to waves of deregulation, privatisation and institutional reforms.

(Hilgers, 2012: 82)

This is the true backdrop to language and poverty in the world today and not language policy, which ultimately may be seen to derive, to a great extent, from the imperatives of neoliberalism.

3 In such a situation, one possible response by parents was to seek to educate their children as if they were living back home. In the home, this led to points of reference such as religion, family and general folk knowledge passed on generationally. Outside, however, there were great obstacles to setting up schools that would cater to Greek children exclusively, Spanish children exclusively or Turkish children exclusively and so on. Castles and Kosack note that at the time of writing, they found very few examples of schools for migrant children that handled the entirety of their education and only the feeble beginnings of what in recent years has become the fairly pervasive network of complementary schools in countries such as the UK (Lytra and Martin, 2010b; see, further, discussion in this chapter). Governments already were reluctant to fund schools that, in effect, socialised children to life in a foreign country. As regards educational authorities in the migrants' home countries, there was generally not enough money on offer to make schools viable in what were more often than not faraway locations.

4 Marketisation refers to a range of processes by which fields or domains of social activity, which had previously been organised according to criteria that had to do with community and institution building, come to be framed in terms of the market, understood as a set of practices involving the exchange of goods and resources according to norms of competitiveness and economic efficiency. Generally government led, marketisation

means that while an area such as education continues to have as its prime function the socialisation of children to the norms and ways of dominant society through the control and disciplining of the content of a range of knowledge domains (and this, despite the ongoing efforts of many academics and educators to make education about reducing inequality in increasingly stratified societies), the ways in which it is planned, delivered and evaluated come to resemble (or, in effect, they are the same as) those which apply in the private sector. Competition and the drive towards ever greater efficiency take over for the basic notions of functionality and public service provision for all. And the content of schooling comes to be aligned more explicitly and integrally with the job market, which presumably awaits individuals on completion of their formal education.

5 In writing this section, I benefited greatly from an extended email conversation with Marnie Holborow about Marx's views on commodities and the prospect of 'language as a commodity', which took place over several days in mid-April 2013.

5

SOCIAL CLASS IN SECOND LANGUAGE ACQUISITION AND LEARNING

Introduction

In previous chapters, I have examined in detail how social class has and has not been a key construct in research taking place under the general umbrellas of sociolinguistics and bi/multilingualism. In this chapter, I continue with my journey through different subareas of applied linguistics, in this case examining second language acquisition and learning research, which, given its general concern with cognition and linguistic development, has traditionally not found much room for social categories and certainly not for social class. And, bearing this in mind, with a view to avoiding the repetition of arguments developed in the previous two chapters, I will keep my discussion here short. As has been the case in previous chapters, I begin with a short presentation of the field of inquiry that will be the focus.

Over the past several decades much has been published under the general headings of second language acquisition (SLA) and second language learning. The two terms will be conflated here into one: second language acquisition/learning – abbreviated as SLA/L – and I will understand this acronym as follows:

> [T]he scholarly field of inquiry that investigates the human capacity to learn languages other than the first, during late childhood, adolescence or adulthood, and once the first language or languages have been acquired. It studies a wide variety of complex influences and phenomena that contribute to the puzzling range of possible outcomes when learning an additional language in a variety of contexts.
>
> *(Ortega, 2009: 1–2)*

Constituting SLA/L are the many applied linguistics and specialised SLA/L conferences organised worldwide every year and most importantly the many publications that appear every year. On the one hand, there are the book chapters and articles in general applied linguistics journals as well as more specialised SLA/L journals, such as *Studies in Second Language Acquisition, Language Learning* and *Second Language Research*. Here one finds a predominance of publications from a cognitive-linguistic perspective and social class in second language acquisition and social issues in general seldom get a look-in. Indeed, if I examine the content of articles published over the past decade in these three journals, as well as others that publish articles on SLA/L, I find no mention of social class except when it is listed as a factor to bear in mind, but with no effective discussion of what it might mean and exactly how it might be a factor. An exception to this trend is an article I published in *Language Teaching Research* in 2012, which serves as the basis for my discussion of a Colombian second language learner living in London (see later).

Meanwhile, if we move to consider the numerous research monographs published every year, we see the same trend. And of course, there are the textbooks examining the field as a whole (e.g. Ellis, 2008; Gass, Beheney and Plonsky, 2013; Lightbown and Spada, 2013; Meisl, 2011; Mitchell, Myles and Marsden, 2013; Ortega, 2009; Saville-Troike, 2012), as well as edited volumes doing the same (Atkinson, 2011; Gass and Mackey, 2012; Macaro, 2012; Ritchie and Bhatia, 2009). Thus, a general survey of such publications shows how class has never been, and is still not today, on the SLA/L agenda to any significant degree. In the next section, I develop this point in more detail.

Social class in SLA/L research[1]

In most SLA/L textbooks, there is no mention whatsoever of class, although in Ortega (2009) 'social class' is mentioned on one page (p. 247). Here there is a reference to Celeste Kinginger's (2004) study of an American student on a study abroad programme in France whom she calls Alice. Ortega examines how a series of factors in Alice's life came together to constitute her as a lower class subject with middle class aspirations, which, in turn, led to her relative success as a study abroad student. As I note elsewhere (Block, 2007a), this relative success came about, in part, because she was an outsider in her study abroad group, someone who could not afford to participate in activities such as leisurely travel and skiing. Thus, while they were solidly middle class and even wealthy in some cases, Alice was from a relatively poor background and had been raised by a single parent (her mother). However, beyond a mention that class might have been a factor in Alice's case, Ortega goes into no further discussion of class and how it might have an impact on second language learning.

Elsewhere, Ellis (2008) does better than the other cited authors in this regard, providing two pages on 'social class' as a possible shaping factor. Helpfully, he begins his discussion by making clear what he means by the construct:

> An individual's social class is typically determined by means of a composite measure that takes into account of [sic] income, level of education, and

occupation. It is customary to distinguish four groups: lower class, working class, lower middle class, and upper middle class. Finer distinctions (e.g. 'upper working class') are also sometimes made.

(Ellis, 2008: 316)

To his credit, Ellis does attempt a definition of social class, although this definition follows rather closely the survey-based research of Lockwood, Goldthorpe and others (e.g. Goldthorpe *et al.*, 1969) discussed in Chapter 2, as well as Labov's (1966) early work, discussed in Chapter 3. As I noted in these chapters, this approach to social class is limited in that it does not take on board the lived experience of social class, remaining at the level of the statistical aggregate and fixed categories.

Moving to research on the intersection of class and second language learning processes, Ellis is able to provide what can only be seen as slim pickings. He goes through research findings from publications and studies carried out in the 1970s and 80s, such as Preston's (1989, 2002) discussion of a sociolinguistic frame for SLA and Burstall's (1975) research examining uptake and engagement with foreign language learning among working class and middle class secondary school students in the UK. He also briefly discusses a study conducted by Olshtain *et al.* (1990) of the relative English language proficiencies of Israeli adolescents, classified as 'advantaged' (middle class) and 'disadvantaged' (lower class). The researchers drew on Cummins's (2000) work on cognitive academic level proficiency (CALP) and found that the advantaged children had higher CALP, which, in turn, correlated highly with better performance in their English classes. There is an obvious link here to the discussion in Chapter 3 of Bernstein's work on elaborated and restricted code (Bernstein, 1971, 1973) and Bourdieu's work on educational capital (1984, 1993), as middle class children come to the task of education in schools (as institutional settings), and specifically the task of second language learning, with language proficiencies and educational capital more consonant with what schools expect than children from working class and poorer backgrounds. However, no such link is made.

Thus, in the SLA/L literature, there is not at present, neither does there appear to have been in the past, anything resembling a line of research exploring the possible links between social class and the processes and outcomes of second language learning in both formal and informal settings. Given this situation, it is perhaps easy to understand why Ellis concludes his short section on social class by stating: 'It is possible, then, that class is less important for success in language learning than it has been in the past' (Ellis, 2008: 318). This conclusion obeys a certain logic, according to which one can judge the importance of a factor mediating SLA/L by how much this factor comes up in published research. Here the argument seems to be that the lack of research on social class in SLA/L shows that it is not relevant or useful. I have no doubt that for researchers who subscribe to the view that SLA/L is only about cognition and linguistic development, the only element of interest in the world outside the individual mind is the kind of linguistic input with which learners are provided. However, given what I have written in Chapters 1 and 2, I find it hard to accept that social class is not relevant to a wide range of socio-psychological processes in which human beings engage.

As much of the research in SLA/L has focused on formal learning contexts in primary and secondary schools and in further and higher education around the world (what we might call in shorthand form 'foreign language classrooms'), it is worth thinking about how class-based analysis might be brought into these contexts. In Chapter 4, I framed the learning of English as an international language as L1(s) + English bi/multilingualism. I made the point that social class mediates English in such contexts both in terms of how middle and upper class children and adults have the most and best quality access to English and how English language competence, once acquired, tends to index and mediate a middle or upper class position in a variety of contexts around the world. However, there is nothing in what I have mentioned thus far which is about class-based experiences taking place in second language classrooms and within second language classroom interactions. This is because, as far as I can tell, there has been no research that has actually adopted this focus. Indeed, the closest example of what I have in mind is a study that I carried out some years ago, documented in my book *Second Language Identities* (Block, 2007a). It involved my interview-based study of Silvia, a wealthy woman in her mid-30s studying English in Barcelona in the early 1990s.

Social class in an English language classroom

At the time of my contact with her, Silvia was following a Cambridge First Certificate (FCE) exam preparation course, which met two days a week over a period of 10 weeks and the two of us met once a week to discuss issues relating to her English language learning. However, during these meetings we did not just talk about matters such as how she was learning vocabulary and the exact nature of the activities she undertook in her lessons; there was also a great deal of talk about the affective side of teaching and learning and this took place around two key themes: first, there was Silvia's struggle to develop an English-mediated identity, primarily through her essay writing and her teacher's comments on her progress; second, there was her ongoing contact with fellow students, in particular one named Rosa, for whom she expressed dislike and even disdain. I now examine each of these two themes in turn, showing how they relate to Silvia's ongoing construction of her upper class identity.

In a series of interviews, Silvia discussed how her teacher corrected her written work and how she generally focused on what was wrong with it, seldom writing positive comments of encouragement. Struggling to find a clear explanation for why this was the case, in one interview Silvia came to the conclusion that it might be because English language teachers (and by this she meant teachers from the United States, the UK, Australia, Canada, New Zealand and Ireland) think that they are better than their students because they possess a complete command of English and their students do not:

S = Silvia; D = David Block
[Transcription conventions in Appendix 3]

s: the only thing is that sometimes (.5) I think that teachers / because they speak English and you don't / they are above you / and this infuriates me actually / because I don't know / but you get this feeling a little / and I've mentioned it to other people / and they've told me I'm right / I mean it's not just my thing / I'm not going to have any kind of inferiority complex / it's just it's a little =

D: = what? / that I have something you don't have? =

s: = that I don't have / and it's costing me a lot to have it / and for this reason / look =

D: = *look down on* /

s: that's right /

D: I've never thought about that (.5) but don't you think that it's also mixed up with the power relation that there might be between teacher and student? /

s: yes / of course / there is always a power relation between the teacher and the student / and at times it has bothered me / and you say / well who do you think you are? / you're just a teacher / it's true / you might know a lot of English / but I know a lot of other things / (Silvia-2/6/93)

(Block, 2007: 129; re-transcribed for this discussion)

s: lo único es que a veces (.5) pienso que los profesores / por el hecho de hablar inglés / y que tu no lo hables / están un poco por encima de ti / y esto da un poco de rabia la verdad / porque / no sé / pero da un poco esta sensación / y le he comentado con alguna otra persona / y me han dicho que sí / o sea que no es cosa mía / que no voy a tener ningún complejo de inferioridad / es que es un poco la =

D: = ¿qué?/ ¿Que yo tengo algo que tu no tienes? =

s: = que yo no tengo / y que a mi me está costando mucho tenerlo / y por eso / *look* =

D: = *look down on* /

s: eso es /

D: nunca lo había pensado (.5) ¿pero no crees que esto también está intermezclado un poco con la relación de poder que puede haber entre profesor y alumno?/

s: sí / claro/ siempre hay una relación de poder entre el profesor y alumno/ y a mi a veces me ha molestado / y dices / ¿pero qué te has creido? / si tu solo eres un profesor / Claro / es que es verdad / sabrás mucho inglés/ pero yo sé muchas otras cosas/

(Block, 2007: 129; re-transcribed for this discussion)

Leaving to the side my rather disingenuous 'I've never thought about it', we see here that although she does not articulate matters strictly speaking in class terms here, Silvia does make reference to something class like. As I note in Block (2007a: 129–30):

Here Silvia makes reference to what seems to be a question of social class. A well-educated woman from a wealthy family, with a law degree and a home in one of Barcelona's most exclusive residential areas – in short, someone with an excess of economic, cultural and social capital – certainly does not have to take certain things from someone who is 'just a teacher'. She seems to resent the fact that the classroom situation puts her in a less powerful position, albeit for only four hours a week.

Elsewhere in the interviews, Silvia invokes class more explicitly when discussing one of her classmates, Rosa, for whom, as explained already, she professed a degree of dislike.

> so / this girl / they had told me that in her first course here / she had a lot of problems with the class / that she ended up falling out with half the class / and at first I thought / she's not that bad / that it must have been the other people's fault and not hers / but now I think it's her fault / I mean / I have no doubt that if she fell out with everyone / it's down to her / because she's (.5) I think she is a self-made person / and when people face adverse circumstances / they become more demanding and more (.5) if you have things easy in life / more or less / you are more condescending / but if you have them a little (.5) then you're very demanding I think / and I think that's what's going on with this girl / (Silvia-5/5/93)
>
> *(Block, 2007: 133–34; re-transcribed for this discussion)*

> bueno / esta chica / a mi me habían comentado que el curso que ella empezó aquí / tuvo muchos problemas con la clase / que acabó peleada con media clase / y yo al principio pensé / bueno no es para tanto / que sería culpa de la gente y no de ella / pero ahora pienso que es culpa de ella / o sea / no me cabe duda en absoluto que si acabó mal con la clase / es por ella / porque es (.5) me parece que es una persona que se ha hecho a si misma / y cuando las personas tienen las circunstancias adversas / se vuelven más exigentes y más (.5) si tu tienes las cosas fáciles en la vida / más o menos / eres más condescendiente / pero si las has tenido un poco (.5) luego eres muy exigente creo / y creo que es lo que le pasa un poco a esta chica /
>
> *(Block, 2007: 133–34; re-transcribed for this discussion)*

Interestingly in this case, Silvia moves from describing Rosa as a difficult person to deal with to an attribution of this difficulty to her status as someone who was not born into wealth and who has had to fight her way to the top: 'She is a self-made person.' For Silvia, such a person betrays her relatively humble background through her behaviour and her treatment of others. To make this point, she describes Rosa as 'demanding', attributing this characteristic to the fact that she has faced 'adverse circumstances', which presumably she has overcome. In addition, or perhaps as a result, she lacks the kind of *noblesse oblige* of the upper classes, as she is not as 'condescending' as she should be.

Silvia goes further in her analysis of Rosa when she cites an example of how she tries too hard to impress others. Rosa, it seems, had Swiss nationality and spoke some German. And according to Silvia, she displayed this circumstance whenever she could as a symbol of status: being Swiss – that is, being the citizen of a country with one of the highest standards of living in the world – is superior to being just Spanish, and speaking German, it would seem, indexes high culture. However, Silvia was not at all impressed with this type of behaviour as the following excerpt shows:

> she is all the time excusing herself / because she says words in German (.5) and sometimes I think she does it a little on purpose / but (.5) and I think that this girl also does it sometimes / because she likes to show off that she was in Switzerland / that she has Swiss nationality / and I don't know (.5) that the Swiss are so perfect / I don't know (.5) and that her son speaks German (.5) everyone has their things / but I don't go around telling everyone (.5) normally if they don't ask me / I don't go (.5) go around boasting / (Silvia-26/5/93)
>
> *(Block, 2007: 134–35; re-transcribed for this discussion)*

> todo el rato se está excusando / porque dice palabras en alemán (.5) y a veces pienso que quizás lo hace un poco a propósito / pero(.5) y yo creo que esta chica a veces también lo hace / porque le gusta presumir de que ella estaba en Suiza / que tiene la nacionalidad suiza / y que no sé (.5). que los suizos son tan perfectos / no sé (.5) y que su hijo habla alemán / y (.5) cada uno tiene sus cosas / pero yo no voy contando por ahí (.5) normalmente si no me preguntan / no voy (.5) alardeando por ahí /
>
> *(Block, 2007: 134–35; re-transcribed for this discussion)*

In this sense, Silvia presents what she sees as Rosa's boasting about herself as the mark of a 'parvenu', which Bourdieu described as follows:

> [T]he parvenus who presume to join the group of legitimate, i.e. hereditary, possessors of the legitimate manner, without being the product of the same social conditions, are trapped, whatever they do, in a choice between anxious hyper-identification and the negativity which admits its defeat in its very revolt: either the conformity of an 'assumed' behaviour whose very correctness or hyper-correctness betrays an imitation, or the ostentatious assertion of difference which is bound to appear as an admission of inability to identify.
>
> *(Bourdieu, 1984: 95)*

It was thus Rosa's 'anxious hypercorrection', a behavioural hypercorrection which parallels the linguistic hypercorrection described by Labov (1966; see Chapter 3), which did not sit well with Silvia. For her, there were the *real* members of the

Barcelona upper class, who like Silvia could claim a distinguished family background and who had had a privileged upbringing in the *zona alta* of Barcelona. And then there were the new rich, passing as upper class, those who had earned their money (an admirable feat to be sure), but who could never make up for what they had never lived: the years of upper class education and the embodiment and inculcation of élite *structures of feeling* (Williams, 1977; see Chapter 2), which are the exclusive domain of those who not only belong to the upper classes, but also know how to occupy this station in an appropriate manner. In citing her Swiss nationality and German speaking son, Rosa was achieving the opposite of her intentions, as her attempts at distinction 'betray[ed] an imitation, or the ostentatious assertion of difference which ... [was] bound to appear as an admission of inability to identify' (Bourdieu, 1984: 95).

What I have written thus far is the invocation of social class as a big category, for Rampton a 'secondary representation [...] ... [in terms of] discourses *about* social groups, about the relations of power between them, and about their different experiences of material conditions and practical activity' (Rampton, 2006: 223; see Chapter 3). But what about something more micro level, in the realm of 'everyday discourses, activities and practices' (Rampton, 2006: 222)? Is there anything in Silvia's speech that would be categorisable as indexing social class?

In a transcription of this kind, there are a few worthwhile things to be gleaned as regards *how* Silvia said what she said as Silvia's way of speaking continuously indexed her social class position. First, it is important to note that Silvia and I spoke in Spanish and not Catalan against the backdrop of Catalan/Spanish bilingualism in Barcelona in the early 1990s and our respective individual ethnolinguistic affiliations. Regarding the latter, I could be classified as a privileged immigrant from North America, someone who had come to feel far more affiliated to Catalan than Spanish. By contrast, Silvia was born and raised in a wealthy Barcelona family during the 1960s and 1970s at a time when the Catalan upper class was split between those who used Catalan regularly and those who self-identified far more with Spanish (Woolard, 1986, 1989). From what I could tell, based on my contacts with her as well as conversations I observed her participating in with third parties, Silvia preferred to speak Spanish. In any case, when I told her that we could do the interviews in either Catalan or Spanish and made clear my preference for the former, she chose Spanish. Of course, I cannot rule out that she did this thinking that Spanish would be easier for me given that the sociolinguistic rules of code switching at the time were basically that outsiders were not expected to learn the most inside of languages, Catalan. But certainly, her choice to speak in Spanish was a definite social class marker. However, establishing that Silvia spoke Spanish does not tell us *how* she spoke it. Her Spanish could be identified as Catalan accented and inflected, or in any case, unmistakably from Barcelona to people from other parts of Spain. As I noted earlier, it was Spanish that was highly indexical of an upper class position in Catalan society of the period, of a particular part of that upper class which for generations had identified far more with Spain than with Catalonia and which had marked this preference by speaking Spanish instead of

Catalan where this was possible (Woolard, 1986, 1989). It also marked the area where she grew up (the *zona alta* of Barcelona) and the people with whom she spent most of her time (members of the upper class of Barcleona, educated in the same or similar private schools).

The long and the short of this admittedly very sketchy and partial analysis, based to a great extent on my knowledge of the sociolinguistics of Catalan and Spanish in Catalonia, is that social class is alive and well in the language classroom or, in any case, in students' understandings of what is going on in the language classroom with regard to their relationships with fellow students. If we take a view of the classroom which is ecological (van Lier, 2004), then we see that a multitude of factors intersect to constitute what are moment-to-moment communicative events. Silvia's descriptions of her interactions with her teacher and fellow students led her to invoke *class in itself* as *class for itself* in her analyses of why her relationships with her teacher and her fellow student Rosa were not good. That is, she took the objective state of class relations in society (her class position contrasted with her teacher's and Rosa's) and invoked these relations in her display of her own class consciousness. In addition, the way that Silvia self-presented, in particular the way that she spoke Spanish, provided another way for her to convey class, albeit one that was considerably less self-conscious than how she positioned her teacher and Rosa in class terms. My point here is that all individuals are classed and that classrooms as fields of social activity serve as grounds on which class politics and practices get played out.

In line with what I have argued in previous chapters with reference to sociolinguistics and bi/multilingualism research, I believe that social class can be a useful construct in SLA/L research. But as is the case with so many social constructs, it cannot inform us about how the mind is working, the individual psychology of second language learning. However, it can help us to understand issues such as relative access to different types of input across groups defined in terms of their class position in society. And it can provide us with some insight into how particular attitudes and dispositions impact on second language learning processes, that is, how social class embodied in habitus shapes how learners orient to and engage with second language learning processes. By contrast, it cannot be used as a stable variable that can be linked to second language learning in terms of statistical probability and predictability, as some researchers do with attitudes, motivation, learning style and other learner variables (Dörnyei, 2009; Ellis, 2008). It is, in this sense, more like gender, ethnicity, nationality and race, all identity inscriptions that have made their way into SLA/L research, albeit not in a way recognised to any significant extent by the authors of books about SLA/L cited earlier. In this regard, Ellis (2008) again does somewhat better than other authors as he deals with identity on several occasions in his book. In particular, he has a section entitled 'Social Identity theory' in which he reviews the work of Bonny Norton, surely the researcher most responsible for introducing identity to applied linguistics as a whole and one of the few identity researchers in applied linguistics to include some discussion of social class in her work.

Second language identities and social class

In the mid-1990s Bonny Norton (then Bonny Norton Peirce) published a ground-breaking paper, 'Social identity, investment and language learning' in which she lamented the lack of a more social sensitivity in SLA/L research with little on the experiential side of second language learning and learners themselves positioned as more than just language learners. As she put it: 'SLA theorists have not developed a comprehensive theory of social identity that integrates the language learner and the language learning context' and she added that there was a need to develop 'a comprehensive theory of identity that integrates the language learner and the language learning context' (Norton Peirce, 1995: 12). At roughly the same time, Tara Goldstein's (1997) *Two Languages at Work: Bilingual Life on the Production Floor* appeared and in it the author did manage to move from explanations of learning outcomes in terms of cognition and linguistic factors to a consideration of identity issues that link the second language learner to the second language learning context. Goldstein conducted an in-depth, long-term ethnographic study exploring the language use patterns of 27 Portuguese immigrant women working in a factory in Toronto between January 1988 and March 1990. Through contacts with her informants, via observation and interviews, Goldstein was able to show how most of the women in the study used Portuguese for most of their day-to-day activities, which ranged from the workplace to community and family. All of this occurred against a backdrop of efforts by the Canadian government to provide English language instruction to all immigrants, the official thinking being that learning English would facilitate integration into Canadian society.

Looking back at Goldstein's study after all of these years, I see how it throws up numerous issues that might be linked to social class, but which are not fully explored in detail as such by the author. In particular, there is the way in which the near exclusive use of Portuguese across domains of social activity comes to index a certain acquiescence to a working class position in Canadian society. In this sense, albeit in very different ways, these women were not dissimilar to Willis's (1977) lads, discussed in Chapter 2: while the lads did not take school seriously because they were already oriented towards factory jobs they would have on leaving school, Goldstein's Portuguese Canadian women seemed to renounce upward mobility in favour of maintaining community and family ties, all of which were mediated by Portuguese and not English. Indeed, Goldstein's study provides a good example of intersectionality, as it combines gender issues with class issues against the historical–national backdrop of the Azores Islands, from where all of these women had migrated. Elsewhere, I sum up this intersectionality as follows:

> Goldstein's study is mainly about Portuguese immigrant feminine subject positions and how the key focal point in the lives of these women is the family: childcare, financial obligations to the family and acceptance of masculine hegemony, both inside and outside the home. Mixed in are classed subject positions emergent from the minimal formal education of the women

(often only four years in the Azores, as noted above) and their at-best moderate professional skills, which left them with few prospects for jobs outside of Stone Specialties. And finally, there is a patriarchal Portuguese culture which relegates women to subordinate positions in all aspects of their lives, which has seemingly been transferred intact from villages in the Azores to urban Toronto.

(Block, 2007a: 85)

Nevertheless, social class is not a key construct in Goldstein's account of her informants' lives and for such an analysis we have to look elsewhere in second language identities studies. In *Identity and Language Learning*, Norton (2000) does much better in this regard as she examines the interrelationship between identity and power and how these impact on access to English in classroom and naturalistic settings. Norton focused on the trials and tribulations of five immigrant women in Canada over a period of 15 months in 1990–91. In two of the examined cases, she invokes class as a key mediating factor in the relative access that her informants had to English speaking networks – and presumably English language development.

Katarina was a Polish woman in her mid-thirties at the time of the study, who had recently immigrated with her husband. Katarina had an MA in Biology and she claimed proficiency in Czech, Slovak, Russian and German. However, she spoke no English on her arrival in Canada and she was only able to find employment as kitchen help in a German restaurant. Here she found herself working with Canadians and fellow immigrants who were far younger than she. However, the key issue for her was the fact that she was unable to use her qualifications and her multilingualism, the latter being of little use to her because English was not among the languages that she could speak. As Norton explains, Katarina was all too aware of her situation and the role of English in it, as 'she was very eager to learn it so that she would become part of a social network of people who would value the professional status she had acquired in Poland' (Norton, 2000: 92). To make matters worse, Katarina's husband was in the same position, as a professional for whom the move to Canada had left him declassed due to a lack of English language competence. Both parents' lack of English language proficiency meant that they had to rely on their children to help them with difficult situations mediated by English. Katarina's case shows the hidden injuries of declassing, of the feelings of inadequacy and anomie which come with the type of migrant experience she found herself in.

Meanwhile Felicia, a Peruvian woman in her mid-forties, had moved to Canada with her husband and three children because the family was afraid of 'terrorism'. She was like Katarina in that she also felt that she had given up a great deal in terms of wealth and status in the move to Canada. Felicia had a BA in education and had worked as a teacher in her home country, although at the time of her departure she was a homemaker. Her husband, a successful businessman, had provided the family with a high standard of living, which included a home in an exclusive neighbourhood in Lima, a second home at the beach, extensive holiday travel and private schools for their three children. However, he struggled to find a job with a high profile in Canada and Felicia described the family situation as follows:

> We downed our standard of living in Canada. We used to have a relaxed life in our country. My husband had a very good job. Canada doesn't give my husband the opportunity to work. I never will understand why the government gave him the professional visa.
>
> *(Norton, 2000: 102)*

The mention of 'relaxed life' in Peru somewhat contradicts the fear of terrorism, which Felicia cited as the reason for the family leaving that country. However, she no doubt refers here to the aforementioned status and wealth – both leading to comfortable lifestyle – which her family enjoyed due to her husband's successful business.

Felicia worked as a babysitter and delivered newspapers, but what bothered her most was her lost status as someone to be reckoned with and respected. In Canada, she found that she was nobody and, what was worse, she was positioned by Canadian citizens as an 'immigrant'. She explained her situation as follows:

> Canada can be a very good country for some kinds of immigrants; people who lived in countries under communism are happy here or people who never had anything in their countries. Here, they can work in any kind of work and get things. But professional people and wealthy people lose a lot coming to Canada. They are not welcome here as the Canadian Consul told them in their countries. They spend a lot of their money here and is not easy to come back when they have children looking for their way in life. Opportunities are very difficult to find for them, and life goes without emotion. The only thing I find is good, is that there is no terrorism and many thiefs here.
>
> *(Norton, 2000: 56)*

One aspect of the experiences of these two women is declassing, which is often a factor in migration. There is also an element of the 'hidden injuries of class' (Sennett and Cobb, 1972), or more generally the affective side of class, discussed in Chapter 2. Katarina and Felicia were very different people: the former perhaps more middle class in Poland in educational and occupational terms, the latter more upper class in Peru in economic and consumer terms, even if her class position derived above all from her husband's occupation and income. However, they shared a certain feeling of shame deriving from the feeling of having had income, possessions, status and recognition in their home countries and of having none of these things to a sufficient degree in their adopted home, Canada.

About a decade ago, in a study that also focused on adults, I found a somewhat different immigrant experience in my contacts with Carlos, a middle class Colombian man living in the UK.[2] Carlos lived in London with his English wife, and although he held a PhD in Philosophy and had worked at a university in Colombia, he had never devoted very much time to the study of English, which, as he acknowledged in one of our first conversations, made him different from most well-educated Colombians. He and his wife tended to use Spanish far more than English, both in the home and with their friends, most of whom were middle class speakers of Spanish from Argentina, Colombia, Spain and other Spanish speaking countries. Carlos's lack of English language proficiency, which did not seem to concern him, meant that he had to work in jobs far below what he had done in Colombia and when I met him he was working as a porter in a large building in central London. Thus, like Katarina and Felicia, he experienced declassing when he moved to London over a year before we met 2003. However, in his contacts with me, he did not manifest any feelings of injury, as was the case with Katarina and Felicia. As I note elsewhere (Block, 2006, 2007a, 2007c, 2012), he had a rich life away from work as regards pastimes, including reading, going to the cinema and relatively frequent weekend trips to European cities. All of this was possible because he and his wife were both in full-time employment, they had savings and they owned two properties in greater London, which they rented out. Well educated and not suffering economically, Carlos went through life with the confidence that Bourdieu (1984, 1993) noted in the French middle class, a confidence that comes with cultural capital and a middle class habitus.

In the workplace, however, matters were very different, not least because he had to use English with his colleagues, all of whom were working class white Englishmen who spoke a London English which included most of the features outlined by Rampton (2006) as typical of Cockney English (see discussion in Chapter 3). In the following excerpt, taken from a longer conversation recorded by Carlos himself, Carlos is talking to Dan, a recently retired former colleague. The main topic introduced by Carlos is the trials and tribulations of Chelsea Football Club during the 2003–4 season. Transcription conventions can be found in Appendix 3.

      C = Carlos; D = Dan

1 C: they can run for the championship /
2 D: yeah I'd love to see em do some/f/in' this season / they haven' won i/?/
      for donkey's bloody years [you know
3 C: [did you see the match? /
4 D: I saw i/?/ Sunday when they won 5-nil /
5 C: you used to go to the stadium and all /
6 D: yeah =
7 C: = to the Stamford Bridge /
8 D: yeah ehr (.5) I haven' been yet this season / but the boys rung me up the
      other day / we're gonna try and get tickets (.5) coz see / you know Bill Bailey
      / he can' get down very [often
9 C: [yeah =
10 D: = but he's next on the ((xxx)) / and he's gonna try and get tickets when
      we play Charlton [which
11 C: [ehrm =

12 D: = I only go about once a season now coz (.5) I mean I could go if I wan/ʔ/ed /
    but wi/f/ 'im livin' up north / 'e 'e can' afford to come down to London very
    often / and what wi/f/ the price of the ticket / it's too expensive for 'im =
13 C: more than thirty pounds =
14 D: o:oh ye:ah / some of the tickets / [some of 'em
15 C: [the price of the tickets change when /
        it depends on =
16 D: = wha/ʔ/ match yeah / Charlton is one of the [cheaper matches
17 C: [a:h =
18 D: = but it's still about /f/ir/ʔ/y one pounds =
19 C: = forty one /
20 D: well some of 'em are for/ʔ/y odd pounds / all depends [wha/ʔ/
21 C: [but you're a rich
        man Dan / come on you can [spend
22 D: [wo:ah =
23 C: = couple of pounds for old Chelsea / < Carlos laughing >
24 D: cos/ʔ/ a bloody fortune now football does / < Carlos continues laughing
        while Dan prepares to leave >
25 C: OK Dan nice to see [you
26 D: [see you again =
27 C: OK see you before Christmas.

It is possible that Carlos perhaps did not understand some of the things that Dan said in
this conversation, as during the course of my contacts with him he often told me that he
had trouble following Dan and his other work colleagues because of their working class
Cockney speech (although he did not describe their speech in this manner, saying
instead that he thought that Dan's speech 'was very closed'). A close examination of the
transcription reveals numerous features of Cockney English, as outlined above: glottal
stops, voiced labiodental fricatives, voiceless labiodental fricatives and h dropping. If we
examine the exchange turn by turn, we see that it moves along quickly as regards shifts
in topic: from Chelsea's poor performance during the season, to the frequency with
which Dan attends matches, to the rising cost of tickets. In my view, there are two episodes that are worthy of comment, as they show how social class is made in interaction.

The first episode occurs in turns 18 and 19, when in reference to the ticket prices
for a Chelsea–Charlton match, Dan says 'but it's still about /f/ir/ʔ/y one pounds'
(i.e. 31 pounds) and Carlos follows Dan's assertion by saying 'forty one'. Clearly,
when saying '30', Dan uses a voiceless labiodental fricative (/f/) instead of a more
standard voiceless dental fricative (/θ/) and this has wrong-footed Carlos, who has
understood '40'. As we observed in Chapter 3, this pronunciation feature is typical
of Cockney working class speech, even if, as we also observed in Chapter 3, some
of these features of traditional Cockney are being taken up by a cross section of
Londoners as they speak 'multicultural London English' (Cheshire *et al.*, 2011). In this
episode, therefore, Dan makes his class position through his speech and Carlos conveys
his outsider status, not only as a foreigner, but as 'non-English working class'.

Just after this misunderstanding due to Dan's pronunciation, there is a second episode in which social class is constructed. In turns 21 and 23, Carlos reprimands Dan for being worried about the cost of tickets, since he is a 'rich man [who can] spend a couple of pounds for old Chelsea'. In doing so, he engages in the kind of playful banter said to be central to the making of working class culture in the UK. As Willis explains:

> Many verbal exchanges on the shopfloor are not serious or about work activities. They are jokes, or 'pisstakes', or 'kiddings' or 'windups'. There is a real skill in being able to use this language with fluency: to identify the points on which you are being 'kidded' and to have appropriate responses ready in order to avoid further baiting.
>
> *(Willis, 1977: 55)*

As it is, in response to Carlos's 'windup', Dan only manages to interject a tame 'wo:ah' in turn 22 and a coda to close down the topic in turn 24: 'cos/?/ a bloody fortune now football does', using notably London working class syntax in doing so.

In addition to these two episodes, social class may be seen to be made in a third way in this exchange. I refer here to the main topic, football. However, before pursuing this line of argument, I should acknowledge that there is recent research that challenges the traditional interpretation of talk about football as an index of working class positioning in the context of twenty-first-century Britain. Crompton writes on this very issue as follows:

> The erosion of the 'traditional' working class fan base and football's growing attraction for the middle classes meant that the successful clubs became increasingly attractive in financial terms, grounds were improved, and ticket prices rose dramatically. The really big change, however, came in 1992 when the sale of television rights, at a stroke, massively increased the money available to the clubs, particularly the more successful clubs … The leading clubs have become global brands, and local links have to a large extent disappeared.
>
> *(Crompton, 2008: 4)*

Crompton's point about what amounts to the middle class takeover of football in Britain notwithstanding, it could still be argued that given his age and upbringing, and the way that he has lived his adult life, Dan speaks about football from a working class position. Indeed, conversations about football in the workplace with his work colleagues over several decades were as much a part of the making of working class culture as the 'pisstakes', 'kiddings' and 'windups' (Willis, 1977). As for Carlos, football occupied a very different psychological and social space. In Colombia, it has traditionally been more of a cross-class phenomenon than has been the case in the UK. But, more importantly, Carlos himself saw football as a safe topic to take on with his work colleagues, explaining to me on occasion that he could not talk about politics or his interest in cinema and travel with them as easily.

Ultimately, this kind of surface analysis of speech and topic can only get us so far if our goal is to develop an in-depth understanding of Carlos's class position vis-à-vis languages in his life. As stated already, Carlos worked in a job well below his qualifications and therefore had experienced, in his move to London, a form of occupational declassing that often comes with migration, as we saw above in the case of Katarina (Norton, 2000). However, he showed very little concern about this declassing or even his lower income, because, as I explained above, he and his wife worked, had savings and rented out two properties in Greater London, all of which allowed them to maintain a middle class lifestyle. This middle class lifestyle was evident in the couple's consumption patterns and symbolic behaviour (Bennett *et al.*, 2009). First, as noted earlier, Carlos was interested in reading and cinema. In addition, in his conversations with me, and as I observed when in his home, he was middle class in the way that he talked about food, the way that he bought food and the way that he enjoyed cooking for his friends and family. As we observed in Chapter 2, researchers ranging from Bourdieu (1984) to Lakoff (2006) have noted how food choice, cooking and eating are all class markers. A final activity that indexed Carlos's middle class habitus was travel, in particular the way in which he and his wife made short weekend trips to European cities whenever they could. Adam Jaworski and Crispin Thurlow (2010) examine what they call 'elite tourism', in which the individual always travels with a good amount of knowledge about the destination, acting as a cosmopolitan traveller (Hannerz, 1996) who seeks opportunities to interact with local people, who eats local food specialities and who knows what art exhibitions are in town. By travelling in this way, Carlos and his wife exercised a kind of mobility that distinguishes the middle and upper classes from the working class and poor (see my discussion of how mobility relates to class position in Chapter 2).

In the end, Carlos's middle class lifestyle served to distance him from his work colleagues. In sum, as I note elsewhere:

> Carlos' generally middle class habitus – acquired via his studies, as well as his friendship networks with middle class people throughout his adult years – led him to feel ambivalence in the workplace: he could not identify with his workmates and he found himself relatively ill-equipped to be 'one of the lads'. This state of affairs was no doubt due in part to his somewhat limited English language skills, but it was surely also due to his middle class habitus, which kept him at a certain distance from the very interlocutors from whom he stood the best chance of learning the most English. However, it was also probably due to the fact that Carlos was not willing to invest too much effort in conversations with speakers of what he knew was a non-standard variety of English (see his comments about Dan's English above). Indeed, across all of the conversations which he recorded, Carlos seldom used colloquialisms and there are no cases in which he used taboo words like 'fuck' or 'shit', which did occur with some frequency in his interlocutors' speech.
>
> *(Block, 2012a: 201)*

Nevertheless, it is also worthwhile to highlight that there were other factors involved in this distancing of Carlos from his work colleagues. First, he was a foreigner, and from Colombia, a country his work colleagues associated with drugs and violence. Second, he was, in British census terms, mixed race (his father was black and his mother was *indígena*), when his colleagues were all white. Third, and finally, he simply did not share anything in the way of history with his work colleagues, as his upbringing in a coastal city in Colombia was very different from the kind of upbringing they would have had in London. It is not surprising, then, that a survey of Carlos's conversations recorded over a period of 12 months reveals that he only on rare occasions achieved the kind of working class authenticity, and in the process a degree of integration with his work colleagues, that we see in the exchange with Dan. He normally kept a certain distance from his work colleagues, a distance that was not just attributable to his class habitus, but the other factors mentioned above: nationality, race and history. Still, social class surely loomed large as a factor intersecting with these other dimensions, as a shaper of Carlos's interactions and relationships with his work colleagues as well as with his dealings with the outside world. And it is impossible to understand his language practices in these contexts without taking his class position into account.

Conclusion

For many SLA/L researchers, the kind of research that I have discussed in the last two-thirds of this chapter does not really go to the heart of second language learning, which they see as involving factors such as the kinds of activity that individuals engage in (deemed to be about language *learning* and not language *use*); the nature of the input that learners are exposed to in their interactions in both formal and informal settings; the cognitive processing that goes on as learners come into contact with the target language; and, finally, the kind of linguistic development that takes place as a result of interaction and cognition. These interests are dominant in the SLA/L textbooks cited at the outset, as well as SLA/L journals, and can be said to be foundational to mainstream SLA/L. Against this backdrop, what, if anything, can I say about these issues based on what Silvia told me about her lessons on a week-to-week basis? Or what about the immigrant women in Norton's study? Or Carlos in mine?

Such questions take us back to debates over the past two decades over whether or not SLA/L should, and even can, have a more social side (e.g. Block, 2003; Firth and Wagner, 1997; Lafford, 2007; Norton Peirce, 1995), one which would include the kind of social class issues that I note in this chapter. These issues are, in turn, about bigger identity issues, in that 'who language learners are' is surely a factor that needs to be taken into account in addition to the cognitive-linguistic side of SLA/L processes. And if, as seems to be the case, many SLA/L researchers simply do not see the point in examining such issues, then little can be done. Nevertheless, as was noted in Chapter 4, in English language classrooms around the world, social class is present as regards the kinds of access children, adolescents and adults have to different quantities and qualities of instruction. And as we observed earlier, the access question exists as well when it comes to the kinds of contact that migrants have with the language of the host community in which they are living.

As I noted in the introduction to this chapter, my aim is not to go on forever examining areas of applied linguistics as regards whether or not, and to what extent, social class has been used as a construct. It is my hope that my lengthy discussions of sociolinguistics in Chapter 3 and bi/multilingualism research in Chapter 4, along with my shorter treatment of SLA/L in this chapter, suffice to make the more general point that social class has experienced erasure over the past several decades in applied linguistics and that it would be a useful construct to include in future research. Its inclusion, however, would depend on a major shift in how applied linguists go about answering the big questions in 'the study of real world problems in which language is a central issue' (Brumfit, 1991: 46), a point made in Block *et al.* (2012: 12), where a call is made for an applied linguistics that is 'more interdisciplinary, more politically engaged and indeed, more fit for the times in which we live'. It remains to be seen if some, many, or most applied linguists are willing and/or able to make such a move.

Notes

1 This is an expanded version of my discussion of social class in SLA/L in Block (2012a).
2 This is a revamped and expanded version of my discussion of Carlos in Block (2007c, 2012a).

EPILOGUE

An epilogue can serve many purposes, from being an opportunity to summarise the content of all previous chapters in a book, reminding the reader what he/she has read, to being an opportunity to try to deal with some of the issues arising from the content of the chapters in a book. In this epilogue, I will dispense with a lengthy version of the former function, providing a short one, before devoting a few pages to a couple of issues arising.

The content of this book

I began the main body of this book with Chapter 1, in which I attempted to provide a context for later chapters. In this chapter, I moved from a presentation of my life story inflected by social class, to weightier matters such as globalisation, neoliberalism, political economy and critical realism – the first three covered as essential background to the content of the book and the last as an epistemological position that arises from my understanding of this background. Then, in Chapter 2, I took the reader on a personal journey through my readings in political economy and sociology in recent years. My aim here was to provide the reader with a glimpse of my reasoning about social class covering key scholars and their work in a more or less chronological manner. In Chapters 3, 4 and 5, I examined three general areas of applied linguistics – sociolinguistics, bi/multilingualism research and second language acquisition/learning (SLA/L). I had considerably more to say about the first two than the last one, but in the end, the message running through these chapters is similar and fairly clear. Social class has not figured prominently, or even much at all, in different areas of applied linguistics, although in sociolinguistics it has had a certain presence over the decades. Applied linguistics is impoverished by this omission, or *erasure*, because in the neoliberal times in which we live, and above all in the midst of the economic crisis wrought by neoliberalism, it is only able to examine and analyse the inequality arising from this crisis in terms of recognition and not in terms of redistribution (Fraser, 2003). If the last few years have taught us anything, it is the importance of the economic base of our existence and one does not have to be a fully paid-up Marxist to come to this realisation. Finally, as I note in my personal narrative in Chapter 1, and as I hope is clear by the examples and discussions that I provide in all five of the preceding chapters, there is social class *in itself* and it is inextricably linked with relations of power in society and the life chances of individuals and collectives whose lives are shaped by these relations. We are unwise (to use a charitable term) if we do not take this reality on board.

Social class elsewhere in applied linguistics

In this book, I have been selective in my coverage of applied linguistics, focusing on just three major areas – sociolinguistics, bi/multilingualism and second language acquisition (SLA/L). However, as I have noted along the way, I have framed these three areas rather liberally and my discussions in Chapters 3, 4 and 5 have spread into what some readers will consider entirely separate areas of applied linguistics such as world Englishes in Chapter 4 or second language identities in Chapter 5. Of course, in following this kind of interdisciplinary creep, I am merely reflecting the way applied linguistics is an amalgam of loosely defined subareas that often bleed into one another. Nevertheless, for some readers, the major problem with how I have proceeded is more likely to be that I have left entire areas of research out of my discussions.

One good example is language education in general and more specifically issues around teacher education in language teaching (e.g. Bailey, 2006; Clarke, 2010; Farrell, 2007; Heilbronn, 2008; Johnson, 2009; Malderez and Wedell, 2007; Tedick, 2004; Tsui, 2003). A quick way to dispatch my inattention to this area of research is to say that, once again, there is little mention of social class in such work. The main issue seems to be about the content of teacher training courses and how teachers inhabit a teacher identity. For example, in research examining the former, there is preoccupation with how and the extent to which courses expose trainees to a knowledge base that might be deemed theoretical, including for example coverage of SLA/L research and curriculum theory and the role of teaching practice in such courses. In this work, there is a good deal of attention to how language teaching methodology emerges through the doing of teaching and so-called 'reflective practice' becomes important as a means through which trainee teachers come to formulate and articulate their own theories of second language teaching. And in this kind of formulation of teacher training, there does not seem to be much space for conversations about political economic issues and even less so about social class.

Making this point in a conversation with Brian Morgan about 'class blindness' and critical pedagogies in TESOL (Ramanathan and Morgan, 2009), Vaidei Ramanathan writes that:

> [w]hile our field has over the years heightened our awareness of the impor-
> tance of addressing English teaching to sociopolitical issues, especially those
> relating to issues of sexuality ... , ethnicity ... , race ... , and caste ... , it has
> tended to avoid addressing class.
>
> *(Ramanathan and Morgan, 2009: 154–55)*

To this statement, Morgan adds a call for 'articulation', which would allow TESOL
researchers 'to recognize ... [the] embeddedness [of social class] in "non-classlike"
phenomena like race, ethnicity, religion, gender, geography and so on' (Ramanathan
and Morgan, 2009: 160). However, in language teacher education on the whole,
there seems to be little space for conversations about the eventual class position in
society of second language teachers or how teachers might incorporate into their
teaching the raising of class consciousness among their students. The latter alternative is, quite likely, far too subversive a practice for an institutionalised teacher
education programme, embedded in the power structure of society, to take on.
Why would it? But this is not to say that individual teachers and collectives of
teachers do not take this tack – they do, under the general heading of critical
pedagogy (e.g. Giroux, 2011). Meanwhile, the former alternative, broaching the
class position of teachers in society, seems tame enough for inclusion in teacher
training programmes. However, it does not appear anywhere as far as I can see.

Somewhat of an exception is to be found in recent work I have done with John
Gray (a chapter in Block *et al.*, 2012; Block and Gray, in preparation). Drawing on
Marx to some extent, but also on more recent work by scholars such as Harry
Braverman (1974) and George Ritzer (1996, 2007), we examine how neoliberalism
and the marketisation of education (see Chapter 4, note 4, for a definition) have
come together to change the meaning of *skill* in second language teaching, and
how such a development impacts on teachers. Through an examination of the
history of second language teacher programmes and actual practices on the ground
involving teacher trainers interacting with their trainees, we are able to document
how skill, as was observed in Chapter 4, is no longer something tied to the teacher's
sense of self, his/her sense of craft, and a source of pride; rather, it is now a disciplined, disembodied, well-defined, discrete package of activity, disembedded
from teaching viewed holistically and separate from other disciplined, disembodied,
well-defined, discrete packages of activity. We believe there is scope for more
research along these lines, which combines a sensitivity to the political economic
backdrop of teacher training and development, while maintaining a focus on how
the latter take space on the ground.

Indeed, attention to social class can be brought into more areas of applied linguistics,
but I will not elaborate on this point further. Suffice it to say that research in areas such
as hip hop literacies (e.g. Alim, 2007; Alim, Ibrahim and Pennycook, 2009: Pennycook 2007; Richardson, 2007), which have shown a near exclusive interest in race and
ethnicity as mediators of the semiotic activities and practices of this cultural form,
would benefit from a class-based analysis that would allow discussion and analysis
of *hard* working class and outcast masculinities and femininities.[1] Elsewhere,

language policy research, which tends to be situated within debates about multi-culturalism and identity (e.g. Liddicoat, 2013; May, 2012), would also benefit from greater attention to the economic bases of language policy and practice. This would mean a focus on class implications of taking one decision or another as regards the treatment and roles of languages in an education system and society at large. Finally, research on language and identity would benefit from the more extensive inclusion of social class as a key construct in analysis. In this sense, there is reason to examine work in sociology and political philosophy on the intersections of race, gender and class by Skeggs (e.g. 2004) and Fraser (2003, 2013), respectively.

However, regarding the mention of language and identity, it would be unfair to end this short discussion without mentioning some research in sociolinguistics that does situate social class more centrally in analysis and in a more complete way. This research tends to take on identity issues while showing a sensitivity to political economy issues. For example, Carmen Fought (2006) follows up Labov's research on AAVE, which, as we observed earlier, straddled an interest in race and ethnicity, class and linguistic variation. She provides us with a more socially nuanced, conflict-based discussion of the interrelationship between social class and AAVE. Fought begins with the very appropriate point that researchers have tended to focus on AAVE as 'vernacular' and have, in the process, focused on working and lower class speakers, leaving middle class speakers out of the equation. However, these researchers seldom make clear that this is what they are doing, thus reinforcing a stereotype of all African Americans speaking in the same way, as if there were some racial chip that impelled them to do just this. Fought (2006: 62) argues that a more class-based focus 'has the potential to address intriguing issues in the study of language and ethnicity'. She explains:

> It is possible for working class African-Americans to grow up in segregated areas where a strong majority of their interactions, and consequently the influences on their culture and speech, involve other African-Americans … On the other hand, middle-class African-Americans are more likely to have a variety of contacts with people of different ethnic backgrounds. They are also more likely to encounter pressure to assimilate to mainstream norms, including language norms, as part of their participation in various professional fields. Among the effects of this pressure is the fact that most of them will need to command some version of 'standard' English as a professional or personal resource.
>
> *(Fought, 2006: 62)*

Fought goes on to discuss key elements at the crossroads of African American ethnic and racial identity and social class in American society, noting for example how standard English, a middle class phenomenon, is positioned as 'white'. This, of course, puts African Americans who are middle class, and primarily users of standard English, in the difficult position of being labelled 'white' or being accused of 'selling out'. In this case, a middle class position is conflated into a racial status constituted by a racial phenotype and a culture associated with it in American society (Urciuola, 1996). And the latter, in effect, trumps the middle class position and thus, seemingly, there is 'race for itself' but not 'class for itself'. Meanwhile, the middle class position, 'class in itself', exists objectively, emanating from and enduring in the kinds of circumstance that Fought outlines, as seen earlier: the differentiable occupations, housing, socialising patterns and so on, all of which index class position.

Elsewhere, Pia Pichler (2009), draws on earlier work in sociology on gender and social class (e.g. Skeggs, 1997, 2004; Walkerdine, Lucey and Melody, 2001), integrating the latter into her focus on the construction of gendered identities among female secondary school students in London. Pichler focuses on three cohorts: 'cool and socially aware private-school girls'; 'sheltered but independent East End girls'; and 'tough and respectable British Bangladeshi girls'. While the first group was made up of four distinctly upper middle class girls, the last two groups were working class in composition in terms of family income, family dwelling, neighbourhood, parenting at home, the kinds of activity that they engaged in and the kind of talk that they produced.

The private school girls positioned themselves in multiple domains of activities ranging from their studies to music and sex. Pichler found these girls to be more overtly aware of class than the girls in the other two cohorts, which contradicts the notion that social class is relatively invisible among those who occupy higher positions in society and a far greater preoccupation among those at the lower end of society (hooks, 2000). Pichler sums up the way that class is indexed in what the girls choose to talk about and how they talk about it:

> Their talk about poems and mines, dance clubs and their clientele, London's West and East End, state-school students, A-levels and future university degrees, and public perception of 'over-privileged' private school girls indexes social class both directly and indirectly via 'cultural concepts' (Silverstein, 2004), and cultural tastes and capital (Bourdieu, 1984).
>
> *(Pichler, 2009: 61)*[2]

The sheltered girls manifested 'an (unexpressed) awareness of a range of pathologising discourses about working class adolescents and families, especially about single mothers' (Pichler, 2009: 65), which they 'disidentified' with. Instead they positioned themselves as 'respectable' and, further to this, 'sheltered', that is, as living under the constant vigilance and care of their single mothers (and, as Pichler notes, their absent fathers). Ultimately, they came across as 'responsible with regard to their schooling/education, boyfriends and sexual experiences and as compliant with the mostly strict but loving parenting they experience at home' (Pichler, 2009: 65). Meanwhile, the Bangladeshi girls achieved the toughness that Pichler attributes to them 'by the adoption of anti-school and taunting stances ... and ... verbal challenges and insults in the form of teasing and boasting' (Pichler, 2009: 109), all practices 'that appear influenced by ideologies of and norms of British lad(ette)/ working class culture' (Pichler, 2009: 147), as observed in Willis's (1977) 'lads' (see Chapter 2).

To conclude, research of this kind shows a way forward as it works in an intersectional manner, integrating class-based analysis into discussions of what are two of the most researched identity inscriptions, race and gender. Nevertheless, it should be noted that while Fought and Pichler do a good job of making clear the intersection of social class with race and gender, they do not, to my mind, go far enough and even, to some extent, leave social class as an add-on to more important issues arising in race and gender in society.

A final comment about *erasure*

One major theme running through this book is that social class has been *erased* or marginalised as a way of thinking about society and that this marginalisation has occurred in society at large, in the social sciences in general and in applied linguistics. What I have not taken on is why this might be the case. As I noted in Chapter 2, there is a long tradition, especially pronounced in the most developed economies of the world, of either arguing that everyone is middle class or arguing that class is no longer a useful construct. Savage, Silva and Ward (2010) provide an interesting discussion of what they call 'class dis-identification', a term that captures well the idea that 'people are generally reluctant to identify themselves unambiguously as members of social classes and class identities do not necessarily seem highly meaningful to them' (Savage *et al.*, 2010: 61). In this sense, for many people, Marx's (2005) *class for itself* is not a reality in their lives.

According to Savage *et al.* (2010), there are many different reasons for individuals to claim no class position or consciousness when asked to do so. First, there is the problem with how such views are elicited, which tends to be in face-to-face interviews. Asking people point blank about their social class position might look good intuitively (if you want to know something, just ask it), but it can prove to be counterproductive in that it is not always easy to answer such complex questions so suddenly (see Bourdieu, 1999, for an interesting discussion of interviews in field work). In addition, there is the issue of how exactly social class is being defined, the idea being that while a more upgraded multilevelled version of social class might inspire people to talk about it, trying to shoehorn people into cardboard categories, around occupation, education and income, may well prove to be counterproductive. Still another reason for dis-identification comes from the need for middle and upper class people to 'efface their own distinctive privileges' (Savage *et al.*, 2010: 72). From this perspective, it is relatively 'uncool' (my term, not that of Savage *et al.*) to embrace overtly middle class or upper class positions in society when there is so much debate about inequality and rising poverty.

But moving back to applied linguistics and applied linguists, we find a curious form of dis-identification with social class in the form of a generalised disengagement from and *erasure* of class across applied linguistics, a phenomenon that

I identified in the Prologue and then subsequently have explored in detail in Chapters 1–5. There are all kinds of reasons why this *erasure* has taken place and we might look to Savage *et al.* once again for some reasons. Here I would like to focus on just one and it begins with the fact that whatever their background in their formative years, all applied linguists, as academics, are middle class if we situate them according to the dimensions of class outlined in Chapter 2.[3] And it is this middle class part of their being, the 'structures of feeling' (Williams, 1977; see Chapter 2) of being middle class, which comes to be important when researchers focus on a topic like identity.

It is by now a fairly widely accepted notion (albeit one I have come across more informally – and therefore anecdotally – and not via empirical research) that our research interests are shaped directly by our personal and individual life stories and trajectories. As an important aspect of researchers' life stories and trajectories is their middle class condition, it is not surprising that there is often a tendency to impose on research a view of the world that emanates from and reflects a middle class position in society (see Bourdieu 1990, 2000, for thoughts on what he calls, respectively, 'intellectualcentricism' and the 'scholastic fallacy'). This means that when focusing on identity, as a lot of applied linguists have done in recent years, there is a strong tendency to focus on issues around gender, race, religion and sexuality because these are the dimensions of identity that are most salient to applied linguists in their daily lives and middle class people in multicultural societies.

This is the point that I made repeatedly in this book, drawing on Fraser's (2003, 2008) work on recognition and redistribution. Once again, it is worth mentioning that Fraser is not trivialising recognition-based battles against discrimination that have taken place in many parts of the world over the past several decades (and continue in the present). However, she is questioning whether affirmative action policies go deep enough in tackling the roots of discrimination (NB she uses the term 'affirmative action' to refer to measures that deal with the surface level of discrimination; see Chapter 2). She proposes paying greater attention to economic and material bases of human existence, going deep as regards these issues so as to achieve a transformation of the economy and of society.

Thus academics live in a middle class world, a world in which injustice and inequality tend to be framed in terms of what differentiates one academic from another, as opposed to what differentiates academics from other members of society at large. And the dimensions that are integral to discussions of diversity and difference in such an environment revolve around gender, race, sexuality, nationality, disability and so on. This is not to say that social class is never discussed among academics; neither is it the case that all academics come from middle class backgrounds (as I stated earlier) and therefore have no direct line into the cultures of working class and poor people. However, it is to say that a possible explanation for why so many academics in the social sciences and applied linguistics have so little to say about social class is that it is not a dimension of human existence that is immediately obvious to them. In addition, as Fraser (2003, 2008) and others have noted, progressive elements in societies have shifted from a concern with redistribution and class issues to a concern with recognition and identity issues. My point is that this shift should be corrected and that redistribution should be put on the agenda of applied linguistics research and social class should figure as a key construct in research being carried out.

Notes

1 It should be noted that in the work of Elaine Richardson (e.g. 2007) there is a focus on *hard* femininities and race in hip hop in the United States. However, Richardson's very interesting intersectional work, establishing links between race and gender, leaves class relatively under-theorised and effectively out of the equation.

2 A couple of clarifications are in order here. The reference to 'mines' occurred in a conversation in which one of the girls contrasted her life, studying poetry, with 'other people [who] have gotta like … go down mines' (Pichler, 2009: 26). Meanwhile, for those unversed in the British educational system, 'A levels' are 'advanced-level' examinations usually taken during the final year of secondary school. Depending on the result, the student has more or less choice as regards the university he/she will eventually attend.

3 I perhaps should add here that it is primarily senior academics who mark and set the dominant research trends in fields of inquiry and that these individuals tend to be very well established as middle class in the societies in which they live.

APPENDIX 1

Goldthorpe's class categories

TABLE A.1 Goldthorpe's class categories

I	Higher grade professionals, administrators, and officials; managers in large industrial establishments; large proprietors
II	Lower grade professionals, administrators, and officials, higher grade technicians; managers in small industrial establishments; supervisors of non-manual employees
IIIa	Routine non-manual employees, higher grade (administration and commerce)
IIIb	Routine non-manual employees, lower grade (sales and services)
IVa	Small proprietors, artisans, etc., with employees
IVb	Small proprietors, artisans, etc., without employees
IVc	Farmers and smallholders; other self-employed workers in primary production
V	Lower grade technicians; supervisors of manual workers
VI	Skilled manual workers
VIIa	Semi-skilled and unskilled manual workers (not in agriculture, etc.)
VIIb	Agricultural and other workers in primary production

Source: Erikson and Goldthorpe, 1992

APPENDIX 2

NS-SEC analytic classes, operational categories and subcategories 2010

TABLE A.2 NS-SEC analytic classes, operational categories and subcategories, 2010

Analytic classes	Operational categories and subcategories classes
1.1	L1 Employers in large establishments
	L2 Higher managerial and administrative occupations
1.2	L3 Higher professional occupations
	L3.1 'Traditional' employees
	L3.2 'New' employees
	L3.3 'Traditional' self-employed
	L3.4 'New' self-employed
2	L4 Lower professional and higher technical occupations
	L4.1 'Traditional' employees
	L4.2 'New' employees
	L4.3 'Traditional' self-employed
	L4.4 'New' self-employed
	L5 Lower managerial and administrative occupations
	L6 Higher supervisory occupations
3	L7 Intermediate occupations
	L7.1 Intermediate clerical and administrative occupations
	L7.2 Intermediate sales and service occupations
	L7.3 Intermediate technical and auxiliary occupations
	L7.4 Intermediate engineering occupations
4	L8 Employers in small organisations
	L8.1 Employers in small establishments in industry, commerce, services etc.
	L8.2 Employers in small establishments in agriculture
	L9 Own account workers
	L9.1 Own account workers (non-professional)
	L9.2 Own account workers (agriculture)

TABLE A.2 (CONTINUED)

Analytic classes	Operational categories and subcategories classes
5	L10 Lower supervisory occupations
	L11 Lower technical occupations
	L11.1 Lower technical craft occupations
	L11.2 Lower technical process operative occupations
6	L12 Semi-routine occupations
	L12.1 Semi-routine sales occupations
	L12.2 Semi-routine service occupations
	L12.3 Semi-routine technical occupations
	L12.4 Semi-routine operative occupations
	L12.5 Semi-routine agricultural occupations
	L12.6 Semi-routine clerical occupations
	L12.7 Semi routine childcare occupations
7	L13 Routine occupations
	L13.1 Routine sales and service occupations
	L13.2 Routine production occupations
	L13.3 Routine technical occupations
	L13.4 Routine operative occupations
	L13.5 Routine agricultural occupations
8	L14 Never worked and long-term unemployed
	L14.1 Never worked
	L14.2 Long-term unemployed
*	L15 Full-time students
*	L16 Occupations not stated or inadequately described
*	L17 Not classifiable for other reasons

Source: www.ons.gov.uk/ons/guide-method/classifications/current-standard-classifications/soc
2010/soc2010-volume-3-ns-sec-rebased-on-soc2010–user-manual/index.html
Notes
* For complete coverage, categories L15, L16 and L17 are added as 'Not classified'. The composition of 'Not classified' will be dependent on the data source.
5.2 L14 is an optional category while L15, L16 and L17 are the residual categories that are excluded when the classification is collapsed into classes.
5.3 The operational subcategories are required for bridging and continuity in relation to SC and SEG, rather than being necessary in terms of the conceptual base of the NS-SEC. See 6 for detailed descriptions of the categories and subcategories, and 8 for more information about continuity with SC and SEG.
5.4 The categories describe different forms of employment relations, not skill levels, so the category names deliberately do not refer to 'skill'.

APPENDIX 3

Transcription conventions

- Slash (/) shows the end of a chunk of talk, normally paced
- Question mark (?) indicates question intonation
- Pauses are timed to the nearest second and the number of seconds is put in brackets: (.5)
- Square brackets ([) aligned across two lines indicate the point where speakers overlap
- Equals sign (=) at the end of one utterance and the start of the next speaker's utterance indicates that there was no audible gap between speakers
- Double brackets around 'x's shows that the speaker's utterance is inaudible or cannot be made out: ((xxx))
- Phrases or words in angled brackets (< ... >) is an additional comment by the transcriber on what is happening at the time or the way in which something is said
- Colon (:) indicates an elongated vowel (e.g. no:o)
- Glottal stop for voiceless dental plosive /t/ is indicated as /ʔ/
- Voiced labiodental fricative for voiced dental fricative /ð/ = /v/
- Voiceless labiodental fricative for voiceless dental fricative /θ/ = /f/
- H and other consonant dropping = (')

REFERENCES

Abelmann, N., Park, S. J. and Kim, H. (2009) 'College rank and neo-liberal subjectivity in South Korea: The burden of self-development', *Inter-Asia Cultural Studies*, 10 (2): 229–47.

Albright, J. and Luke, A (eds) (2008) *Pierre Bourdieu and Literacy Education*, London: Routledge.

Alim, S. (2007) *Roc the Mic Right: The Language of Hip Hop Culture*, London: Routledge.

Alim, S., Ibrahim, A. and Pennycook, A. (eds) (2009) *Global Linguistic Flows: Hip Hop Cultures, Youth Identities, and the Politics of Language*, London: Routledge.

Althusser, L. (2008 [1971]) *On Ideology*, London: Verso.

Aron, R. (1969) 'Two definitions of class', in A. Béteille (ed.), *Social Inequality* (pp. 67–78), Harmondsworth: Penguin.

Arrighi, G. (2010) *The Long Twentieth Century: Money, Power and the Origins of Our Times*, new edition, London: Verso.

Atkinson, D. (ed.) (2011) *Alternative Approaches to Second Language Acquisition*, London: Routledge.

Atkinson, P. (1985) *Language, Structure and Reproduction: An Introduction to the Sociology of Basil Bernstein*, London: Methuen.

Atkinson, P., Davies, B. and Delamont, S. (eds) (1995) *Discourse and Reproduction: Essays in Honor of Basil Bernstein*, Cresskill, NJ: Hampton Press.

Auer, P. and Li Wei (eds) (2007) *Multilingualism and Multilingual Communication. Handbook of Applied Linguistics, Volume 5*, Berlin: Mouton de Gruyter.

Bailey, K. (2006) *Language Teacher Supervision: A Case-based Approach*, Cambridge: Cambridge University Press.

Baker, C. (2011) *Foundations of Bilingual Education and Bilingualism*, 5th edition, Clevedon: Multilingual Matters.

Baker, C. and Prys Jones, S. (eds) (1998) *Encyclopedia of Bilingualism and Bilingual Education*, Clevedon: Multilingual Matters.

Ball, S. (2007) *Education Plc: Understanding Private Sector Participation in Public Sector Education*, new edition, London: Routledge.

——(2008) *The Education Debate: Policy and Politics in the Twenty-First Century*, London: Policy Press.

Baran, P. A. and Sweezy, P. M. (1966) *Monopoly Capital: An Essay on the American Economic and Social Order*, Harmondsworth: Penguin.

Bauman, Z. (2000) *Liquid Modernity*, Cambridge: Polity.

——(2007) *Consuming Life*, Cambridge: Polity.

Beck, U. (1992) *Risk Society: Towards a New Modernity*, London: Sage.

Benn Michaels, W. (2006) *The Trouble with Diversity: How We Learned to Love Identity and Ignore Inequality*, New York: Metropolitan Books.

Bennett, T., Savage, M., Silva, E., Warde, A., Gayo-Cal, M. and Wright, D. (2009) *Culture, Class, Distinction*, London: Routledge.

Bereiter, C. and Engelmann, S. (1966) *Teaching Disadvantaged Children in the Preschool*, Englewood Cliffs, NJ: Prentice-Hall.

Berger, P. L. and Luckman, T. (1966) *The Social Construction of Reality*, Harmondsworth: Penguin.

Bernstein, B. (1971) *Class, Codes and Control, Volume 1: Theoretical Studies Towards a Sociology of Language*, London: Routledge & Kegan Paul.

——(ed.) (1973) *Class, Codes and Control, Volume 2: Applied Studies Towards a Sociology of Language*, London: Routledge & Kegan Paul.

——(1975) *Class, Codes and Control, Volume 3: Towards a Theory of Educational Transmissions*, London: Routledge & Kegan Paul.

——(1990) *Class, Codes and Control, Volume 4: The Structuring of Pedagogic Discourse*, London: Routledge & Kegan Paul.

——(1996) *Pedagogy, Symbolic Control and Identity: Theory, Research, Critique*, London: Routledge & Kegan Paul.

——(2000) *Pedagogy, Symbolic Control and Identity: Theory, Research, Critique*, 2nd edition, London: Rowman & Littlefield.

Bhaskar, R. (1998) *The Possibility of Naturalism*, 3rd edition, London: Routledge.

——(2002) *From Science to Emancipation: Alienation and the Actuality of Enlightenment*, London: Sage.

Bhatia, T. K. and Ritchie, W. (eds) (2003). *The Handbook of Bilingualism*, Oxford: Blackwell.

Bialystok, E. (2001) *Bilingualism in Development: Language, Literacy, and Cognition*, New York: Cambridge University Press.

Bigelow, M. (2010) *Mogadishu on the Mississippi: Language, Racialized Identity, and Education in a New Land*, Oxford: Blackwell.

Blackledge, A. and Creese, A. (2008) 'Contesting "language" as "heritage": Negotiation of identities in late modernity', *Applied Linguistics*, 29 (4): 533–54.

——(2010) *Multilingualism: A Critical Perspective*, London: Continuum.

Block, D. (2001) 'Foreign nationals on a PGCE modern languages course: Questions of national identity', *European Journal of Teacher Education*, 24: 291–311.

——(2002) 'Destabilized identities across language and cultural borders: Japanese and Taiwanese experiences', *Hong Kong Journal of Applied Linguistics*, 7 (2): 1–19.

——(2003) *The Social Turn in Second Language Acquisition*, Edinburgh: Edinburgh University Press.

——(2005) 'Convergence and resistance in the construction of personal and professional identities: Four French modern language teachers in London', in S. A. Canagarajah (ed.), *Reclaiming the Local in Language Policy and Practice* (pp. 167–96), Mahwah, NJ: Lawrence Erlbaum.

——(2006) *Multilingual Identities in a Global City: London Stories*, London: Palgrave.

——(2007a) *Second Language Identities*, London: Continuum.

——(2007b) 'The rise of identity in SLA research, post Firth and Wagner (1997)', *Modern Language Journal*, 91 (5): 861–74.

——(2007c) '"Socialising" second language acquisition', in Zhu Hua, P. Seedhouse, Li Wei and V. Cook (eds), *Language Learning and Teaching as Social Interaction* (pp. 89–102), London: Palgrave.

——(2009) 'Identity in applied linguistics: The need for conceptual exploration', in Li Wei and V. Cook (eds), *Contemporary Applied Linguistics Volume 1* (pp. 215–32), London: Continuum.

——(2010a) 'Researching language and identity', in B. Paltridge and A. Phakiti (eds), *Continuum Companion to Second Language Research Methods* (pp. 337–49), London: Continuum.

——(2010b) 'Engaging with human sociality: Thoughts on communication and embodiment', *Applied Linguistics Review*, 1 (1): 45–56.

——(2011) 'Citizenship, education and global spaces', *Language and Intercultural Communication*, 11 (2): 162–70.

——(2012a) 'Class and second language acquisition research', *Language Teaching Research*, 16 (2): 188–205.

——(2012b) 'Unpicking agency in sociolinguistic research with migrants', in M. Martin-Jones and S. Gardner (eds), *Multilingualism, Discourse and Ethnography* (pp.47–60), London: Routledge.

——(2013a) 'The structure and agency dilemma in identity and intercultural communication research', *Language and Intercultural Communication*, 13 (2): 126–47.

——(2013b) 'Moving beyond "lingualism": Multilingual embodiment and multimodality in SLA', in S. May (ed.) *Addressing the Multilingual Turn: Implications for SLA, TESOL and Bilingual Education* (pp. 54–77), London: Routledge.

Block, D. and Gray, J. (forthcoming) 'Marketisation and language teacher training'.

Block, D., Gray, J. and Holborow, M. (2012) *Neoliberalism and Applied Linguistics*, London Routledge.

Blommaert, J. (2003) 'Commentary: A sociolinguistics of globalization', *Journal of Sociolinguistics*, 7 (4): 607–23.

——(2005) *Discourse*, Cambridge: Cambridge University Press.

——(2010) *The Sociolinguistics of Globalization*, Cambridge: Cambridge University Press.

Blommaert, J. and Makoe, P. (2011) 'Class in class: Ideological processes of class in deseg-regated classrooms in South Africa', *Working Papers in Urban Language & Literacies*, 80, King's College London/Tilbrug University.

Bloomfield, L. (1933) *Language*, New York: Holt, Rinehart, & Winston.

Boltanski, L. and Chiapello, E. (2007) *The New Spirit of Capitalism*, London: Verso.

Bosc, S. (2008) *Stratification et classes sociales (La société française en mutation)*, 7th edition, Paris: Armand Colin.

Boterro, W. (2005) *Stratification: Social Division and Inequality*, London: Routledge.

Bourdieu, P. (1977a) *Outline of a Theory of Practice*, Cambridge: Cambridge University Press.

——(1977b) 'The economics of linguistic exchanges', *Social Science Information*, 16 (6): 645–68.

——(1984) *Distinction*, London: Routledge.

——(1986) 'The forms of capital', in J. F. Richardson (ed.), *Handbook of Theory of Research for Sociology of Education* (pp. 241–58), New York: Greenwood Press.

——(1990) *The Logic of Practice*, Palo Alto, CA: Stanford University Press.

——(1991) *Language and Symbolic Power*, Cambridge: Polity.

——(1993) *The Field of Cultural Production: Essays on Art and Literature*, Cambridge: Polity.

——(1996) *The State Nobility*, Cambridge: Polity.

——(2000) *Pascalian Meditations*, Cambridge: Polity.

——(2001) *Masculine Domination*, Cambridge: Polity.

——(2005) *The Social Structures of the Economy*, Cambridge: Cambridge University Press.

Bourdieu, P. et al. (1999) *The Weight of the World*, Cambridge: Polity.

Bouzou, N. (2011) *Le chagrin des classes moyennes*, Paris: Jean-Claude Lattès.

Bradley, H. (1996) *Fractured Identities: Changing Patterns of Inequality*. Cambridge: Polity.

Braudel, F. (1972 [1949]) *The Mediterranean and the Mediterranean World in the Age of Phiippe II, Volume 1*, London: Collins.

Braverman, H. (1974) *Labor and Monopoly Capital*, New York: Monthly Review Press.

Breen, R. (2005) 'Foundations of a neo-Weberian class analysis', in E. O. Wright (ed.) *Approaches to Class Analysis* (pp. 31–50), Cambridge: Cambridge University Press.

Brenner, R. (1977) 'The origins of capitalist development: A critique of neo-Smithian Marxism', *New Left Review*, 104: 25–92.

Brooks, D. (2001) *Bobos in Paradise: The New Upper Class and How They Got There*, New York: Simon & Schuster.

Brumfit, C. (1991) 'Applied linguistics in higher education: Riding the storm', *BAAL Newsletter*, 38: 45–49.

Burstall, C. (1975) 'Factors affecting foreign-language learning: A consideration of some relevant research findings', *Language Teaching and Linguistics Abstracts*, 8: 105–25.

Buruwoy, M. (2003) 'For a sociological Marxism: The complementary convergence of Antonio Gramsci and Karl Polanyi', *Politics & Society*, 31 (2): 193–261.

Butler, C. and Hamnett, C. (2011) *Ethnicity, Class and Aspiration: Understanding London's New East End*, London: Policy Press.

Byrd-Clark, J. (2009) *Multilingualism, Citizenship, and Identity: Voices of Youth and Symbolic Investments in an Urban, Globalized World*, London: Continuum.

Callinicos, A. (1995) *Marx*, Cambridge: Polity.

——(2010) *Bonfire of Illusions*, Cambridge: Polity.

Cameron, D. (2000) *Good to Talk? Living and Working in a Communication Culture*, London: Sage.

——(2005) 'Language, gender, and sexuality: Current issues and new directions', *Applied Linguistics*, 26 (4): 482–502.

Canagarajah, S. (1999) *Resisting Linguistic Imperialism in English Teaching*, Oxford: Oxford University Press.

——(2013) *Translingual Practice: Global Englishes and Cosmopolitan Relations: Lingua Franca English and Global Citizenship*, London: Routledge.

Carrasquillo, A. L. and Rodriguez, V. (2002) *Language Minority Students in the Mainstream Classroom*, 2nd edition, Clevedon: Multilingual Matters.

Carroll, W. K. (2010) *The Making of a Transnational Capitalist Class: Corporate Power in the 21st Century*, London: Zed Books.

Castells, M. (1996) *The Rise of the Network Society: The Information Age: Economy, Society and Culture Vol 1*, Oxford: Blackwell.

Castles, S. and Kosack, G. (1973) *Immigrant Workers and Class Structure in Western Europe*, Oxford: Oxford University Press.

Cheshire, J., Fox, S., Kerswill, P. and Torgersen, E. (2008) 'Ethnicity, friendship network and social practices as the motor of dialect change: Linguistic innovation in London', *Sociolinguistica*, 22: 1–23.

Cheshire, J., Kerswill, P., Fox, S. and Torgersen, T. (2011) 'Contact, the feature pool and the speech community: The emergence of multicultural London English', *Journal of Sociolinguistics*, 15: 151–96.

Clarke, M. (2010) *Language Teacher Identities: Co-Constructing Discourse and Community*, Clevedon: Multilingual Matters.

Cohen, N. (2007) *What's Left? How Liberals Lost Their Way*, London: Harper Perennial.

Cole, M. (2009) *Critical Race Theory and Education: A Marxist Response*, London: Palgrave.

Collins, J. (2006) 'Where's class in second language learning?', *Working Papers in Urban Language and Literacies*, 41, King's College London.

Collins, M. (2004) *The Likes of Us*, London: Granta Books.

Collins, R. (1975) *Conflict Sociology: Toward an Explanatory Science*, New York: Academic Press.

Conteh, J., Martin, P. and Robertson, L. H. (eds) (2007) *Multilingual Learning: Stories from Schools and Communities in Britain*, Stoke on Trent: Trentham Books.

Cook, G. (2003) *Applied Linguistics*, Oxford: Oxford University Press.

Cook, V. J. and Bassetti, B. (eds) (2011) *Language and Bilingual Cognition*, Hove: Psychology Press.

Cook-Gumperz, J. (ed.) (1973) *Social Control and Socialization: A Study of Social Class Differences in the Language of Maternal Control*, London, Routledge & Kegan Paul.

Coupland, N. (2007) *Style*, Cambridge: Cambridge University Press.

Crenshaw, K. (1991) 'Mapping the margins: Intersectionality, identity politics, and violence against women of color', *Stanford Law Review*, 43 (6): 1241–99.

Critcher, C. (1979) 'Sociology, cultural studies and the post-war working class', in J. Clarke, C. Critcher and R. Johnson (eds), *Working Class Culture: Studies in History and Theory* (pp. 13–40), London: Hutchinson.

Crompton, R. (2008) *Class and Stratification*, 3rd edition, Cambridge: Polity.

Crouch, C. (2011) *The Strange Non-Death of Neoliberalism*, Cambridge: Polity.

Cummins, J. (1996) *Negotiating Identities: Education for Empowerment in a Diverse Society*, Los Angeles: California Association for Bilingual Education.

——(2000) *Language, Power and Pedagogy: Bilingual Children in the Crossfire*, Clevedon: Multilingual Matters.

——(2009) 'Fundamental psychological and sociological principles underlying educational success for linguistic minority students', in T. Skutnabb-Kangas, R. Phillipson, A. Mohanty and M. Panda (eds) *Social Justice Through Multilingual Education* (pp. 19–35), Clevedon: Multilingual Matters.

Dahrendorf, R. (1959) *Class and Class Conflict in Industrial Society*, London: Routledge & Kegan Paul.

Davies, A. (2007) *An Introduction to Applied Linguistics: From Practice to Theory*, Edinburgh: Edinburgh University Press.

Davies, A. and Elder, K. (eds) (2005) *The Handbook of Applied Linguistics*, new edition, Oxford: Wiley Blackwell.

Day, R. (2006) *Community and Everyday Life*, London: Routledge.

De Angelis, G. and DeWaele, J. M. (eds) (2011) *New Trends in Crosslinguistic Influence and Multilingualism Research*, Clevedon: Multilingual Matters.

De Fina, A., Schiffrin, D. and Bamberg, M. (eds) (2006) *Discourse and Identity*, Cambridge University Press.

De Houwer, A. (2009) *An Introduction to Bilingual Development*, Clevedon: Multilingual Matters.

De Mejia, A.-M. (2002) *Power, Prestige and Bilingualism*, Clevedon: Multilingual Matters.

Dennis, N., Henriques, F. and Slaughter, C. (1956) *Coal is Our Life: Analysis of a Yorkshire Mining Community*, London: Tavistock.

Dewaele, J.-M., Housen, A. and Li Wei (eds) (2003) *Bilingualism: Basic Principles and Beyond*, Clevedon: Multilingual Matters.

Doogan, K (2009) *New Capitalism? The Transformation of Work*, Cambridge: Polity.

Dorling, D. (2011) *Injustice: Why Social Inequality Persists*, London: Policy Press.

Dörnyei, Z. (2009) *The Psychology of Second Language Acquisition*, Oxford: Oxford University Press.

Duchêne, A. and Heller, M. (2012) 'Multilingualism and the new economy', in M. Martin-Jones, A. Blackledge and A. Creese (eds), *The Routledge Handbook of Multilingualism* (pp. 369–283), London: Routledge.

——(eds) (2013) *Language in Late Capitalism: Pride and Profit*, London: Routledge.

Duff, P. (2012) 'Issues of identity', in S. Gass and A. Mackey (eds), *The Routledge Handbook of Second Language Acquisition* (pp. 410–26), London: Routledge.

Duménil, G. and Lévy, D. (2011) *The Crisis of Neoliberalism*, Cambridge, MA: Harvard University Press.

Dunn, B. (2009) *Global Political Economy: A Marxist Critique*, London: Pluto Press.

Durkheim, E. (1964 [1895]) *The Rules of Sociological Method*, New York: Free Press.

——(1984 [1893]) *The Division of Labor in Society*, New York: Free Press.

Ebert, T. and Zavarzadeh, M. (2008) *Class in Culture*, Boulder, CO: Paradigm Publishers.

Eckert, P. (1989) *Jocks and Burnouts: Social Categories and Identity in the High School*, New York: Colombia University Press.

——(2004) 'The meaning of style', *Texas Linguistic Forum*, 47: 41–53.

——(2008) 'Variation and the indexical field', *Journal of Sociolinguistics*, 12: 453–76.

——(2012) 'Three waves of variation study: The emergence of meaning in the study of sociolinguistic variation', *Annual Review of Anthropology*, 41: 87–100.

Edwards, A. D. (1976) *Language in Culture and Class*, London: Heinemann.

Edwards, J. (1994) *Multilingualism*, London: Routledge.

——(2009) *Language and Identity*, Cambridge: Cambridge University Press.

——(2010a) *Language Diversity in the Classroom*, Clevedon: Multilingual Matters.

——(2010b) *Minority Languages and Group Identity*, Amsterdam: John Benjamins.

——(2011) *Challenges in the Social Life of Language*, London: Palgrave.

——(2012) *Multilingualism: Understanding Linguistic Diversity*, London: Continuum.

Ehrenreich, B. (2001) *Nickel and Dimed*, London: Granta Books.

Ehrenreich, B. and Hochschild, A. (2003) *Global Woman: Nannies, Maids and Sex Workers in the New Economy*, London: Granta Books.

Elliott, A. and Lemert, C. (2006) *The New Individualism: The Emotional Costs Of Globalization*, London: Routledge.

Elliot, A. and Urry, J. (2010) *Mobile Lives*, London: Routledge.

Ellis, R. (2008) *The Study of Second Language Acquisition*, 2nd edition, Oxford: Oxford University Press.

Englebretson, R. (ed.) (2007) *Stancetaking in Discourse: Subjectivity, Evaluation, Interaction*, Amsterdam: John Benjamins.

Engels, F. (2009 [1845]) *The Condition of the Working Class in England*, Oxford: Oxford University Press.

Erikson, R. and Goldthorpe, J. (1992) *The Constant Flux: A Study of Class Mobility in Industrial Societies*, Oxford: Oxford University Press.

Farrell, T. S. C. (2007) *Reflective Language Teaching: From Research to Practice*, London: Continuum.

Firth, A. and Wagner, J. (eds) (1997) 'On discourse, communication, and (some) fundamental concepts in SLA research', *Modern Language Journal*, Special Issue, 81 (3): 285–300.

Foucault, M. (1962) *The Archaeology of Knowledge*, London: Tavistock.

——(1973) *The Birth of the Clinic. An Archaeology of Medical Perception*, London: Routledge.

Fought, C. (2006) *Language and Ethnicity*, Cambridge: Cambridge University Press.

Fraser, N. (2003) 'Social justice in the age of identity politics: Redistribution, recognition, and participation', in N. Fraser and A. Honneth, *Redistribution or Recognition? A Political-Philosophical Exchange* (pp. 7–109), London: Verso.

——(2008) *Adding Insult to Injury: Nancy Fraser Debates Her Critics?* [edited by K. Olsen], London: Verso.

——(2013) *Fortunes of Feminism: From State-Managed Capitalism to Neoliberal Crisis*, London: Verso.

Friedman, S. (2012) 'Cultural omnivores or culturally homeless? Exploring the shifting cultural identities of the upwardly mobile', *Poetics*, 40: 467–89.

Fuhui Tong and Qing Shi (2012) 'Chinese–English bilingual education in China: A case study of college science majors', *International Journal of Bilingual Education and Bilingualism*, 15 (2): 165–82.

Garcia, O. (2008) *Bilingual Education in the 21st Century: A Global Perspective*, Oxford: Blackwell.

Gass, S., Behney, J. and Plonsky, L. (2013) *Second Language Acquisition: An Introductory Course*, 4th edition, London: Routledge.

Gass, S. and Mackey, A. (eds) (2012) *The Routledge Handbook of Second Language Acquisition*, London: Routledge.

Gee, J. P. (2008) *Social Linguistics and Literacies: Ideology in Discourses*, 3rd edition, London: Falmer.

Gee, J. P., Hull, G. and Lankshear, C. (1996) *The New Work Order: Behind the Language of the New Capitalism*, Cambridge: Polity.

Giddens, A. (1973) *The Class Structure of Advanced Societies*, London: Hutchinson.

——(2000) *Runaway World: How Globalization is Reshaping Our Lives*, 2nd edition, London: Routledge.

Giroux, H. (2011) *On Critical Pedagogy*, London: Bloomsbury.

Goffman, E. (1981) *Forms of Talk*, Oxford: Blackwell.

Goldstein, T. (1997) *Two Languages at Work: Bilingual Life on the Production Floor*, Berlin: Mouton de Gruyter.

Goldthorpe, D., Lockwood, D., Bechhofer, F. and Platt, J. (1969) *The Affluent Worker in the Class Structure*, Cambridge: Cambridge University Press.

Goldthorpe, J. H. and Lockwood, D. (1963) 'Affluence and the British class structure', *Sociological Review*, 11 (2): 133–63.

Goldthorpe, J., Llewellyn, C. and Payne, C. (1980) *Social Mobility and Class Structure in Modern Britain*, Oxford, Clarendon Press.

Gootenberg, P. and Reygadas, L. (eds) (2010) *Inequalities in Latin America. Insights from History, Politics and Culture*, Durham, NC: Duke University Press.

Gorz, A. (1982) *Farewell to the Working Class: An Essay on Post-Industrial Socialism*, London: Pluto Press.

Grabe, W. (2002) 'Applied linguistics: An emerging discipline of the twenty-first century', in R. Kaplan (ed.), *Oxford Handbook of Applied Linguistics* (pp. 3–12), Oxford: Oxford University Press.

Gray, J. and Block, D. (2013) 'All middle class now? Evolving representations of the working class in the neoliberal era – the case of ELT textbooks', in N. Harwood (ed.) *English Language Teaching Textbooks: Content, Consumption, Production* (pp. TBD), London: Palgrave Macmillan.

Grenfell, M. (ed.) (2011) *Bourdieu, Language and Linguistics*, London: Continuum.

Grieco, M. and Urry, J. (eds) (2012) *Mobilities: New Perspectives on Transport and Society*, London: Ashgate.

Grusky, D. and Galescu, G. (2005) 'Foundations of neo-Durkheimian class analysis', in E. O. Wright (ed.), *Approaches to Class Analysis* (pp. 51–81), Cambridge: Cambridge University Press.

Guilherme M. (2002) *Critical Citizens for an Intercultural World: Foreign Language Education as Cultural Politics*, Clevedon: Multilingual Matters.

Halliday, M. (1990) 'New ways of meaning: A challenge to applied linguistics', *Journal of Applied Linguistics*, 6: 7–36.

Hanks, W. (1996) *Language and Communicative Practices*, Boulder, CO: Westview Press.

Hanley, L. (2007) *Estates: An Intimate History*, London: Granta Books

Hannerz, U. (1996) *Transnational Connections: Culture, People, Places*, London: Routledge.

Harbert, W., McConnell-Ginet, S., Miller, A. and Whitman, J. (eds) (2009) *Language and Poverty*, Clevedon: Multilingual Matters.

Harris, R. (2006) *New Ethnicities and Language Use: The Emergence of Brasian Identities*, London: Palgrave.

Harvey, D. (1989) *The Condition of Postmodernity: An Enquiry into the Origins of Cultural Change*, Oxford: Blackwell.

——(2005) *A Brief History of Neoliberalism*, Oxford: Oxford University Press.

——(2010a) *The Enigma of Capital*, Oxford: Oxford University Press.

——(2010b) *A Companion to Marx's Capital*, London: Verso.

Hashimoto, K. (2003) *Class Strucure in Contemporary Japan*, Melbourne: Trans Pacific Press.

Haugen, E. (1953) *The Norwegian Language in America: A Study in Bilingual Behavior*, Philadelphia: University of Pennsylvania Press.

Hayek, F. A. (1960) *The Constitution of Liberty*, Chicago: University of Chicago Press.

Heath S. B. (1983) *Ways with Words*, Cambridge: Cambridge University Press.

Heilbronn, R. (2008) *Teacher Education and the Development of Practical Judgement*, London: Continuum.

Held, D. and McGrew, A. (2007) *Globalization/Anti-Globalization: Beyond the Great Divide*, Cambridge: Polity.

Held, D., McGrew, A., Goldblatt, D. and Perraton, J. (1999) *Global Transformations: Politics, Economics and Culture*, Cambridge: Polity.

Heller, M. (2002) 'Globalization and the commodification of bilingualism in Canada', in D. Block and D. Cameron (eds) *Globalization and Language Teaching* (pp. 47–63), London: Routledge.

——(2003) 'Globalization, the new economy and the commodification of language', *Journal of Sociolinguistics*, 7 (4): 473–92.

——(2006) *Linguistic Minorities and Modernity: A Sociolinguistic Ethnography*, 2nd edition, London: Continuum.

——(2007a) 'Bilingualism as ideology and practice,' in M. Heller (ed.), *Bilingualism: A Social Approach* (pp. 1–22), London: Palgrave.

——(ed.) (2007b) *Bilingualism: A Social Approach*, London: Palgrave.

——(2010) 'The commodification of language', *Annual Review of Anthropology*, 39: 101–14.

——(2011) *Paths to Postnationalism*, Oxford: Oxford University Press.

——(2013) 'Repositioning the multilingual periphery: Class language and transnational markets in Francophone Canada', in S. Pietikäinen and H. Kelly-Holmes (eds), *Multilingualism and the Periphery* (pp. 17–34), Oxford: Oxford University Press.

Hilgers, M. (2012) 'The historicity of the neoliberal state', *Social Anthropology/Anthropologie Sociale*, 20 (1): 80–94.

Hill Collins, P. (1993) 'Toward a new vision: Race, class and gender as categories of analysis and connection', *Race, Sex and Class*, 1 (1): 25–45.

Hoggart, R. (1957) *The Uses of Literacy*, Harmondsworth: Penguin.

Holborow, M, (1999) *The Politics of English: A Marxist View of Language*, London: Sage.

——(2007) 'Language, ideology and neoliberalism', *Journal of Language and Politics*, 6 (1): 51–73.

hooks, b. (2000) *Where We Stand: Class Matters*, London: Routledge.

Hymes, D. (1974) *Foundations of Sociolinguistics*, London: Tavistock.

Ibrahim, A. (1999) 'Becoming black: Rap and hip-hop, race, gender, identity, and the politics of ESL learning', *TESOL Quarterly*, 33 (3): 349–69.

Irvine, J. T. and Gal, S. (2000) 'Language ideology and linguistic differentiation', in P. V. Kroskrity (ed.), *Regimes of Language: Ideologies, Polities, and Identities* (pp. 35–84), Santa Fe: School of American Research Press.

Ishida, H. and Slater D. H. (eds) (2010) *Social Class in Contemporary Japan: Structures, Sorting and Strategies*, London: Routledge.

Issa, T. and Williams, C. (2009) *Realising Potential: Complementary Schools in the UK*, Stoke on Trent: Trentham Books.

Jaffe, A. (ed.) (2009a) *Stance: Sociolinguistic Perspectives*, Oxford: Oxford University Press.

——(2009b) 'Introduction: The sociolinguistics of stance', *Stance: Sociolinguistic Perspectives* (pp. 3–28), Oxford: Oxford University Press.

Jakobson, R. (1990) *On Language*, Cambridge, MA: Harvard University Press.

Jaworski, A. and Thurlow, C. (2010) 'Taking an elitist stance: Ideology and the discursive production of social distinction', in A. Jaffe, (ed.) *Stance: Sociolinguistic Perspectives* (pp. 195–226), Oxford: Oxford University Press.

Jenkins, J. (2009) *World Englishes: A Resource Book for Students*, 2nd edition, London: Routledge.

Jewitt, C. (2009) 'An introduction to multimodality', in C. Jewitt (ed.), *Handbook of Multimodal Analysis* (pp. 14–27), London: Routledge.

——(2011) 'The changing pedagogic landscape of subject English', in K. O'Halloran and B. A. Smith (eds), *Multimodal Studies: Exploring Issues and Domains* (pp. 184–201), London: Routledge.

Johnson, K. (2009) *Second Language Teacher Education: A Sociocultural Perspective*, London: Routledge.

Jones, O. (2012) *Chavs: The Demonization of the Working Class*, London: Verso.

Joseph, J. (2004) *Language and Identity*, London: Palgrave.

Jule, A. (ed.) (2006) *Language and Religious Identity: Women in Discourse*, London: Palgrave.

Kahl, J. (1957) *The American Class Structure*, Belmont, CA: Wadsworth Publishing.

Kamada, L. (2009) *Hybrid Identities and Adolescent Girls: Being 'Half' Japanese*, Clevedon: Multilingual Matters.

Kanno, Y. (2003) *Negotiating Bilingual and Bicultural Identities: Japanese Returnees Betwixt Two Worlds*, Mahwah, NJ: Lawrence Erlbaum.

Kaplan, R. (ed.) (2002) *The Oxford Handbook of Applied Linguistics*, Oxford: Oxford University Press.

Kiesling, S. (2009) 'Style as stance: Can stance be the primary explanation for patterns of sociolinguistic variation?', in A. Jaffe (ed.), *Stance: Sociolinguistic Perspectives* (pp. 171–94), Oxford: Oxford University Press.

Kinginger, C. (2004) 'Alice doesn't live here anymore: Foreign language learning and identity construction', in A. Pavlenko and A. Blackledge (eds), *Negotiation of Identities in Multilingual Contexts* (pp. 219–42), Clevedon: Multilingual Matters.

Kleyn, T. and Adelman Reyes, S. (2011) 'Nobody said it would be easy: Ethnolinguistic group challenges to bilingual and multicultural education in New York City', *International Journal of Bilingual Education and Bilingualism*, 14 (2): 207–24.

Kramsch, C. (2009) *The Multilingual Subject*, Oxford: Oxford University.

Kress, G., Jewitt, C., Bourne, J., Franks, A., Hardcastle, J., Jones, K. and Reid, E. (2005) *English Urban Classrooms: A Multimodal Perspective on Teaching and Learning*, London: Routledge.

Kress, G. and van Leeuwen, T. (2013) *Reading Images: The Grammar of Visual Design*, 3rd edition, London: Routledge.

Labov, W. (1963) 'The social motivation of a sound change', *Word*, 19: 273–309.

——(1966) *The Social Stratification of English in New York City*, Washington, DC: Center for Applied Linguistics.

——(1972 [1969]) 'The logic of nonstandard English', in P. Giglioli (ed.) *Language and Social Context* (pp. 179–215) Harmondsworth: Penguin; originally published in *Georgetown Monographs on Language and Linguistics*, 22, 1–22, 26–31.

——(1984) 'Field methods of the project on linguistic change and variation', in J. Baugh and J. Sherzer (eds), *Language in Use* (pp. 28–53), Englewood Cliffs, NJ: Prentice-Hall.

——(2004 [1972]) 'Academic ignorance and black intelligence', in O. Santa Ana (ed.) *Tongue Tied: The Lives of Multilingual Children in Public Education* (pp. 134–51), Oxford: Rowan & Littlefield; originally published in *The Atlantic Monthly*, 239: 59–67.

——(2006) *The Social Stratification of English in New York City*, 2nd edition, Cambridge: Cambridge University Press.

Lafford, B. (2007) 'Second language acquisition reconceptualized? The impact of Firth and Wagner (1997)', *Modern Language Journal*, 91 (5): 735–56.

Lakoff, R. (2006) 'Identity a la carte; Or, you are what you eat', in A. de Fina, D. Schiffrin and M. Bamberg (eds), *Discourse and Identity* (pp. 142–65), Cambridge: Cambridge University Press.

Lambert, W. E., Hodgson, R.C., Gardner, R.C. and Fillenbaum, S. (1960) 'Evaluational reactions to spoken language', *Journal of Abnormal and Social Psychology*, 60: 44–51.

Lareau, A. (2011) *Unequal Childhoods: Class, Race, and Family Life, Second Edition with an Update a Decade Later*, Berkeley, CA: University of California Press.

Lash, S. and Urry, J. (1994) *Economies of Signs and Space*, London: Sage.

Lave, J. and Wenger, E. (1991) *Situated Learning: Legitimate Peripheral Participation*, Cambridge: Cambridge University Press.

Lee, C. K. (2007) *Against the Law: Labor Protests in China's Rustbelt and Sunbelt*, Berkeley: University of California Press.

Lee, R. E. (2010) 'Critiques and developments in world-systems analysis: An introduction to the special issue', *Journal of Philosophical Economics*, 4 (2): 5–18.

Lenin, V. (1982 [1919]) 'The abolition of classes' [section from 'A great beginning'], in A. Giddens and D. Held (eds), *Classes, Power and Conflict: Classical and Contemporary Debates* (pp. 57–59), Berkeley: University of California Press.

Leung, C., Harris, R. and Rampton, B. (1997) 'The idealised native speaker, reified ethnicities and classroom realities', *TESOL Quarterly*, 31 (3): 543–60.

Li Wei (2006) 'Complementary schools, past, present and future', *Language and Education*, 20 (1): 76–83.

——(ed.) (2009a) *Bilingualism and Multilingualism: Critical Concepts in Linguistics, Volume 1, Linguistic and Developmental Perspectives*, London: Routledge.

——(2009b) *Bilingualism and Multilingualism: Critical Concepts in Linguistics, Volume 2, Psycholinguistic and Neurolinguistic Perspectives*, London: Routledge.

——(2009c) *Bilingualism and Multilingualism: Critical Concepts in Linguistics, Volume 3, Sociolinguistic and Interactional Perspectives*, London: Routledge.

——(2009d) *Bilingualism and Multilingualism: Critical Concepts in Linguistics, Volume 4, Applied Perspectives*, London: Routledge.

Liddicoat, A. (2013) *Intercultural Language Teaching and Learning*, Oxford: Blackwell.

Lightbown, P. and Spada, N. (2008) *How Languages are Learned*, 4th edition, Oxford: Oxford University Press.

Lutz, A. (2002) 'Bilingualism in the USA: Language outcomes and opportunities for Latinos', PhD thesis, University at Albany/SUNY.

Lytra, V. and Martin, P. (eds) (2010a) 'Introduction', in *Sites of Multilingualism: Complementary Schools in Britain Today* (pp. xi–xx), Stoke on Trent: Trentham Books.

——(eds) (2010b) *Sites of Multilingualism: Complementary Schools in Britain Today*, Stoke on Trent: Trentham Books.

Macaro, E. (ed.) (2013) *Continuum Companion to Second Language Acquisition*, London: Continuum.

McElhinny, B. (ed.) (2007) *Words, Worlds and Material Girls*, Berlin: Mouton de Gruyter.

Mackey, W. F. (2003) 'Bilingualism in North America', in T. K. Bhatia and W. Ritchie (eds), *The Handbook of Bilingualism* (pp. 607–41), Oxford: Blackwell.

McLaren, P. and Scatamburlo-D'Annibale, V. (2004) 'Paul Willis, class consciousness, and critical pedagogy: Toward a socialist future', in N. Dolby and G. Dimitriadis (with P. Willis) (eds), *Learning to Labor in New Times* (pp. 41–60), London: Routledge.

Maddison, A. (2007) *Contours of the World Economy, 1–2030 AD: Essays in Macro-Economic History*, Oxford: Oxford University Press.

Mahew, H. (2008 [1851]) *London Labour and the London Poor*, London: Wordsworth Editions.

Malderez, A. and Wedell, M. (2007) *Teaching Teachers: Processes and Practices*, London: Continuum.

Marcuse, H. (1964) *One Dimensional Man: Studies in the Ideology of Advanced Industrial Society*, London: Routledge & Kegan Paul.

Martin-Jones, M., Blackledge, A. and Creese, A. (eds) (2012) *The Routledge Handbook of Multilingualism*, London: Routledge.

Marx, K. (1904 [1859]) *A Contribution to the Critique of Political Economy*, Chicago: Charles H. Kerr.

——(1972 [1852]) 'The eighteenth brumaire of Louis Bonaparte', in R. C. Tucker (ed.), *The Marx-Engels Reader* (pp. 432–525), New York: W.W. Norton.

——(1973 [1858]) *Grundrisse*, Harmondsworth: Penguin.

——(1976 [1867]) *Capital: A Critique of Political Economy, Volume 1*, New York: Vintage Books.

——(1988 [1844]) *Economic and Philosophic Manuscripts of 1844*, Amherst, NY: Prometheus Books.

——(1991 [1865]) *Capital: Volume 3*, Harmondsworth: Penguin.

——(2005 [1847]) *The Poverty of Philosophy*, Buffalo, NY: Prometheus Books.

Marx, K. and Engels, F. (1948 [1846]) *Communist Manifesto*, New York: International Publishers.

——(1998 [1846]) *The German Ideology*, London: Lawrence & Wishart.

May, S. (2012) *Language and Minority Rights: Ethnicity, Nationalism and the Politics of Language*, 2nd edition, London: Routledge.

Meisl, J. (2011) *First and Second Language Acquisition: Parallels and Differences*, Cambridge: Cambridge University Press.

Miller, J. (1983) *Many Voices: Bilingualism, Culture and Education*, London: Routledge.

Mills, C. W. (1951) *White Collar*, Oxford: Oxford University Press.

Milroy, J. (1981) *Regional Accents of English: Belfast*, Belfast: Blackstaff.

——(1987) *Observing and Analysing Natural Language*, Oxford: Blackwell.

——(1991) 'The interpretation of social constraints on variation in Belfast English', in J. Cheshire (ed.), *English Around the World: Sociolinguistic Perspectives* (pp. 75–85), Cambridge: Cambridge University Press.

Milroy, J. and Milroy, L. (1978) 'Belfast: Change and variation in an urban vernacular', in P. Trudgill (ed.), *Sociolinguistic Patterns in British English* (pp. 19–36), London: Arnold.

——(1985) 'Linguistic change, social network, and speaker innovation', *Journal of Linguistics*, 21: 339–84.

Milroy, L. and Milroy, J. (1992) 'Social network and social class: Toward an integrated sociolinguistic model', *Language in Society* 21: 1–26.

Mitchell, R., Myles, F. and Marsden, E. (2013) *Second Language Learning Theories*, 3rd edition, London: Hodder Education.

Moore, E. (2010) 'The interaction between social category and social practice: Explaining was/were variation', *Language Variation and Change*, 22 (3): 347–71.

——(2012) 'The social life of style', *Language and Literature*, 21 (1): 66–83.

Mount, F. (2004) *Mind the Gap: Class in Britain Now*, London: Short Books.

Murray, C. (2012) *Coming Apart: The State of White America, 1960–2010*, New York: Crown Publishers.

Myers-Scotton, C. (2005) *Multiple Voices*, Oxford: Blackwell.

Navarro, V. (2006) *El subdesarrollo social de España. Causas y consecuencias*, Barcelona: Anagrama.

Nederveen Pieterse, J. (1995) 'Globalization as hybridization', in M. Featherstone, S. Lash and R. Robertson (eds), *Global Modernities* (pp. 45–68), London: Sage.

——(2009) *Globalization and Culture: Global Mélange*, 2nd edition, Lantham, MD: Rowman & Littlefield.

Noels, K. A., Yashima, T. and Zhang, R. (2012) 'Language, identity and intercultural communication', in J. Jackson (ed.), *Routledge Handbook of Language and Intercultural Communication* (pp. 52–66), London: Routledge

Norton, B. (2000) *Identity and Language Learning: Gender, Ethnicity and Educational Change*, Harlow: Longman/Pearson Education.

——(2010) 'Language and identity', in N. Hornberger and S. McKay (eds), *Sociolinguistics and Language Education* (pp. 349–69), Clevedon: Multilingual Matters.

——(2011) 'Identity', in J. Simpson (ed.), *Routledge Handbook of Applied Linguistics* (pp. 318–30), London: Routledge.

Norton, B. and Toohey, K. (2011) 'Identity, language learning, and social change', *Language Teaching*, 44 (4): 412–46.

Norton Peirce, B. (1995) 'Social identity, investment, and language learning', *TESOL Quarterly*, 29 (1): 9–31.

Nunan, D. and J. Choi (eds) (2010) *Language and Culture: Reflective Narratives and the Emergence of Identity*, Cambridge: Cambridge University Press.

Ogbu, J. (1988) 'Class stratification, racial stratification, and schooling', in L. Weis (ed.), *Class, Race, and Gender in American Education* (pp. 163–82), Albany, NY: State University of New York Press.

Olshtain, O., Shohamy, E., Kemp, J. and Chatow, R. (1990) 'Factors predicting success in EFL among culturally different learners', *Language Learning*, 20: 23–44.

Omoniyi, T. and White, G. (eds) (2006) *The Sociolinguistics of Identity*, London: Continuum.

Ortega, L. (2009) *Second Language Acquisition*, London: Hodder Education.

Ortner, S. (2006) *Anthropology and Social Theory: Culture, Power, and the Acting Subject*, Durham, NC: Duke University Press.

Pakulski, J. (2005) 'Foundations of a post-class analysis', in E. O. Wright (ed.), *Approaches to Class Analysis* (pp. 152–79), Cambridge: Cambridge University Press.

Pakulski, J. and Waters, J. (1996) *The Death of Class*, London: Sage.

Palmer, D. (2009) 'Middle-class English speakers in a two-way immersion bilingual classroom: "Everybody should be listening to Jonathan right now … "', *TESOL Quarterly*, 43 (2): 177–202.

Park, J. S.-Y. (2009) *The Local Construction of a Global Language: Ideologies of English in South Korea*, Berlin: Mouton de Gruyter.

——(2010) 'Images of "good English" in the Korean conservative press: Three processes of interdiscursivity,' *Pragmatics and Society*, 1 (2): 189–208.

——(2011) 'The promise of English: Linguistic capital and the neoliberal worker in the South Korean job market', *International Journal of Bilingual Education and Bilingualism*, 14 (4): 443–55.

Park, J. S.-Y. and Wee, L. (2012) *Linguistic Capital and Language Policy in a Globalizing World*, London: Routledge.

Park, S. J. and Abelmann, N. (2004) 'Class and cosmopolitan striving: Mothers' management of English education in South Korea', *Anthropological Quarterly*, 77 (4): 645–72.

Parker, D. S. and Walker L. S. (eds) (2013) *Latin America's Middle Class: Unsettled Debates and New Histories*, Lanham, MD: Lexington Books.

Parsons, T. (1951) *The Social System*, London: Routledge & Kegan Paul.

Pavlenko, A. (2009) (ed.) *The Bilingual Mental Lexicon: Interdisciplinary Approaches*, Clevedon: Multilingual Matters.

——(2011) *Thinking and Speaking in Two Languages*, Clevedon: Multilingual Matters.

Pennycook, A. (1994) *The Cultural Politics of English as an International Language*, London: Longman.

——(1998) *English and the Discourses of Colonialism*, London: Routledge.

——(2007) *Global Englishes and Transcultural Flows*, London: Routledge.

——(2012) *Language and Mobility: Unexpected Places*, Clevedon: Multilingual Matters.

Peterson, M. A. (2011) *Connected in Cairo: Growing up Cosmopolitan in the Modern Middle East*, Bloomington, IN: Indiana University Press.

Peterson, R. A. (1992) 'Understanding audience segmentation: From elite and mass to omnivore and univore', *Poetics*, 21, 243–58.

Phillipson, R. (1992) *Linguistic Imperialism*, Oxford: Oxford University Press.

——(2003) *English-Only Europe? Challenging Language Policy*, London: Routledge.

——(2010) *Linguistic Imperialism Continued*, London: Routledge.

Pichler, P. (2009) *Talking Young Femininities*, London: Palgrave.

Pietikainen, S. and Kelly-Holmes, H. (eds) (2013) *Multilingualism and the Periphery*, Oxford: Oxford University Press.

Piller, I. (2012) 'Multilingualism and social inclusion', in M. Martin-Jones, A. Blackledge and A. Creese (eds), *The Routledge Handbook of Multilingualism* (pp. 281–96), London: Routledge.

Piller, I. and Cho, K. (2013) 'Neoliberalism as language policy', *Language in Society*, 42 (1): 23–44.

Platt, L. (2011) *Understanding Inequalities: Stratification and Difference*, Cambridge: Polity.

Politzer, R. (1981) 'Social class and bilingual education: Issues and contradictions', *Bilingual Education Paper Series*, 5 (2): npn.

Polyani, K. (2001 [1944]) *The Great Transformation: The Political and Economic Origins of Our Time*, Boston, MA: Beacon Press.

Preece, S. (2010) *Posh Talk*, London: Palgrave.

Preston, D. (1989) *Sociolinguistics and Second Language Acquisition*, Oxford: Blackwell.

——(2002) 'A variationist perspective on second langue acquisition', in R. Kaplan (ed.), *The Oxford Handbook of Applied Linguistics* (pp. 141–59), Oxford: Oxford University Press.

Pujolar, J. (2007) 'Bilingualism and the nation-state in the post-national era', in M. Heller (ed.), *Bilingualism: A Social Approach* (pp. 71–110), London: Palgrave.

Ramanathan, V. (2005) The English-vernacular Divide: Postcolonial Language Politics and Practice, Clevedon: Multilingual Matters.

Ramanathan, V. and Morgan, B. (2009) 'Global warning? West-based TESOL, class blindness, and the challenge for critical pedagogies', in F. Sharifian (ed.), *English as an International Language: Perspectives and Pedagogical Issues* (pp. 153–68), Clevedon: Multilingual Matters.

Rampton, B. (2003) 'Hegemony, social class and stylisation', *Pragmatics*, 13 (1): 49–84.

——(2006) *Language in Late Modernity: Interaction in an Urban School*, Cambridge: Cambridge University Press.

——(2007) 'Neo-Hymesian linguistic ethnography in the United Kingdom', *Journal of Sociolinguistics*, 11 (5): 584–607.

——(2010) 'Social class and sociolinguistics', *Applied Linguistics Review*, 1: 1–21.

——(2011) 'Style in a second language', *Working Papers in Urban Language & Literacies*, 65, King's College London.

Reed, A. and Chowkwanyun, M. (2012) 'Race, class, crisis: The discourse of racial disparity and its analytical discontents', *Socialist Register*, 48 (1): 149–75.

Reich, R. (1991) *The Work of Nations*, New York: Vintage.

Rex, J. and Tomlinson, S. (1979) *Colonial Immigrants in a British City: A Class Analysis*, London: Routledge & Kegan Paul.

Ricardo, D. (2004 [1817]) *On the Principles of Political Economy and Taxation*, New York: Dover Publications.

Richardson, E. (2006) *Hiphop Literacies*, London: Routledge.

Rickford, J. (1986) 'The need for new approaches to social class in sociolinguistics', *Language and Communication*, 6 (3): 215–21.

Ritchie, W. C. and Bhatia, T. K. (eds) (2009) *New Handbook of Second Language Acquisition*, Bingley: Emerald Group Publishing.

Ritzer, G. (1996) *The McDonaldization of Society*, revised edition, Thousand Oaks, CA: Sage.

——(2007) *The Globlization of Nothing 2*, Thousand Oaks, CA: Sage.

Roberts, K. (2001) *Class in Modern Britain*, London: Palgrave.

Rogaly, B. and Taylor, B. (2009) *Moving Histories of Class and Community: Identity, Place and Belonging in Contemporary England*, London: Palgrave.

Rosen, H. (1972) *Language and Class: A Critical Look at the Theories of Basil Bernstein*, London: Falling Wall Press.

Rubdy, R. and Tan, P. K. W. (eds) (2008) *Language as Commodity: Global Structures, Local Marketplaces*, London: Continuum.

Sadovnik, A. R. (ed.) (1995) *Knowledge and Pedagogy: The Sociology of Basil Bernstein*, Norwood, NJ: Ablex Publishing.

——(2001) 'Basil Bernstein (1924–2000)', *Prospects: The Quarterly Review of Comparative Education*, 31 (4): 687–703.

Sassen, S. (2007) *Sociology of Globalization*, New York: W.W. Norton.

Savage, (2000) *Class Analysis and Social Transformation*, Buckingham: Open University Press.

Savage, M., Silva, E. and Warde, A. (2010) 'Dis-identification and class identity', in E. Silva and A. Warde (eds), A *Cultural Analysis and the Legacy of Bourdieu* (pp. 60–74), London: Routledge.

Saville-Troike, M. (2012) *Introducing Second Language Acquisition*, 2nd edition, Cambridge: Cambridge University Press.

Sayer, A. (2005) *The Moral Significance of Class*, Cambridge: Cambridge University Press.

Schneider, E. W. (2011) *English Around the World: An Introduction*, Cambridge: Cambridge University Press.

Seargeant, P. (2012) *Exploring World Englishes: Language in a Global Context*, London: Routledge.

Sennett, R. and Cobb, J. (1972) *The Hidden Injuries of Class*, New York: W.W. Norton.

Simpson, J. (ed.) (2011a) *The Routledge Handbook of Applied Linguistics*, London: Routledge.

——(2011b) 'Introduction: Applied linguistics in the contemporary world', in *The Routledge Handbook of Applied Linguistics* (pp. 1–8), London: Routledge.

Skeggs, B. (1997) *Formations of Class and Gender: Becoming Respectable*, London: Sage.

——(2004) *Class, Self, Culture*, London: Routledge.

Sklair, L. (2010) 'Transnational practices', in G. Ritzer and Z. Atalay (eds), *Readings in Globalization* (pp. 185–95), Malden, MA: Wiley Blackwell.

Skutnabb-Kangas, T. (2000) *Linguistic Genocide in Education – or Worldwide Diversity and Human Rights?*, London: Routledge.

——(2009) 'Multilingual education for social justice: Issues, approaches, opportunities', in T. Skutnabb-Kangas, R. Phillipson, A. Mohanty and M. Panda (eds) *Social Justice Through Multilingual Education* (pp. 36–62), Clevedon: Multilingual Matters.

Skutnabb-Kangas, T. and Cummins, J. (eds) (1988) *Minority Education: From Shame to Struggle*, Clevedon: Multilingual Matters.

Skutnabb-Kangas, T., Phillipson, R., Mohanty, A. and Panda, M. (eds) (2009) *Social Justice Through Multilingual Education*, Clevedon: Multilingual Matters.

Smart, B. (1999) *Facing Modernity*, London: Sage.

Smith, A. (1982 [1776]) *The Wealth of Nations, Books 1–3*, Harmondsworth: Penguin.

Snell, J. (2009) 'Pronouns, dialect and discourse: A socio-pragmatic account of children's language in Teesside', PhD thesis, University of Leeds.

——(2010) 'From sociolinguistic variation to socially strategic stylisation', *Journal of Sociolinguistics*, 14 (4): 618–44.

——(2013) 'Dialect, interaction and class positioning at school: From deficit to difference to repertoire', *Language and Education*, 27 (2): 110–28.

Spring, J. (2009) *Globalization of Education: An Introduction*, London: Routledge.

Street, B. (1995) *Social Literacies: Critical Approaches to Literacy in Development, Ethnography and Education*, Reading, MA: Addison-Wesley.

Stroud, C. (2007) 'Bilingualism: Colonialism and post colonialism', in M. Heller (ed.), *Bilingualism: A Social Approach* (pp. 25–49), London: Palgrave.

Subirats, M. (2012) *Barcelona: de la necesidad a la libertad: Las clases sociales en los albores del siglo XXI*, Barcelona: Universitat Oberta de Catalunya.

Tedick, D. (ed.) (2004) *Second Language Teacher Education: International Perspectives*, London: Routledge.

Thompson, E. P. (1980 [1963]) *The Making of the English Working Class*, Harmondsworth: Penguin.

Touraine, A. (2007) *A New Paradigm for Understanding Today's World*, Cambridge: Polity.

Toynbee, P. (2003) *Hard Work: Life in Low-pay Britain*, London: Bloomsbury.

Trudgill, P. (1974a) *Sociolinguistics: An Introduction*, Harmondsworth: Penguin.

——(1974b) *The Social Differentiation of English in Norwich*, Cambridge: Cambridge University Press.

Tsui, A. (2003) *Understanding Expertise in Teaching: Case Studies of Second Language Teachers*, Cambridge: Cambridge University Press.

Urciuoli, B. (1996) *Exposing Prejudice: Puerto Rican Experiences of Language, Race, and Class*, Boulder, CO: Westview Press.

——(2008) 'Skills and selves in the new workplace', *American Ethnologist*, 35 (2): 211–28.

Urry, J. (2007) *Mobilities*, Cambridge: Polity.

Valdes, G., Fishman, J., Chavez, R. and Perez, W. (2006) *Developing Minority Language Resources*, Clevedon: Multilingual Matters.

Van Lier, L. (2004) *The Ecology and Semiotics of Language Learning: A Sociocultural Perspective*, Berlin: Springer.

Vandrick, S. (2011) 'Students of the new global elite', *TESOL Quarterly*, 45 (1): 160–69.

Veblen, T. (2007 [1899]) *The Theory of the Leisure Class*, Oxford: Oxford University Press.

Vincent, C. and Ball, S. (2006) *Childcare, Choice and Class Practices: Middle Class Parents and their Children*, London: Routledge.

Volosinov, V. N. (1973) *Marxism and the Philosophy of Language*, New York: Seminar Press.

Wacquant, L. (2008) *Urban Outcasts: A Comparative Sociology of Advanced Marginality*, Cambridge: Polity.

——(2012) 'Three steps to a historical anthropology of actually existing neoliberalism', *Social Anthropology/Anthropologie Sociale*, 20 (1): 66–79.

Walkerdine, V., Lucey, H. and Melody, J. (2001) *Growing Up Girl: Psycho-social Explorations of Gender and Class*, London: Palgrave.

Wallerstein, I. (2004) *World Systems Analysis: An Introduction*, Durham, NC: Duke University Press.

Warde, A., Wright, D. and Gayo-Cal, M. (2007) 'Understanding cultural omnivorousness: Or, the myth of the cultural omnivore', *Cultural Sociology*, 1 (2): 143–64.

Weber, M. (1968 [1922]) *Economy and Society, Volumes 1 & 2*, Berkeley, CA: University of California Press.

——(2002 [1905]) *The Protestant Work Ethic and the Spirit of Capitalism*, Harmondsworth: Penguin.

Weis, L. (ed.) (2008) *The Way Class Works: Readings on School, Family, and the Economy*, London: Routledge.

Wenger, E. (2006) 'Communities of practice: A brief introduction', online. Available at: www.ewenger.com/theory/communities_of_practice_intro.htm

Whyte, W. (1956) *The Organization Man*, Harmondsworth: Penguin.

Williams, G. (1992) *Sociolinguistics: A Sociological Critique*, London: Routledge.

Williams, R. (1976) *Keywords*, London: Fontana.

——(1977) *Marxism and Literature*, new edition, Oxford: Oxford University Press.

——(1980) *Problems in Materialism and Culture: Selected Essays*, London: Verso.

Willis, P. (1977) *Learning to Labour: How Working Class Kids Get Working Class Jobs*, London: Saxon House.

Wills, J., Datta, K., Evans, Y., Herbert, J., May, J. and McIlwaine, C. (2010) *Global Cities at Work: New Migrant Divisions of Labour*, London: Pluto Press.

Woldoff, R. (2011) *White Flight/Black Flight: The Dynamics of Racial Change in an American Neighborhood*, Ithaca, NY: Cornell University Press.

Wood, E. M. (1998) *The Retreat from Class: The New 'True' Socialism*, new edition, London: Verso.

Woolard, K. A. (1985) 'Language variation and cultural hegemony: Toward an integration of sociolinguistic and social theory', *American Ethnologist*, 12 (4): 738–48.

——(1986) 'The "crisis in the concept of identity" in contemporary Catalonia', in G. W. McDonough (ed.) *Conflict in Catalonia. Images of an Urban Society* (pp. 54–71), Gainesville, FL: University of Florida Press.

——(1989) *Double Talk: Bilingualism and the Politics of Ethnicity in Catalonia*, Stanford, CA: Stanford University Press.

Wright, E. O. (1985) *Classes*, London: Verso.

——(2005) 'Foundations of a neo-Marxist class anlsyis', in E. O. Wright (ed.), *Approaches to Class Analysis* (pp. 4–30), Cambridge: Cambridge University Press.

Young, M. and Wilmott, P. (1957) *Family and Kinship in East London*, Harmondsworth: Penguin.

Žižek, S. (2009) *First as Tragedy, then as Farce*, London: Verso.

INDEX

Please note that page numbers relating to Notes will have the letter 'n' following the page number. Page references to Tables will be in *italics*.